DISCARD

P9-CMT-653

COMPLETE
BIKE
MAINTENANCE

NEW AND EXPANDED EDITION

For Road, Mountain & Commuter Bicycles

FRED MILSON

MVP
BOOKS

NEWARK PUBLIC LIBRARY
121 HIGH STREET
NEWARK, NEW YORK 14513

Contents

CHAPTER

CHOOSING
A BIKE

Bikes for adults

There's an enormous range of bikes available now but it boils down to six or seven different types. Ideally you buy a bike to suit the type of riding that you intend to do, but price does come into it as well.

A bike toward the bottom of the price range. Nevertheless, it has 14 Shimano gears and a suspension fork. Bikes like this provide a good introduction to cycling.

Mountain bikes

Originally for plummeting down mountain sides, their versatility makes them suitable for city riders who need to bump up and down curbs and ride through potholes. Some of the cheapest bikes are mountain bikes, particularly if you buy at the big retail stores. They start off with aluminum or steel frames, heavy wheels and tires, and a limited range of gears. Bikes like this are useful for deciding whether you like cycling or not but you're soon likely to want something a bit better.

At the next price level the quality obviously improves. Again, the retail stores have the advantage of buying by the container load, and they've recently improved their assembly standards as well. However, if you go for a "bike in a box," you take full responsibility for the way it's assembled.

City bikes

A mountain bike is in its element off-road, while a city bike takes some parts of an off-road bike and blends them with parts that are more suitable for the road. So it has an upright riding position but also narrower handlebars and lighter wheels and tires than a mountain bike. But the main question for city bike riders concerns the type of gears. You have a choice of derailleur gears, which offer a wide range of ratios but require a certain amount of maintenance. Or a hub gear, which has a relatively small number of ratios, needs the minimum of maintenance, but makes it far more difficult to take the back wheel out of the frame.

This is a city bike equipped with a Shimano eight speed hub gear and a cromoly fork. It also has disc brakes, which have only recently been introduced to this part of the market.

Hybrid bikes

These are like racers but have flat handlebars, with brake and gear levers to match and a choice of fork. Some have a simplified suspension fork made by SR or Suntour but this is not really appropriate. A lightweight steel fork or a carbon fiber item is much more appropriate.

In some ways they are ideal for commuting because the handlebars encourage a more upright riding position, which is good for safety as well as increased comfort. But they keep most of the speed advantage of the racer, with a racing saddle and light wheels while 700 x 28 or 32 tires improve the ride. And a compact chainset is even more desirable than on a racer.

Racing bikes

This is the first bike where the independent bike dealer has a real advantage, able to advise about price versus quality, size and possible upgrades.

Three recent developments are worth looking out for. One is a compact chainset, either 48 or 50 x 34 teeth, which gives much more suitable gearing than the standard 52 or 53 x 39 teeth. The next is a carbon fork. These will be confined to bikes at the top of the price range, but you won't regret spending $250 more. Thirdly, some racers have frames that are more upright at the front, which makes them a good deal more comfortable for ordinary mortals.

The racing heritage of the hybrid can easily be spotted, with a minimum of modifications to make it more comfortable and convenient to use on the road. Also known as a flat bar bike.

GET SOME TRAINING
A professional cycle instructor will help you to improve your bike control skills such as emergency stopping and swerving. They'll also help you to build the confidence needed for basic road use, improve your urban riding technique for more advanced situations, or get a complete beginner quickly up and riding. An instructor will also be able to give you advice on bike fitting, and show you how to check your own bike. Even experienced cyclists can benefit from training, so look for a certified League of America Bicyclists instructor. The advocacy group keeps a register of qualified instructors and training providers, which is available on their website www.bikeleague.org.

Racing bikes are pure speed machines, with only a few concessions to comfort. They're a bit tough to ride in the first place, but once you get used to them even the saddle is comfortable.

Touring bikes

Touring bikes are a sub-category of racing bikes, designed to be outfitted with front and rear carriers for panniers, lots of brazed-on fittings and more comfortable frame angles. In addition, the gears and chainset are often mountain-bike style with 27 gears, and so are the brakes. You can use a touring bike for commuting all year round but they come into their own when traveling long distances and carrying heavy loads.

Touring bikes are now strongly influenced by mountain bikes, but they haven't forgotten their past, with drop handlebars and a near-racing frame.

Fashion bikes

On the other hand, fashion bikes deserve a small slot in this summary as well. They tend to have curved tubes and outrageous frame designs, with the performance of the bike very much secondary to the appearance. They're becoming a good deal more popular.

Let yourself go with a fun bike!

Folding bikes

Folding bikes are another category that is doing well, due at least in part to the increase in bike commuting. However, the cheapest sort of folding bike is a disappointment. They don't fold very well, and they don't ride very well either. If you're going for a folding bike, go for one of the well-known British, German or Far Eastern brands. And try before you buy to check on the folding mechanisms and their qualities as bikes. But if you're particularly tall or short, forget it because these bikes have a limited amount of adjustability.

A folding bike, featuring a folding stem and handlebars plus a frame that hinges in the middle. It's a well equipped bike with eight SRAM derailleur gears, a Truvativ chainset, and vee brakes, so it's among the more expensive of its type.

Trekking bikes

Finally, there are trekking bikes. These are very popular in northern Europe and range from classic bikes with hub gears to bikes with wide derailleur gears and everything bolted on. The emphasis is on their ability to go to the uttermost ends of the earth, rather than lightness, even when they start off with a light frame.

You can make a good case for buying every one of these types, so don't just buy a mountain bike as a default choice. Think what you'll be using your bike for and how much you'll be riding it, and then make your selection.

Trekking bikes are popular in northern Europe but are also becoming better known elsewhere. They provide comfort and the ability to go anywhere. This shows the handlebars, with many different hand positions and the built-in compass.

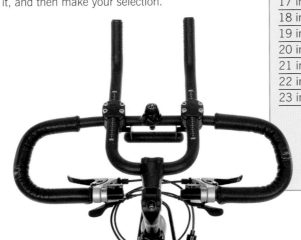

SIZING YOUR BIKE

As a rule of thumb:
MOUNTAIN BIKES There should be a minimum of 3 inches clearance over the top tube when you stand flat-footed on the ground.
ROAD BIKES There should be a minimum of 1 inch clearance over the top tube when you stand flat-footed on the ground. However, some frames follow the compact design with a sloping top tube. These should have between 2 inches and 3 inches of clearance.

Alternatively, stand with your back to a wall, with your feet about 6 inches apart. Get a book and press one side against the wall, while the other presses up into the crotch. Measure from the back of the book to the ground and multiply by 0.66. This gives you the size of frame that you need.

However, bikes have a 1in longer top tube for every 2in increase in frame size. So if you've got unusually long arms or a long trunk it's a good idea to go for the next frame size up. But if you've got unusually long legs, go for a shorter frame and make up for it with a long seat post, if necessary.

Alternatively, you'll find that this table is pretty accurate.

FRAME SIZE	FRAME SIZE IN CM	INSIDE LEG
15 inches	38cm	24in–29in
16 inches	41cm	25in–30in
17 inches	43cm	26in–31in
18 inches	46cm	27in–32in
19 inches	49cm	28in–33in
20 inches	51cm	29in–34in
21 inches	54cm	30in–35in
22 inches	56cm	31in–36in
23 inches	59cm	32in–37in

Set your riding position

Sizing is the first thing that you must get right. Generally speaking people buy bikes that are too large for them, so the handlebars are too far away and they have to push the saddle too far forward to make up for it. Following the rule of thumb, you should buy a frame that will have at least 4in of seat post showing, and preferably 6in or so.

According to the rule of thumb, the standover height on racers and hybrid bikes should be one inch . . .

. . . while on mountain and city bikes it should be three inches.

As for frame sizes, they are usually displayed on the down tube or seat tube. Mountain bikes normally start at 15 inches and go up to 18 or 19 inches, but frames intended for women go smaller. Most city bikes are sized in a similar way, but sometimes start at 14 inches and go up to 19 inches.

Racers generally start at 19 inches or 49cm and go up to 25 inches or 60cm, although 58cm is usually the top size. Alternatively there is a simplified system of XS, S, M, ML, L and XL, which is used by Giant and other companies for their compact frames. The compact design particularly suits female riders, which allows sizes 3XS, 2XS, XS and so on.

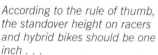

At the shop they make a guess at your riding position and set it to that, but its only when you get your bike home that you can set about adjusting the details. First, reset your saddle height but only after riding for ten minutes or so, when you've settled down on the bike.

Bring the pedals around to the six and twelve o'clock position and adjust the saddle so that your heel just about keeps contact with the lower pedal. Then, when you put the balls of your feet on the pedals, your leg should be very slightly bent. That is more-or-less the correct saddle height, although you might want to raise or lower it by ¼ inch after more experience.

For bikes with rear suspension or a suspension seat post, you also have to take into account the amount of sag when setting the saddle height. If possible get a friend to watch you and mark the exact amount up or down that's required.

Next, you have to get the saddle right in the fore and aft plane. Set the saddle exactly horizontal, then make yourself a little plumb line. Turn the pedals until they are exactly horizontal at three and nine o'clock, then drop the plumb line from the bony projection just below the knee. It should cut across the leading pedal at the pedal axle. If it doesn't, move the saddle forward or backward until you get it right. In addition, you can angle it up or down a couple of degrees, if you find you prefer it that way. The saddle height may need correcting slightly as well if you decide to alter the angle of the saddle.

Now for the stem, which you can only make your mind up about after getting the saddle right. On a mountain bike, you need a stem that allows you to keep your back at roughly 45°. You can vary this using stems of a different length and angle, and by the number of spacers in the headset.

As for a racing bike, the classic position keeps the trunk too close to the horizontal for comfort. So instead, fit a stem that allows you to ride "on the tops" of the handlebars with your back at about 45 degrees and the arms bent at roughly 30 degrees. And position the straight part of the handlebars just below the saddle, unless you are tall. In that case position the handlebars further below the saddle, depending on exactly how tall you are. You should be prepared to change the stem for a shorter or longer one if necessary.

A way of checking the length of the stem on a racer is to get right down on the dropped section of the handlebars. If you then look at the stem, it won't be possible to see the front hub if the length is correct. But if the stem appears to be in front of the hub, the stem is too long. And if the hub can be seen, the stem is too short.

1 This rider first of all places his heels on the pedals, to get the height of the saddle. Then, to confirm the correct saddle height, he has put on cycling shoes and clipped into a pair of pedals. The leg is very slightly bent at the bottom of the pedal stroke.

2 To get the correct fore-and-aft position for the saddle, a weighted string hangs from the bony part just below the knee. The saddle is then adjusted until this improvised plumb line hits the centre of the pedal axle exactly, when the pedal is in the three o'clock position.

Over a period of time you'll be able to refine your position still further. In particular, you start with your foot right on top of the axle but you might find it better if it moves slightly backward. This applies whether you are using toe clips or a clipless system.

Frames on utility and leisure bikes are normally laid far back, so most of your weight inevitably falls on the saddle. There is no way of avoiding this completely but you could try lowering the handlebars or fitting straight ones if you are really uncomfortable. Toe clips are not usually fitted to utilities but you should still try to keep the ball of your foot over the pedal axle so that you can pedal fairly efficiently.

As these bikes are mostly used for short journeys around town, the saddle can be set lower than normal. This allows the rider to plant one foot flat on the ground while sitting in the saddle, which is more comfortable when waiting at traffic lights and other hold ups.

Finally, these instructions only apply to mountain bikes and racers, as they are the two extremes. Adapt them to other bikes as required.

When you've got everything approximately right you can start fine-tuning your position. One of the most important areas here is the foot, which may be better if the pedal axle is just fractionally behind the ball of the foot. You'll have to try it to see.

YOUR RIDING POSITION IS NOT RIGHT IF:

Your bottom is sore after a few miles.
Cure: check that the saddle is the correct height and not far from horizontal. Then try moving it forward a bit. And try a gel saddle.

You slip toward the nose of the saddle.
Cure: lift the nose of the saddle a little.

You feel stretched out over the frame.
Cure: raise the handlebars a bit and fit a shorter stem.

Your neck and shoulders get stiff or ache.
Cure: raise the handlebars so you can look forward without kinking your neck.

Your wrists hurt.
Cure: raise the handlebars or lower the saddle.

Your knees hurt.
Cure: check saddle height is correct. Ensure the pedals turn freely and your feet are not held too firmly in the toe clips.

Your feet hurt.
Cure: stiffer shoes, preferably proper cycling shoes. Do not overtighten your shoe laces or toe straps.

RIDING POSITION ON MOUNTAIN BIKES

Set the basic saddle height in the same way as on a racer. But for cross-country riding, and even more for downhill, allow more bend at the knee so that you can easily put your foot down when it feels as if you are losing control. In addition, the back should be at roughly 45° to the ground. This throws more weight onto the handlebars, holding the front wheel down and helping you to keep control over really rough ground or at high speed.

MOUNTAIN BIKES ON THE ROAD

Many first-time buyers simply go for a mountain bike because they don't really know about the other types. Luckily a mountain bike is very adaptable, so a minimum of change is needed to make them suitable for short or medium distances on the road.

Adaptation number one is to fit the bike with a pair of slick or semi-slick tires, 622 x 1.5in. This cuts down the rolling resistance of the wide mountain bike tires, and allows them to be run at higher pressures. This also reduces the amount of rolling resistance.

Adaptation number two is to reduce the width of the handlebars. This is covered in the "Bars and Saddles" chapter of this book. It makes them more comfortable to handle, and easier to thread through small gaps in traffic.

Finally, adaptation number three is to to change the gears for ones that are more usable on the road. That means changing the cassette for one that gives you an even spread of ratios, instead of a wide range biased toward the very low gears.If you wait until the cassette is worn out this modification will cost you nothing.

Woman specific

Women set up their bikes in exactly the same way as men, but because their proportions tend to be different, they end up with a differently shaped bike. First of all, women are generally shorter and lighter than men, with smaller hands and arms as well. On the other hand women's legs tend to be longer, while the pelvis and the genital organs are a different shape. These are averages, so there are exceptions but they are generally true. Unless these physical differences are taken into account, women will struggle to reach their full potential as cyclists.

Woman Specific Design (WSD) versions of most of the bikes described earlier are available but in addition, there are a couple of types that mostly appeal to women. One is the classic roadster, usually in black, with a very upright riding position and three hub gears. And the saddle is very broad, with springs at the back. Such a bike is fine for short distances in town but that's all.

Then there is the Dutch bike, with an open frame and often equipped with a Shimano Nexave groupset. Typically this has a fairly upright riding position, eight-speed hub gears, and the chain is completely contained by the chaincase. This is also mainly intended for short distance work, but it can be equipped with panniers to act as a trekking bike.

Similar to the Dutch bike is the comfort bike, which is like a hybrid but has 650c wheels and derailleur gears with a rotary gear change. It also features an adjustable stem, a suspension seat post and a gel-filled saddle.

As for the Woman Specific Designs, these are now available in increasing numbers. For mountain bikes, the forks are set to suit a lighter rider and they have narrower handlebars, easy reach brakes,

Dutch bikes tend to be well equipped, with multi-speed hub gears and built-in lighting. They work well over short distances, but you can also use them for touring.

This woman-specific design is inexpensive but presses all the right buttons. But don't just buy a mountain bike . . . consider the other types as well.

A classic roadster bike suits many women who only want to ride short distances in town.

Another woman-specific design, a racing bike is suitable for commuting as well as leisure cycling. However, the top tube makes this design unsuitable for riding in a skirt.

a woman's saddle and they may have shorter cranks. The more expensive ones also have adapted frame geometry and sizing.

For racing bikes, the smaller size frames are fitted with 650c wheels and shorter cranks, only going up to 700c and 170mm cranks on the larger sizes. However, don't jump to the conclusion that they will always be right for you. You have to hop on and see, and it could be that you'll do better adapting a man's bike to fit.

Start off adapting a bike by fitting a female-specific saddle. At one extreme is the racing saddle that is almost as minimal as a man's. At the other is a bouncy gel-filled device, or a Brooks leather saddle with separate springs but whichever type you choose, its broader at the back and shorter overall. You can also fit a longer seat post if that is necessary to cater for long legs but a shorter trunk, or a suspension seat post. That simply increases comfort, at the expense of a small increase in weight.

Then there are the brake levers. On mountain bikes and other flat barred bikes, the brake levers are adjustable for reach, so some adaptation is built-in. For racing bikes, the latest brake levers from both Shimano and SRAM are more suitable for a wide range of hand sizes, including female ones.

As for problems with reaching the handlebars, it's quite easy to change the stem and this is covered on page 162. Finally, if really necessary, you can fit 165mm or even shorter cranks. These are available from women's bike specialists, and so are adaptors to make the cranks even shorter.

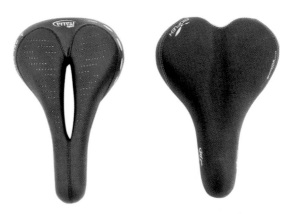

These show the difference between a women's racing saddle (left) and a women's general-purpose saddle (right). They are both broader than male types, but shorter overall as well. Nevertheless, a saddle is such a personal choice that you might have to try several before getting the right one. It's also worth trying the effect of angling the saddle down by a few degrees.

1 An extra-long seat post will allow you to ride a small frame with a short reach, but to accommodate long legs.

2 Nearly all brake levers offer some sort of adjustment for reach. But generally speaking it's only effective on good quality levers.

3 If you want to experiment with your riding position, it's worth trying an adjustable stem. Undoing the bolt allows you to raise or lower the handlebars.

Kids' bikes

When buying a bike for your kids stick roughly to the sizes and ages set out in the table, unless they're unusually big or small for their age. You may be tempted to buy a bike that a child will grow into, but you should resist the impulse. They will find it much more difficult to gain confidence if they can't really control the bike.

Tiny 14in and 16in wheel bikes are usually fitted with a crude headset and bottom bracket, and a one-piece chainset. They are acceptable on bikes of this size, especially if you are buying based on price at a department store or somebody is offering bikes in a box to assemble yourself.

But when it comes to 20in wheels, look for a bike with adult-style components. For this you may well find that a proper cycle retailer is best. They will take the time to find you a bike that has the right components and that fits well. Of course, such a bike will cost you nearly as much as an adult bike of reasonable quality. If this is too much, consider buying second-hand but again, go for adult-style components. You will find it much easier to get parts to fit, and much easier to maintain as well.

When you get to 24in bikes all the same applies only more so. What's more, the kid will be getting to an age when he or she can use the gears sensibly. But remember that they nearly always neglect their brakes, so maintain them yourself to make sure that your kids are safe. This particularly applies if the bike is fitted with Vee brakes.

Avoid getting a bike fitted with either front suspension, or front and rear suspension. Kids' bikes just aren't expensive enough to be fitted with proper suspension components, it'll complicate maintenance and they're heavy as well.

WHEEL SIZE	AGE
14in	2½ to 5
16in	5 to 7
20in	7 to 9
24in	9 to 11
26in	11 plus

24in WHEELS

From nine onward, a scaled-down adult bike is the best choice, with proper bearings in the headset and bottom bracket plus gears. Equipped with this sort of bike a youngster can take part in all family expeditions and keep up with adults most of the time. If you go for a bike with a 14 or 15in frame and a sloping down tube there will be good step-over clearance for the youngest rider but it'll still be the right size in two or three years' time. Later on you can fit a longer seat post, and even toe clips from 11 years onward, to extend its life into the middle school years.

BMX 16in WHEEL BIKES

BMX bikes are very popular, fitting kids from about eight onward but with no upper limit since they're very adjustable. They're particularly valuable for developing bike skills off-road.

16in WHEEL BIKES

One step after play bikes, a 16in wheel machine starts to give kids real mobility when the family goes out. Mountain bike styling gives this bike a robust character but training wheels, if used at all, should only be left on for a very short time.

PLAY BIKES WITH 14in WHEELS

From 2½ to 5 years. Training wheels are OK initially but take them off by the time the bike is getting too small at 4 or 5. A bike of this kind gives very young children a taste for cycling.

20in WHEELS

Suitable for girls and boys aged seven to nine, this size of bike can either have a single gear for low maintenance and crash resistance, or a derailleur gear that mimics adult bikes but probably won't work for long. The picture shows a bike with an immensely strong Y-frame.

Kids' bike set-up

Parents report that training wheels are a good thing on starter bikes. But think about removing training wheels from a child's bike when they are four or five, though this can vary a bit from child to child. Leaving it much later than this means it will take longer for them to learn to balance.

Beginners of any age learn most quickly and safely if they are supported by another person until they can balance themselves. This can be done by holding the saddle rails, or the shoulders of the learner. It's important that braking is taught before concentrating on balancing, particularly as most falls happen once the rider can balance but fails to stop for an obstacle. Make sure the learner rides with their fingers on the brake levers, ready to stop if need be.

If you have trouble teaching somebody how to ride, consider using a professional cycle instructor. They will be well trained, and should be able to get a complete beginner riding within an hour or so.

Once they are riding properly you can adjust the saddle height to give 2in of clearance over the top tube of a conventional frame, or 3in on a sloping tube frame. If you can't get that clearance you'll have to put the bike to one side for the moment because it's too big. Keep your eye on the riding position because it will need adjusting every few months to keep up with their growth.

When the child is ready to ride a 24in bike you can set the saddle as you would an adult's. However, whatever their age you must encourage your child to sit upright because that way they'll find it easier to look ahead down the road.

Encourage your child to wear a helmet at all times as well. So far as adults are concerned helmets are controversial, but no such considerations affect children.

Finally, your kids will need some training. In some cases it will be organized by their school and all you'll have to do is lay on plenty of encouragement.

SPECIAL PARTS
Most kids' bikes are small versions of an adult's bike. But some have special headsets and one-piece chainsets that are quite awkward to put on. The headsets are similar to the Aheadset featured on page 182, while the chainset and special bottom bracket are covered on page 147.

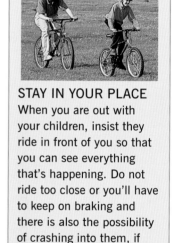

STAY IN YOUR PLACE
When you are out with your children, insist they ride in front of you so that you can see everything that's happening. Do not ride too close or you'll have to keep on braking and there is also the possibility of crashing into them, if somebody in front stops unexpectedly.

ADULT-STYLE FEATURES
This bike has proper headset and bottom bracket bearings, so it'll last for two or three generations of children. If the gears go seriously wrong you can just shorten the chain with a chain tool and do away with them. The bike will work fine on the middle sprocket and the big ring. Note that the saddle height is easily adjustable.

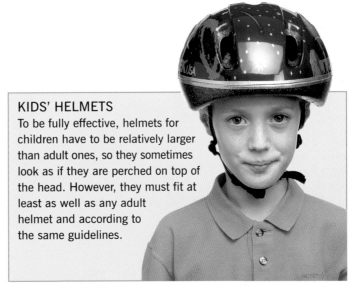

KIDS' HELMETS
To be fully effective, helmets for children have to be relatively larger than adult ones, so they sometimes look as if they are perched on top of the head. However, they must fit at least as well as any adult helmet and according to the same guidelines.

FEET FLAT ON THE GROUND
Until a child develops really secure bike control the saddle should be adjusted so that it's lower than it would normally be. That way they can get their feet down quickly when necessary. This will help to prevent scraped knees and maybe damage to the bike as well.

SLOPING TOP TUBE
The sloping top tube is almost a unisex design, giving plenty of standover height for younger children. Adjust the saddle lower than strictly necessary when they're just starting to develop their bike skills.

TINY BIKES FOR TINIES
An enclosed space or yard is best for very young riders, where they can pick up self confidence in complete safety. Lay out slalom tracks and figure eight steering tests for fun and to develop and improve control skills.

Safety and security

D on't rush in and buy a helmet at the first store you come to. Find one instead that has a good selection of helmets from a wide variety of different makers and employs experienced staff. Then ask them to advise you about the suitability of the different designs for your kind of cycling.

Try on plenty of types and makes of helmet and don't give up until you find one with a really good fit. One test is that if you are able to move the helmet backward and forward with your hands when the chin strap is properly adjusted and fastened, it is too big. Not only will it be uncomfortable, it will also give you much less protection and may even slip off if it is ever put to the test.

Look particularly for ways of adjusting the fit, such as interchangeable pads of varying thickness

to fit in pockets around the edge of the helmet. The other feature to look for is a nape strap or retention bracket at the back of the neck. Apart from the fit of the helmet, the other main factor governing rider comfort is ventilation. Make sure there are plenty of air channels running from front to back because although a helmet may not feel hot in the shop, it certainly will after ten miles of hard pedalling. However, too many full-length ventilation channels can weaken a helmet, so make sure there are plenty of strengthening elements running across the helmet as well.

The minimum legal requirement for any cycle helmet sold in the U.S. is that it must conform to the standard of the Consumer Product Safety Commission.

Safety clothing

1 You will need a waterproof jacket sooner or later. It will only be used in bad weather, so a fluorescent yellow one with strips of reflective material is the best choice as it will help you to be seen.

Bike security

1 Bike security is only relative because if somebody is determined to steal your bike, chances are that they will succeed. Here are three locks: a simple cable lock, a reasonably priced D-lock and a D-lock for a really expensive bike. Cable locks will stop an opportunist thief but not a professional. A D-lock will resist for a good deal longer, unless the thief is well equipped.

Crash helmets

1 Make sure you buy a well-fitting helmet. If the fit is right, the helmet will sit low on your brow but high enough to allow unobstructed vision when you're looking upward or sideways.

2 Inside the helmet, if a retention bracket is fitted, the touch-and-close fastening system enables you to position the bracket accurately, just below the bulge of the skull.

2 Proper cyclists' gloves are a good investment. Go for ones with gel-padded palms. The gel reduces vibration from the road while the glove protects your hands from abrasions in a crash.

3 Cycling gear for children is available in all sorts of designs. But the important thing is to buy a helmet that is endorsed by their particular hero, or their favorite story, so they wear it willingly.

4 The best value in bike safety is a reflective belt and matching arm bands. They are effective night and day. But reflectors on the pedals are even more effective because they move all the time.

5 A reflective vest is a very good value as well, acting as both a reflective garment and something to keep the worst of the weather at bay. They are particularly valuable if you wear dark clothes.

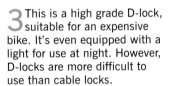

2 Always lock your bicycle to something, preferably an official bike stand. And if you can, take the front wheel out of the bike and lock it with the back wheel and the frame.

3 This is a high grade D-lock, suitable for an expensive bike. It's even equipped with a light for use at night. However, D-locks are more difficult to use than cable locks.

CRASHED HAT

The foam shock absorbing material in a helmet compresses during a crash and doesn't regenerate. As a result, some manufacturers offer to inspect a helmet after a crash. The foam also becomes less effective over a period of time, so it is best to replace any helmet that has been in an accident, however slight. To encourage this, some makes offer free replacement after an accident. However, bear in mind that if you leave the cheapest helmets aside, paying a higher price does not necessarily get you a better product.

3 When properly adjusted, a retention bracket prevents the helmet from tipping backward. If this happens, it is irritating and reduces the effectiveness of the helmet in a crash.

4 The straps must fit naturally on either side of the ears. If they don't, go for a different helmet. The adjusters should sit below the ear lobes and the buckle tucks under the chin.

5 Some helmets are fitted with an external adjuster to get the fit exactly right. But most manufacturers rely on interchangeable pads of varying thickness to do this.

2

INSTANT
BIKE CARE

NEWARK PUBLIC LIBRARY
121 HIGH STREET
NEWARK, NEW YORK 14513

Name that part

OTHER STYLES OF SADDLE

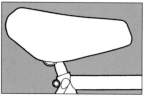

WOMEN'S SADDLE
Specially designed saddle, can be fitted to almost any bike.

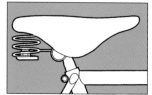

MATTRESS SADDLE
For utility bikes only.

SADDLE

SEAT POST

REAR BRAKE

CABLE ST

WHEEL NUTS

MULTIPLE FREEWHEEL
OR CASSETTE

SEAT TU

FRONT ME

ALTERNATIVE GEARING SYSTEMS

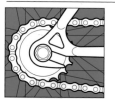

SINGLE SPEED
Mainly used on kids' bikes and BMX, but some adults as well.

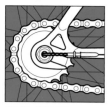

HUB GEARS
As used on most utility bikes.

PED

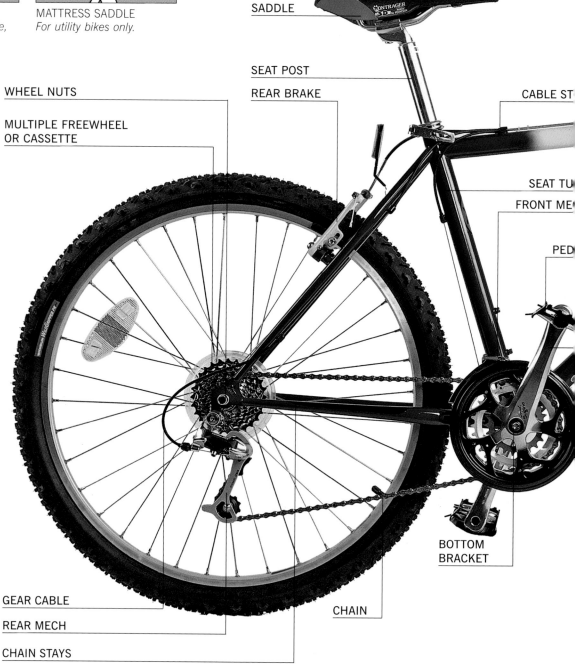

GEAR CABLE

REAR MECH

CHAIN STAYS

CHAIN

BOTTOM
BRACKET

ALTERNATIVE HANDLEBARS

DROP HANDLEBARS
For racing, sports and touring bikes.

FLATS
For hybrids, utilities and Fast Road bikes.

RISER BARS
Used on utility bikes and MTBs.

BAR ENDS

STEM

TOP TUBE

DOWN TUBE

CRANKS

HAINRINGS

HANDLEBARS

BRAKE LEVER

HEADSET

HEAD TUBE

FRONT BRAKE

FRONT WHEEL

SPOKE

TIRE

FORKS

RIM

HUB

QUICK RELEASE

TIRE VALVE

VARIOUS TYPES OF TIRES

KNOBBLY TIRES
For off-road mountain bikes.

MOUNTAIN BIKE SLICKS
For use on the road.

700c and 27in
Tires for racers, tourers, hybrids and flat bar bikes.

Basic tool kit

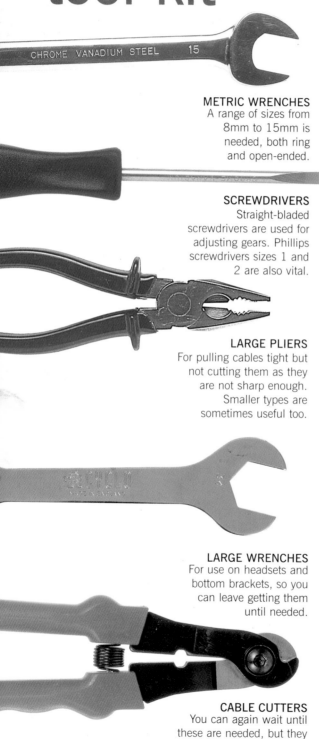

These are the tools and equipment that you will need to maintain your bike. Some of it, like the Allen wrenches and the other wrenches, you will need right away. Other items, like the large wrenches, the cable cutters and the chain tool, can wait until you have to do particular jobs.

Ideally, you need a set of ring wrenches and a separate set of open-ended wrenches. That way you can use one from each set when you are dealing with a nut and bolt of the same size.

As far as lubricants are concerned, you can use old-fashioned cycle oil for the chain, as well as for all the other parts that need oiling from time to time. However, other lubricants are much better and they'll last longer. In particular, wax-based lubricants are good for the chain because they will help to keep it clean.

After you wash your bike, remember to use a lubricant that will keep the water out of the chain and other parts first. Then follow up with a normal product.

METRIC WRENCHES
A range of sizes from 8mm to 15mm is needed, both ring and open-ended.

SCREWDRIVERS
Straight-bladed screwdrivers are used for adjusting gears. Phillips screwdrivers sizes 1 and 2 are also vital.

LARGE PLIERS
For pulling cables tight but not cutting them as they are not sharp enough. Smaller types are sometimes useful too.

LARGE WRENCHES
For use on headsets and bottom brackets, so you can leave getting them until needed.

CABLE CUTTERS
You can again wait until these are needed, but they are vital for the special job of cutting cables.

CHAIN CLEANING MACHINE

DRY LUBRICANT

CLEANING BRUSH

TEFLON-BASED AEROSOL LUBRICANT

SPECIALIZED CHAIN LUBE

CYCLE OIL

SPROCKET BRUSH/RAKE

CHAIN TOOL
Vital for fitting a new chain. Also known as a chain cutter or chain breaker.

PUNCTURE KIT
The most vital part of your tool kit.

OILS AND GREASES

HIGH QUALITY SPRAY LUBE
PTFE is a solid lubricant, so this is a "dry" product.

TOOTHBRUSH
You will sometimes find it easier and quicker to degrease components with a toothbrush than anything else.

UTILITY KNIFE
For cutting handlebar tape, electrical insulation and cable tidies.

ALLEN WRENCHES
The long ball-ended type is shown here. Use the ball-end for working in awkward corners and the plain end when you have to undo something really tight.

PTFE-BASED SPRAY LUBRICANT
Forces water away from chain and gears after washing.

COPPER-BASED ANTI-SEIZE GREASE

GREASE INJECTOR PACK
For use on bearings and brake pivots.

WATERPROOF GREASE
For packing bearings.

ENGINEER'S HAMMER
A 16oz or 20oz hammer is excellent for sharp, accurate blows. This type of hammer is much less likely to slip than others.

TORQUE WRENCH
Component and bike manufacturers now say that you should use a torque wrench when working on some of their products. This fairly expensive tool ($50 plus) is fitted with standard socket wrenches and makes a loud click when you have applied a set amount of force to the nut or bolt. The $3/8$in version is best for working on bikes. Check the component manufacturer's table for how much torque should be used for a particular nut or bolt. The guarantee may be invalidated if you do not use a torque wrench on certain components.

MULTI-TOOL
The most useful sizes of Allen wrenches, plus a Phillips screwdriver and a Torx 25 Tool. For use in the workshop and outdoors.

How to use tools

Using the right tools in the correct way will make the job easier. Nuts and bolts have a six-sided shape, usually called a hexagon. If you damage the hexagon with an ill-fitting wrench, it will be a nuisance until the day you replace it. To avoid this, use a tight ring wrench whenever you can. If you have to use an open-ended wrench and it feels loose on the hexagon, find one with a better fit.

The length of each wrench is related to the amount of force needed to tighten each size of nut, so there is no need to use a lot of muscle. You should be able to tighten up anything sufficiently using the pull of three fingers. If the amount of effort required to tighten a nut or bolt suddenly increases, stop tightening immediately as the bolt is probably about to break or you are damaging the thread.

You can apply a bit of extra force when tightening a nut or bolt that keeps on coming loose. But here it is better to fit a self-locking nut, a spring washer or use Loctite thread-locking compound.

Socket head bolts (usually known as Allen screws) look great because they are so neat. But, unlike nuts or bolts, which you can always remove one way or another, damaged Allen wrench fixings are very difficult to remove. So check that the socket is clean to ensure that the Allen wrench goes to the bottom of the socket and make sure also that the Allen wrench is an exact fit. Do not use cheap silver-painted Allen wrenches as they are too soft. If you have a handful of various Allen wrenches and not a complete set, only use the ones with a metric size engraved on the side. That should ensure they are strong enough.

Phillips screwdrivers are quite likely to damage the screw heads unless you use one with a hardened tip. And push hard on the end of the handle to prevent it from slipping.

As for dealing with cables, it is vital to get a proper cable cutter to trim them to length. Improvised tools like pliers will only squash and fray the cable, reducing its life. Cable cutters can also be used for fitting a cable end, which is a soft metal cap. It is clamped around a cable to prevent it from fraying. Fit a cable end and you greatly extend the life of a cable.

GOOD WRENCH WORK

Always try to pull a wrench toward you as that reduces the chances of injury if the wrench slips. When you push a wrench away from you and it slips, your hand can end up anywhere, gouging a chunk out of your knuckle on the way.

1 Whenever possible, use a ring wrench or socket in preference to any other type. They grip a nut or bolt on all six flats, so if you are careful, there is little chance of the wrench slipping and damaging the hexagon.

2 Compared to a ring wrench, an open-ended one is more likely to slip because they only grip on two flats. When you have to use an open-ended, try to prevent it from slipping by steadying your hand against another component nearby.

7 Phillips screws often crop up on gear mechs and pedals. Check that the screwdriver isn't worn and position it in a straight line with the screw before you apply pressure, or it might slip and make it difficult to remove the fixing at all.

8 To cut inner cable, place between the jaws and squeeze. But to cut brake outer cable, let the jaws cut the plastic first and only then the metal inner. To cut outer cable for gears, a quick squeeze should be enough.

3 A set of open-ended wrenches comes in very useful when you need to hold a bolt still while you undo the nut. You have to do this when a bolt turns before the nut comes undone, and when working on some cable clamps.

4 Socket sets are not usually regarded as bike tools but they are ideal where the nut is buried. On some pedals you can only reach the cone lock nut with a socket and extension. They are also good on crank bolts and BMX stunt pegs.

5 Socket head fixings tend to fill with mud. So clean them out and check that the Allen wrench goes all the way to the base of the socket, before using any force. Otherwise the Allen wrench may slip around in the socket and damage it.

6 When a socket head fixing is buried deep in a component, you will only be able to reach it with the long leg of an Allen wrench. Slip a close-fitting length of tubing over the shorter end, so you have enough leverage.

9 Leave about 2 inches of spare cable, bent slightly so that it cannot get caught up in the mechanism of the gear or brake. You can fit a cable end either with pliers or a cable cutter, but they are strictly for one use only.

10 When you are making up your own outer cables, they should be fitted with a metal ferrule at each end. This ensures that the outer cable is correctly seated in the cable stops and does not fray or start to unwind.

11 The outer gear cable is slightly thinner than the outer brake cable. But more important, it is made so that it will not fold in under pressure and prevent the indexing from working accurately. Brake outer cables will compress slightly as they are wound around a spiral.

12 When steel gets distorted, it is often possible to bend it back again, gripping it in a vice or using a couple of adjustable wrenches. But this rearranges all the molecules in the metal and tends to harden it. This work-hardening process takes effect right away, so it is always best to put the damage right in one go. Try to avoid using a series of separate small adjustments.

Quick lube routine

As they whiz around, chains tend to throw off any oil you put on them. They also get covered with dust and any oil that manages to cling on will get washed off by the rain eventually.

If a chain is then allowed to run dry, the chain, chainring and sprockets will all wear out much faster than if they were lubricated. It will also become harder and harder to change the gears. You can prevent this by lubing (lubricating) the chain frequently and by cleaning it thoroughly, as soon as you can see dirt and dust starting to build up on the links. If you spot a similar build-up on the jockey wheels of the rear gear mechanism, you have left it for too long. Full instructions on cleaning chains appear on page 40.

For regular commuters, this frequently means once a week in winter, maybe once every two weeks in summer. Back this up by drying and spraying the chain with water dispersing lubricant when you have been riding in the rain. Leisure riders should lube their bikes after any cross-country trip and soon after any ride over 40 miles on the road.

That leaves the question of when to lube the other points on your bike. If you're just an occasional user, you should go through the whole lube routine every time you lube your chain. But if you use your bike regularly, doing it every three or four times you oil your chain should be enough. Wipe off any surplus lubricant that collects on the surface.

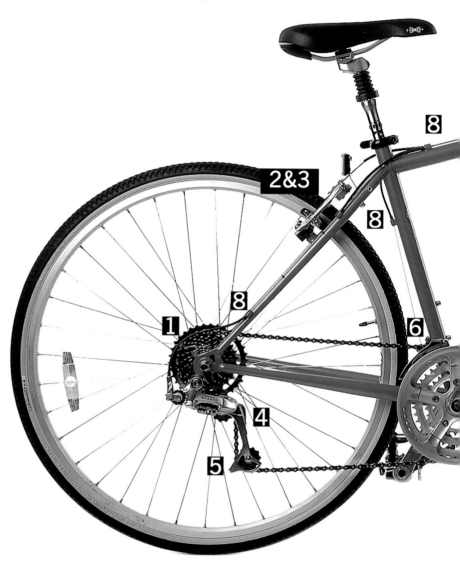

1 Lubricating the chain and sprockets is the number one priority. And scrape any dirt off the sprockets and chainring with a small screwdriver, wipe with a cloth and then lube.

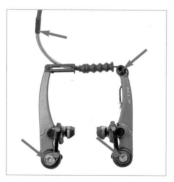

2 Vee brake pivots should be assembled with a spot of grease but need spray lube to keep water and rust at bay. Give the cable attachments and the cable noodle a shot as well.

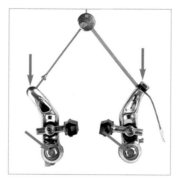

3 Standard cantilevers also need a shot of lube to protect the pivots and just a trace to ensure that the straddle cable does not seize or fray where it joins the brake arms.

4 Rear gear mechanisms need a shot of lube on each of the main pivots, the top pivot and the chain cage pivot. In other words – if it moves, spray it, but only lightly.

7

8

2&3

BRUSH OFF

When using your bike in dry weather, dust collects in all the nooks and crannies. If you do not have time to wash the bike before starting the lube routine, remove all the dust with a dry, one-inch paint brush, but be careful to cover the chain while you do so. This prevents any abrasive dust from being carried into the chain bushes and inner links when you lube the chain.

SLOTS AND STOPS

Most recent bikes have slotted cable stops so you can pull out the outer cables without undoing the inners. This makes it easier to squirt lubricant down the outer cable.

5 Jockey wheels do not pick up much oil from the chain. So they need a squirt to shift any dirt, a wipe and a second shot on the bearings to keep them turning smoothly.

6 The front mech needs a squirt on all the pivots, then a quick wipe around the chain cage. Lube the gear shifters and also wipe any bare inner cable with an oily rag.

7 The brake levers need a shot on the pivots, on the inner cable with the lever pulled back for access and on the cable adjusters. Also check the brake pads for wear.

8 Give all inner cables a squirt where they exit from the outers, especially the rear mech cable. Where necessary, free the outer cables from the stops and fire lube down them.

10-minute safety check – the M Check

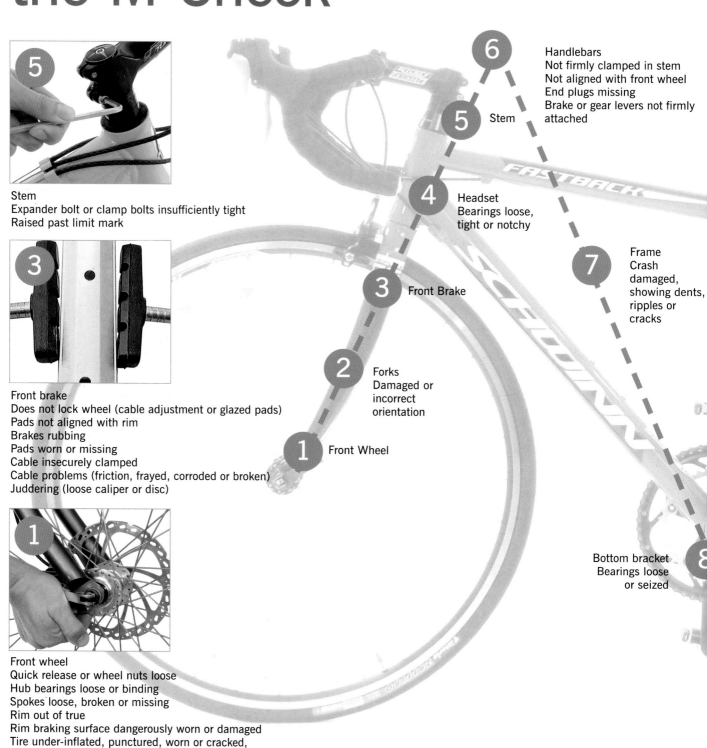

Stem
Expander bolt or clamp bolts insufficiently tight
Raised past limit mark

Front brake
Does not lock wheel (cable adjustment or glazed pads)
Pads not aligned with rim
Brakes rubbing
Pads worn or missing
Cable insecurely clamped
Cable problems (friction, frayed, corroded or broken)
Juddering (loose caliper or disc)

Front wheel
Quick release or wheel nuts loose
Hub bearings loose or binding
Spokes loose, broken or missing
Rim out of true
Rim braking surface dangerously worn or damaged
Tire under-inflated, punctured, worn or cracked, damaged side wall, inner tube not straight

6 Handlebars
Not firmly clamped in stem
Not aligned with front wheel
End plugs missing
Brake or gear levers not firmly attached

5 Stem

4 Headset
Bearings loose, tight or notchy

3 Front Brake

7 Frame
Crash damaged, showing dents, ripples or cracks

2 Forks
Damaged or incorrect orientation

1 Front Wheel

8 Bottom bracket
Bearings loose or seized

The M Check is a good method for carrying out a roadworthiness and safety check, as it minimizes the possibility of missing problems. Start with the front hub and work along the "M." Do this check when you take over a second-hand bike, and roughly every three months as a matter of routine.

There's also a 10-second check on tires and brakes, which you should do every time you ride.

The next two spreads are devoted to wheel checks, because more specialized knowledge is needed in order to carry them out.

Front gears
Not indexed
Limit screws set wrong
Not shifting (defective cable, defective components)

Rear wheel, brake and tire
7 checks on rear brake, as front brake 6 checks on rear wheel, as front wheel

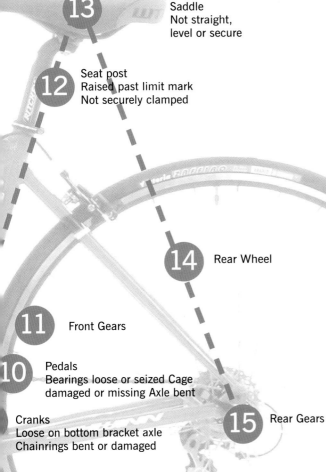

Saddle
Not straight, level or secure

Seat post
Raised past limit mark
Not securely clamped

Rear Wheel

Front Gears

Pedals
Bearings loose or seized Cage damaged or missing Axle bent

Cranks
Loose on bottom bracket axle
Chainrings bent or damaged

Rear Gears

Rear gears
Not indexed
Limit screws set wrong
Defective or incompatible components
Cable friction
Bent gear hanger
Gears jumping (worn components, stiff link)

16

Finally, check for any unsafe accessories like mudguards, racks, locks, chainguards or kickstands.

10-SECOND CHECK, BEFORE EVERY RIDE

Inspect your tires and, if necessary, pump them up.

Make sure your brakes feel OK, and adjust if required.

Removing wheels

When removing or refitting wheels, first operate the quick release on the brakes so there is room for the tire to fit between the brake pads – see page 49. This is particularly important on mountain bikes with their massive tires. Then select the top gear so that the chain is running on the smallest sprocket. If you have a workstand, you can remove the wheels with the bike the normal way up. If not, or you are fixing it by the roadside, turn the bike upside down.

Quick-release hubs are easy to work with, but if you do not tighten them enough, they can come loose and cause an accident. You have to develop an instinct about how hard you have to turn the quick release lever to lock it. If the lever leaves a slight mark on your palm when you have closed it, that is probably tight enough.

Remember that recent bikes have a safety device on the forks that prevents the front wheel from dropping out, even if the quick-release lever is not closed. On these, you have to undo the friction nut several turns before the wheel can be removed.

Most modern bikes are fitted with vertical or semi-vertical rear drop-outs, which are quite easy to use. But older bikes, with horizontal drop-outs, are more of a problem so they are shown here.

When refitting a wheel with hub nuts, the problem is to keep it centralized between the chain stays while you tighten the nuts at the same time. Try steadying the axle with one hand and holding the wrench with the other, then swap, although it is usually easier if you use two wrenches. Then give the wheel nuts a final tightening, using three fingers on the wrench and lots of force.

Wheels fitted with brake discs need extra care. And if they are hydraulic discs, do not touch the brake levers when the wheels are out or you may push the pistons right out of the caliper.

WHEN YOU NEED TO DO THIS JOB:
■ Tire has punctured.
■ Hub bearings need maintenance.
■ Back wheel has pulled over to one side.

TIME:
■ 10 seconds to remove and refit front wheel.
■ 20 seconds to remove a back wheel.
■ 60 seconds to refit back wheel with nuts.

DIFFICULTY:
■ There is a bit of a knack to getting the chain on the sprockets and getting it past the rear mech.
■ Tightening the back wheel nuts alternately, half-a-turn at a time each, while keeping the wheel centralized, is also a knack. You may find it easier using a wrench in each hand.

BACK WHEEL SAFETY SYSTEMS
Watch out for the wheel safety retention system on the back wheel of some bikes with hub nuts. One system uses a pear-shaped washer that fits between the hub nut and the drop-out. The tab on the pear-shaped washer has to be fitted into a slot in the fork end before you fit the hub nut. Both hub nuts are then tightened in the normal way. However, the wheel cannot fall out, even if you have not tightened up the hub nuts enough.

An alternative system is based on dished or conical washers. One washer is fitted under each hub nut, with the serrated side A next to the nuts. A third washer is fitted on the chain side only, between the drop-out and the axle. This time the dogged side B sits next to the frame. Tighten the hub nuts in the usual way.

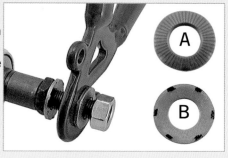

Bolt-in wheels

1 First change to the smallest sprocket, then undo both hub nuts three or four turns. Good-quality hub nuts – usually known as track nuts – have a built-in toothed washer to grip the frame and help prevent the wheel from being pulled to one side. Change to this type if your bike only has plain wheel nuts with a separate washer.

2 Pull the rear mech backward so that the chain cage pivots right out of the way. That will allow the wheel to slide forward out of the drop-outs, although it will be tight. Give the tire a hefty push with your free hand if it sticks.

3 As the wheel drops out of the frame, it will bring the chain with it. So let the rear mech return to normal position and try to lift the wheel away. If it will not come, you will have to lift the chain off the sprocket with your fingers.

4 When you are ready to refit the wheel, pivot the rear mech backward again and pick up the top run of the chain with the top sprocket. Lift the wheel into the mouth of the drop-out, taking care to bring the chain with it.

5 Pull the wheel back into the drop-out and let the rear mech spring back. Next, check that the wheel is centered and fit any safety washers. Tighten the nuts up to finger tightness, check that the rim is centered again and then finally tighten the nuts.

Quick-release wheels

1 For safety reasons, the front fork drop-out on recent bikes has a lip that prevents the front wheel from falling out, even if the quick-release is undone. On older bikes, the front wheel usually drops out as soon as you operate the quick-release.

2 Release the brake, then operate the quick-release. Then hold the friction nut still with one hand while you unscrew the quick-release lever with the other. After a few turns, there will be enough room for you to guide the wheel past the lip.

3 When refitting the wheel, you may have to spread the forks a little to fit the axle into the drop-outs. Then hold the friction nut again and turn the lever clockwise until you have taken nearly all the play out of the quick-release.

4 Initially the quick-release lever requires very little pressure. By halfway, it should need more force and the final locking stage should take quite a push with your palm. If not, tighten the friction nut a little more. Re-set the brake.

WHEELS WITH DISCS

When refitting the wheel, take great care to fit the disc between the brake pads held in the caliper. If you do not, it will simply be impossible to get the wheel back in again. If you have problems, try gently levering the pads apart using a medium-size screwdriver, so there is enough room between them for the disc.

Tire and wheel care

When you spin the front wheel, it should keep on turning for a while and there should not be any kind of grinding or cracking noise. If it seems to slow quite quickly or you can hear odd noises, the hub probably needs stripping down and regreasing. If you can feel any side-to-side movement at the rim, the hub bearings need adjusting – see page 152.

As the wheel turns, use the brake pads or use your thumb to check if the wheel rim moves from side to side or up and down. If you can see that the rim is buckled, see page 156. In addition, all the spokes in a wheel should be at roughly the same tension. If there is a buckle, some of the spokes will probably be loose, but if they all seem to be slack, the wheel needs completely re-tensioning or even re-building by a professional bike mechanic.

No tire runs absolutely true but if the tread wanders from side to side a lot or the tire bulges, try taking it off and refitting it more carefully. If that does not improve things, the tread of the tire may have been put on crooked during manufacture or it may have been damaged. Whatever the explanation, the only solution is a new tire.

When you are checking the tire tread for flints, look also for sponginess, deep cuts and an excessive number of cuts. If there are more than half a dozen or so cuts, or you can see the individual threads in the sidewall, the tire is coming to the end of its days. At that stage, punctures are much more likely.

You may have trouble pumping up a tire with a Presta valve, particularly when using a push-on adaptor. If so, undo the knurled brass valve nut two thirds of the way, then push in the valve stalk for a second, just in case it is stuck. Push the adaptor onto the valve, check it is straight and hold the pump horizontal. Finally, wrap your index finger around the valve to hold the pump in the correct position.

Inflating tires

1 To pump up a Presta valve tube, undo the knurled nut all the way and push in the stalk a fraction until you hear a hiss of escaping air. This ensures that the valve is not stuck. Try wiggling the stalk if it is hard to pump up the tire.

Five-minute tire and wheel check

1 Lift the front and then the back wheel off the ground and give it a spin to check the hub bearings. Then use the brake pads as a fixed point so you can gauge if the rim or tire is not running straight. If disc brakes are fitted, carefully position your thumb close to the rim and use that as the fixed point.

Pumps

1 If you get tired of pumping up tires with a conventional pump, a track pump will do the job much faster.

2 You can usually inflate both Schrader and Presta valves with the adaptor that is fitted to a track pump.

3 As an alternative to a normal mini-pump, you can get a miniature track pump that packs away.

2 Utility and mountain bikes often use a Schrader valve, which is much fatter than a Presta. Some pumps fit both types but you may need an adaptor, so check. Don't use garage air lines on Schrader valves – it is dangerous.

3 Most pumps just push onto the valve but the air will escape if you push the adaptor on too far. If you're having trouble, check that the adaptor is squarely on the valve and steady your hand with a finger around the valve or a spoke.

4 When you have fully inflated a tire with a Presta valve, check that the valve is at right angles to the rim and tighten the valve nut to finger tightness. Don't tighten it more than that as it might cause the valve to leak. Then fit the dust cap.

5 Pump up MTB tires until they are firm, not hard. Set them to the figure on the tire wall, typically 45psi, with a tire pressure gauge. Hybrid tires should be harder (50 to 70psi) but sports bike tires should hardly dent (90 to 120psi). See the table on the next spread.

2 If the tire isn't running straight, take it off and refit it, fitting the beads right into the well of the rim. Then, whether the wheel is buckled or not, stretch each pair of spokes with finger and thumb to see if their tension is equal.

3 Go around the tire with a small screwdriver next, prying out any flints stuck in the tread. Look out for deep cuts, whether or not there is a flint embedded in them. It is best to fit a new tire if there is any serious damage.

4 The tire wall may be covered by a thin coat of colored waterproof rubber, or maybe tread rubber. If the fabric is showing or there are any cuts or splits, let the tire down so you can see how bad the damage is.

5 Try turning the axle with your fingers. If it feels gritty or tight, strip and regrease. If it feels like the bearings are dragging but are running smoothly, run two drops of oil into the bearing or, better still, strip and regrease.

Changing tires

When you decide to renew your tires, go for ones with a Kevlar carcass. They cost a little more but resist punctures so well that it's worth the extra cost. Kevlar is an enormously strong composite fiber that is made into a tape and placed under the tread. There it resists glass and gravel, only letting the sharpest materials through to cause a puncture. There are other puncture-resisting layers as well, such as a foam-like material that is placed under the tread. Again they cost a little but are worth a lot, preventing punctures from things like nails and screws which may enter the foam layer but usually aren't long enough to penetrate

But like anything else, tire rubber tends to perish over time. So if you are bringing a bike back into use after four or five years, you should budget for new tires, even if the tread appears to be good.

When you're fitting a new tire, a lot of people fit a new tube as well, just in case. But don't use tire levers unless you absolutely have to, because they're responsible for a lot of punctures. If you do have to use them, make sure the ends are nicely rounded and watch closely what you do. Putting the end of the tire lever on the tube is a guarantee that you'll cause a puncture.

Removing a tire

1 This tire is vulnerable to punctures. Let the tire down by unscrewing and pressing a Presta valve or pressing the center stalk of a Schrader valve.

2 Push the rounded end of a tire lever under the edge of the tire, opposite the valve. Pull the tire lever down hard to lift the bead over the edge of the rim, then hook it onto a spoke. Repeat about four or five inches apart.

3 Once the first part of the tire is off, take the rest off by putting your hand under the tire and moving it around in a sweeping movement.

4 When one side of the tire is fully off, pull out the tube.

Fitting a new tire

1 Slip one side of the tire onto the rim. If there's an arrow on the sidewall, it must point the way the bike is going.

2 Pump up the inner tube so that it takes a shape but no more. If it forms a circle, it's probably over-inflated.

3 Start putting in the tube at the valve, pressing down hard to seat the valve properly in the rim. Keep the valve at right angles to the rim.

4 Tuck the rest of the tube into the tire, keeping it straight. Lift the tire into position at the valve with your thumbs. Then fit the bead about two thirds of the way around.

Tire carcasses and rim tapes

It's not unknown for tires to need changing, before the tread is worn out. Here are a couple of reasons to change tires prematurely but there are many others as well.

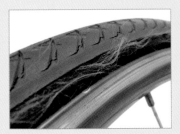

This tire is very old. As a result, the carcass suffers from micro-cracking and some of the yarn that makes up the carcass is escaping from the sides. The tread is fine but one day, this tire will fail disastrously.

Again, this tire is old and the waterproofing on the sidewall has gone. But the real problem is that the carcass has been damaged and is starting to balloon. One day this tire will blow-out quite suddenly.

This shows a plastic rim tape in nearly new condition. Rim tapes cost so little that you should replace them if their condition is ever in doubt. Go for the plastic type, or preferably the stick-on variety.

5 When you reach the valve, push the bead back over the rim and pull the valve out of the rim.

6 You can now pull off the other side of the tire.

7 Check around the rim tape and the spoke nipples, making sure that none can penetrate the tube. File the spoke nipple(s) flat and fit a new rim tape if necessary.

Tire pressures

Heavier riders will need higher pressures.

Racer and Hybrid

Tire Width	Max Pressure	
	bar	psi
23mm	9.5	140
25mm	9	130
28mm	8	120
32mm	7	100

Mountain/City/Comfort

	bar	psi
1.50in/37mm	6	90
1.75in/45mm	5.2	75
2.00in/51mm	4.3	60
2.30in/58mm	3.35	50

5 This is crucial . . . seat the tire into the rim and stretch it around. This takes some doing, so you may have to repeat it several times.

6 If you've stretched the tire correctly, you'll be able to lift the final part of the tire over the rim with your thumbs. Only use tire levers as a last resort.

7 Check that the tire is seated correctly all around and that the valve is at right angles with the rim. Spin the wheel to confirm all is well.

8 Inflate the tire slightly more, checking that it's centered on the rim and seated correctly around the valve. If it's right, inflate fully.

Fixing punctures

The easiest way to find a puncture is to pump the tire up before removing it and listening for the hiss of escaping air. Alternatively, see if you can feel the air on your lips or cheek. If that doesn't work, take out the tube and pump it up a little. Then dunk it in a bowl of water, if you are at home, and watch for the string of bubbles. That will indicate exactly the location of the puncture, however small it is. If you're forced to repair a puncture by the roadside, look for a suitable puddle or even a stream.

Once you've located the puncture, figure out what caused it and fix that as well as the puncture itself. There is nothing worse than fixing a puncture and refitting the tube, only to find that it happens again because you haven't fixed whatever the cause is.

In general, the best safeguard against punctures is to keep the tires well-inflated, see previous page. But if the rim tapes are in a questionable state, you'll go on getting punctures until you replace them.

Many riders go for the adhesive cloth sort but the plastic type is very good too. On the other hand, if you've allowed the brake pad to contact the sidewall, there's nothing for it but to fit a new tire and tube. And adjust the position of the brake pads.

You might be tempted to use self-adhesive patches. But they don't seem to stick as well as the others, so treat them as just a get-you-home device. Many riders also regard a repaired tube as a get-you-home measure, replacing them whenever they are punctured. Some even carry a spare tube. However, it's unwise to rely totally on a spare tube as you sometimes pick up more than one puncture on a ride.

There are also various sealing solutions that you put in the tire, and special tapes that go next to the tube, all to stop punctures. But the real way is first of all to keep your tires in good shape. Secondly, to fit tires with Kevlar carcasses. And thirdly, if you are going off-road or travelling on urban roads littered with broken glass and so on, fit tires with a protective belt under the tread as well as a Kevlar carcass.

When repairing a puncture on the back wheel, do it from the non-chain side to avoid the oil on the chain side. And fit butyl tubes because they are slightly puncture-resistant, are easier to fit and hold the air better. Latex tubes are lighter so they're mainly for racing.

Plastic rim tapes.

A modern puncture kit, with feather-edge patches that blend into the tube, plus a tire patch. But unlike traditional puncture kits, it doesn't have either a crayon for marking the tube or talcum powder.

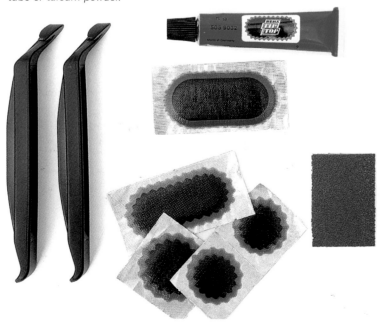

BUBBLE TROUBLE

If a tire keeps going down but you cannot find the puncture, the valve may be slowly leaking air. This will show up if you remove the tube and dunk it in water, but there is a way of checking without going that far. Just fill a small cup or clean yogurt container with water and dip the valve in. If there is a stream of bubbles, you will have to fit a new tube if it is a Presta valve, or screw in a new insert if it is a Schrader.

Repairing punctures

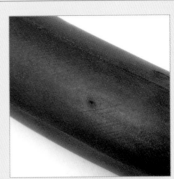

1 Locate the puncture. Then lay the tube out on the tire, so that you can figure out from the tube where it may be punctured or damaged.

2 It turns out that the puncture was caused by a screw penetrating the tread and making a hole in it. Leave the screw in place for now.

CAUSES OF PUNCTURES

There are five main causes of punctures, although the first two are responsible for the vast majority:

1. Simple puncture. Where something penetrates the tread or the sidewall. Usually the tire is undamaged, or has repairable damage, unless the sidewall fails.

2. Snakebite puncture. When the tire is under-inflated, a big bump causes the edges of the rim to trap the tube. It causes two simultaneous punctures across the tube.

3. Tire worn out. Not a cause of punctures as such, more a reason for tread or sidewall punctures. See previous page.

4. Rim tape. A puncture on the underside of the tube, caused by a defective or non-existent rim tape.

5. Brake pads. An uneven, elongated puncture in the side of the tube. Caused by the brake pads touching the tire and eventually wearing through. Usually the tire needs replacing and the brake pads repositioning.

Before you try to fix a puncture, examine the tube and then lay it out on the tire. You should be able to diagnose the type of puncture from its position, and figure out whether the tire is OK or needs to be tossed.

3 The tube was roughened with the sandpaper supplied in the puncture kit, then rubber solution is applied and spread evenly.

4 When the rubber solution has dried, check where the puncture is, stick the patch on and rub it down from the center toward the edges.

5 When the edges are stuck down, break the transparent covering by folding it in half and peel it away from the middle.

6 The tread has been damaged, so remove the cause and apply a repair patch. It's stuck to the tire in exactly the same way as a puncture patch on a tube. Then replace the tube in the tire and pump it up to full pressure, see the previous page. If you get a lot of punctures, you are doing something wrong. Either not replacing the tire or the rim tape when they are worn out. Or not pumping up the tires enough or perhaps buying the wrong tires in the first place.

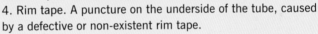
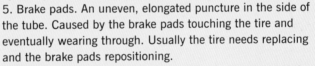
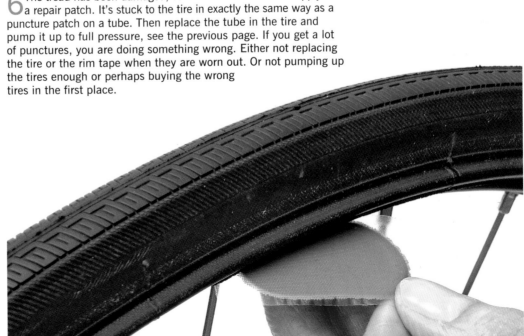

Chain and gears

Chains need frequent attention if they are to keep working efficiently. We have already covered lubing the chain, but it does no harm to repeat that it must be done frequently. However, cleaning the chain is almost as vital, followed once again by lubrication.

How often you need to clean a chain will vary according to use. For mountain bikes used across country, it should be done after every ride. For bikes used on the road, 500 miles is a general guide. However, if it is raining constantly during the winter or spring, and you have to keep putting lube on the chain, it's probably worth cleaning it every 250 miles.

You also need to keep an eye open for chain wear. Test the chain by pulling a link away from a tooth on the chainwheel. If you can move it away more than an eighth of an inch, it needs investigating, see page 113.

But the chain problem that demands swift attention is a stiff link. This shows up as a slight jump or glitch in the driveline, or a slight click or cough in the chain, occurring every two or three turns of the pedal. You need a chain tool to correct it, though the hardest job is finding the stiff link. If you don't find it, chances are that the chain will break eventually.

As for the gears, you can usually get the indexing working by just increasing the tension on the cable by something like half a turn of the cable adjuster. If not, chances are that the outer cable between the frame and the rear mech needs attention. A quick flush with solvent may be enough but if not, fit a new one. You can make one yourself, or ready-made ones are available at any bike shop. Remember that gear outer cable is slightly thinner than brake outer cable, and isn't interchangeable.

On the other hand, if you tip the chain down between the sprockets and the frame, or the other way, between the sprockets and the wheel, the high limit screw (marked H) or the low limit screw (marked L) require attention, see page 77.

Chain care

1 This is the latest type of chain cleaning machine. It comes with a can of aerosol chain cleaner, so you just open up the chain machine.

HOW TO USE YOUR GEARS

REMEMBER:
The low gears are for climbing hills. Middle gears are for flat ground. Top gear is strictly for descents.

AT THE BACK WHEEL:
The small sprocket is top gear, the largest sprocket is bottom gear.

BUT AT THE FRONT:
The small chainring is low gear, and the biggest ring is high gear.

Automatic chain cleaner

If you have to service your bike in the house or somewhere else where it is vital to keep the floor clean, a chain cleaning machine is very useful. First, you take the top off and position the machine on the bottom run of chain, near the rear mech. Then you hook the arm behind the bottom jockey wheel and refit the top. The machine must now be filled with solvent. To help this process, there is an automatic measuring system.

Finally, you just turn the pedals backward and as the chain runs through the machine, it is scrubbed clean by several sets of revolving brushes. Dispose of the used solvent responsibly.

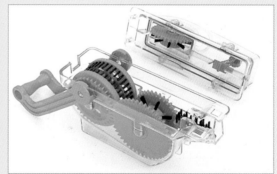

2 Then clamp it on the bottom run of the chain and turn the pedals backward. Don't just throw the used solvent down the drain.

3 To gauge the amount of chain wear, lift the chain off the chainring. The more wear, the further it will lift away until it reaches ⅛ inch.

4 You can detect a stiff link by the regular jump or cough every two or three turns of the pedals. The chain'll break if you leave it.

5 Put the chain on the nearside guides, and then turn the handle about ¹⁄₁₀ of a turn. If that doesn't work, repeat the process.

Rear mech

1 When the indexing goes astray, the first thing is to increase the tension on the gear cable via the cable adjuster. In general, on racing bikes and hybrids it's on the rear mech but on every other type it's on the handlebars at the gear shifter. Adjust the cable tension by turning ¼ or ½ turn at a time.

2 If that doesn't work, free the cable from the rear mech and slip it out of the cable stop. Spray it with WD-40, and flush the outer cable to clean it.

3 Wipe it carefully with a rag, lubricate and then fit it back onto the rear mech. Give it a test ride. If that hasn't worked, fit a new outer cable.

4 If you don't have a ready made cable handy, you can fit a homemade alternative. Remember to fit cable ferrules at both ends of the outer.

5 Check that the limit screws are adjusted correctly, particularly the one for top gear. Then re-attach to the rear mech and road test.

Wash and polish

If your bike is really dirty, the first thing to do is to deal with the mud. When it's fresh you can probably just brush it off. But if it's had a chance to dry out, dampen it thoroughly before you attempt to clean the bike.

Then go for an alkaline or neutral general-purpose cleaner. It's a simple spray-on job that cuts through dirt, oil and pretty well every other sort of contaminant. Then apply a spray that will repel any water in parts like the chain and the gears, and leave a protective PTFE finish.

Alternatively, if your bike is generally soiled but isn't really dirty, you can just wash it with warm water and car shampoo.

Sometimes the chain, the gears and the bottom bracket are covered in oil. In that case, you will need to back up the general-purpose cleaner with a specially made degreaser. This is sprayed on, scrubbed with a brush and flushed away with water. Racing mechanics place the bike in a bike stand first. Then the chain and associated parts get a dose of degreaser, followed by several sponges of warm water to flush it away. The process is finished off with a special chain lubricant.

If your bike is fitted with disc brakes, you'll find that oil, grease and pad residue all tend to get baked-on. Again it's a spray-on job, with a specially formulated cleaner which will bring the disc surface back to new.

Don't wash your bike in the sun as the water will dry off too quickly. And don't use a pressure washer either, as bike bearings aren't designed to keep out water under pressure. For the same reason, if you use a hose let the water cascade down over the bike but don't squirt it directly at the hubs, headset, bottom bracket or gears. Keep the bike upright as well, either standing on its own wheels or in a bike stand.

Disc brakes generate high temperatures when used in anger, which tends to bake on the dirt. Remove it all and get back to a plain metal surface with a special cleaner.

Using bike cleaner

1 Remove the first layer of dirt with a brush, so the cleaner can go to work on the bike itself later.

2 Now spray the bike with a slightly alkaline cleaner. Scrub with a brush wherever the bike is particularly dirty.

3 Wash off the cleaner with plenty of water, preferably warm or hot. Then apply the PTFE-based finish.

4 The finished bike is shiny and the PTFE spray polish protects against water getting in anywhere.

Using car shampoo

1 Squirt some car shampoo into a bucket of hot water. Apply a first coat to the whole bike using an old sponge or dishwashing brush, but give it time to work. Then give it a second coat, using an old dishwashing brush or something similar.

2 If you have time, get a bucket of clean warm water and rinse the foam away. Use a sponge to cascade water over the frame, the mudguards and the hubs if necessary. Look for any areas that have been missed or need extra attention.

3 Wherever the foam seems to form droplets and roll off, use a degreaser to break down the film of oil. Work it with a brush to ensure the dirt and oil mixes with the degreaser. Then flush it away with plenty of water, particularly the chain and gears.

4 Dry the frame, mudguards, saddle and handlebars with a clean rag or a chamois. Then squirt PTFE-based lube over the chain, gears, hubs and headset to drive out any water that has gotten in. Lube the chain with a special lubricant.

CHAPTER

BRAKING
SYSTEMS

Types of brake

Although there are many different designs, most braking systems work by pressing a pad against the braking surface on the wall of the wheel rim. How well this works depends on how hard the pad is forced against the rim, how flat the braking surface of the rim is and how well the pad material bites on it.

Brake pads wear fairly fast but do not forget that the braking surface of a wheel rim also wears. However, if the pad material is kept clean, it wears very slowly. Only if the rim is allowed to become seriously worn is there a real danger of the wheel collapsing without warning.

Luckily, most rims are now equipped with a wear line. So long as the wear line is visible, you are safe. However, older bikes don't have a wear line, and you have to rely on your own judgement. In this case, check the condition of the rims when you change the brake pads and occasionally during use. Have the wheel rebuilt with a new rim when wear reaches 1.5mm.

Disc brakes are the big exception to all this, but they can only be fitted if the wheels and frame are suitable. Discs work much better than rim brakes in bad weather and deep mud, so they are ideal on MTBs. And they rule out any problems with worn wheel rims.

Hub brakes are now becoming more popular as well. Their big advantages are that they need little in the way of maintenance and are pretty well waterproof. They are covered in Chapter 5.

CANTILEVER BRAKES
Fitted to older mountain bikes, and a few cyclocross and touring bikes as well.
This is a sound design that has now been overtaken on mountain bikes by vee brakes, leaving specialized use only. Nevertheless, standard cantis combine low weight, powerful stopping and plenty of clearance for mud.

DUAL PIVOT BRAKES
Now standard on road bikes, except for Campagnolo, who have gone back to side pull brakes at the rear. Each brake arm moves independently on a separate backplate. Once correctly set up, the brake pads stay at an equal distance from the wheel rim, without constant fiddling. Most are 49mm deep but 57mm ones are available for bikes that require a deeper caliper.

HUB BRAKES
Several types of hub brake are on the market, usually fitted to city bikes. This type is a roller brake, which needs practically no maintenance. Other types like a standard hub brake are stand-alone, or are combined with a hub gear or dynamo. This type of brake is covered in Chapter 5.

VEE BRAKES

Standard on moderately priced MTBs and some hybrids, Vee brakes require less effort at the lever than cantilevers, and are more powerful. But they need careful setting up after replacing cables and pads and this often gets forgotten. As a result, they often perform far below their potential. Special BMX versions are also on the market.

DISC BRAKES

For mountain bikes, but also a few city bikes as well, where their low maintenance is attractive. Probably the most effective braking system, especially in wet conditions. Hydraulic disc brakes need very little effort at the brake lever but cable-operated discs are not quite as effective.

SIDE PULL BRAKES

Largely replaced by dual pivot brakes, there are still many in use on older road bikes. The type shown has a 57mm deep caliper to reach around mudguards and wide tires. Shallow, 49mm versions are also available. Side pulls are fiddly to work on and not very powerful.

Brakes: inspection and lube

There is nearly always a lot of give when you pull the brake lever. Some of it is cable stretch, the lever itself also flexes a little and so do the brake arms. However, brake arms should be quite stiff. If you notice they flex more than a few millimeters, consider upgrading to better quality brakes. If you have standard cantis, that usually means fitting Vee brakes.

Road bike brake arms are longer and thinner than the ones fitted to MTBs, so they usually flex more. Side pull brakes are particularly bad for this, and it is also very difficult to keep them centered correctly. Dual pivot road brakes do not suffer from these problems, so they are much more effective.

If you notice that you pull the brake levers fairly close in to the handlebars when braking normally, cable stretch and pad wear has reached the point where servicing is well overdue.

Test, inspect and adjust

1 Test the brakes by pulling the brake lever. It should not take much effort at first, then the pads will hit the rim. If you then pull harder, it will just stretch the cable a bit more. If the brake lever ends up close to the handlebar, adjustment is needed urgently.

2 Check for worn brake pads, for contamination on the pad surface and wear ridges as well. If the slots are nearly worn away or the wear line is almost gone, fit new pads. Do the same if you cannot remove the contamina-tion or the wear ridges go deep into the rubber.

Brake lubrication

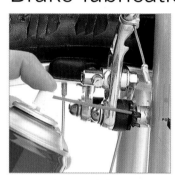 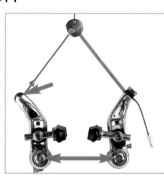

1 If the frame has slotted cable stops, pull the outer cable out of the slot so you can fire lube down the outer cable. If not, just lube the inner cable. On standard cantilevers, aim one shot of lube at the back of each pivot, where it will protect the spring from rust.

2 Standard cantis need another shot for the front of the pivots (double arrow) and just a drip on the free end of the straddle cable. This is to prevent it from getting stuck in its slot. Remember that the brake levers also need a drip of spray lube on the pivot.

QUICK-RELEASE
If the quick-release does not work or is missing, try screwing the cable adjuster in clockwise as far as possible. That should slacken off the cable enough to let you remove the wheel. If it is still not possible to remove the wheel, try letting the tire down. When fitting new cables, it is a good idea to set the cable adjuster in the middle of its travel so that you can use it as a quick-release if necessary.

THE BRAKING SURFACE
The braking surface formed by the wall of the wheel rim is the forgotten part of the braking system. First of all, the brake pad must be compatible with the material that the rim is made of. Most rims are made of aluminum alloy, and you should have no trouble buying pads to suit. But some utility bikes have chrome-plated steel rims and alloy-compatible pads just will not grip on them. If you notice the braking has become lumpy and uneven, that's a sign that the rims are wearing out.

Some rims have a wear line that indicates how far the rim has to go before it should be rebuilt, but on bikes without a wear line use your fingernail as a guide. Surface marks don't matter, but if the lines are so deep that you can catch your nail in them they need replacing. Alternatively, replace them when the wear reaches 1.5mm.

3 Now adjust the cables using the cable adjuster on the brake lever, on MTBs. Undo the thin locknut using pliers if it is stiff. Try tightening the adjuster two turns counter-clockwise but always leave three full threads in the lever for safety, to prevent it from coming out.

4 On road bikes, undo the locknut and screw the adjuster out one turn. Test the amount of brake lever travel and readjust if necessary. Where there is not enough adjustment left, loosen the cable clamp, pull some cable through and then re-tighten.

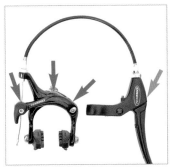

3 On Vee brakes, the cables and brake levers need the same treatment. The pivots need a squirt of lube on each side of the brake arm and so does the slotted link between pivot and pad, where fitted. Finally, give the cable holder and noodle a few drops.

4 Dual pivot brakes need a touch of lubricant where the spring touches the arm, and on both of the pivots, plus the brake lever. On the other hand side pull brakes tend to have a lot of friction, so in addition to lubricating the spring and the central pivot, clean the brake arms as well. If that doesn't work, try fitting a new cable.

TAKE CARE WITH THE OIL CAN

When lubricating the braking system, take care not to drip oil or aerosol lube onto the rims or pads. It is OK to wipe oil off the braking surface, provided you do it thoroughly. But oil will sometimes contaminate the brake pads permanently.

Quick releases

Most braking systems have a quick-release device to increase the pad clearance when removing a wheel.

1 Vee brakes have a fiddly quick-release. First grasp the top of the brake arms and squeeze them together. Then try to steady the cable holder with your thumb while you pull and lift the cable pipe, or noodle, and cable away from the cable holder. You have to lift the inner cable out of a narrow slot in the cable holder, so do not use force.

2 On cantilevers, squeeze the brake arms together with one hand while you unhook the loose end of the straddle wire with the other. If it will not budge, slacken the cable off with the adjuster, then use a pair of pliers.

3 Most road bikes have a quick-release near the cable adjuster. You pull it up when changing the wheel and push it down to close the pads up against the rim. Sometimes, you turn the cable holder through 90°.

4 On Campag Ergopower brake levers, the quick-release button is on the brake lever. Push it in for more clearance. It resets automatically when you next use the brakes.

Vee brakes

Vee brakes are close relatives of the standard cantilever but nearly all the problems of the ordinary canti are removed. They are light enough to operate with two fingers, because the extended brake arms give more leverage. Fitting and adjustment is easier because there is only one cable. And they are more powerful, partly because of the extra leverage and partly because the brake cable works at 90° to the brake arms.

As a result, they have a very direct or linear effect, meaning that the amount of pull on the brake lever is translated directly into the same amount of pull on the brakes. If you used Vee brake levers with cantilever brakes, braking effect would be hard to control and braking power would be inadequate. Conversely, cantilever brake levers used with Vee brakes would not offer enough cable pull to operate the brakes correctly. Worse still, if the brakes *did* contact the rims, the excessive leverage would risk locking the wheels. Both combinations are potentially dangerous; never mix Vee brake and cantilever parts. One other warning – you must use Vee brakes very gently to start with. They stop you so fast, compared with ordinary bike brakes, that you must get used to them before using their full power.

If your bike has cantis, it's easy to upgrade to vee brakes. But your frame must be fitted with brake bosses 80mm from center to center. Check this measurement if the bosses look bent or you can't get Vee brakes to work well.

For fitting Vee brake pads, see pages 64–65. Make sure you fit the cables correctly because the majority of Vee brakes in daily use are incorrectly fitted. Many are even being used with the cable pipe or noodle missing, so they are almost useless. Luckily, spare cable noodles are now supplied separately by Fibrax and other firms selling brake pads and cables, so it's easy to fix.

1 Most vee brakes are operated by combined gear and brake levers. There is a normal cable adjuster but Servo Wave brake levers also have a device to regulate the amount of pull needed. Do not alter this setting yourself.

6 Lube the cable noodle and pull the inner cable through until the slack is taken up. Fit the inner through the slot in the cable holder and position the end of the cable noodle in the cable holder as well. Pull the inner cable tight

BRAKE LEVERS
The angle of the brake levers can easily be changed. Just locate the single screw that holds them in place, loosen, reset the angle and tighten. You can also adjust the reach of the brake levers in most cases: if there is a tiny screw set in the angle between the cable and the fixed part of the lever, screw it in or out to alter the reach.

2 First of all, test fit the brake arms on the pivots. If they seem tight, remove any paint or polish the metal with a light abrasive and test again. Once the brake arms move easily on the pivots but without any slop, apply a little grease.

3 Each brake arm has a small coil spring with a stopper pin on the end. Fit this pin into the middle hole of the boss – do not use the other two. Then push the brake arm onto the pivot and screw the fixing bolt into place.

4 Make sure that the long part of the spring is on the frame side of the brake arm, where it sits up against a metal lug. Next, tighten the fixing bolt, which presses the brake arm onto the pivot, and then fit the other brake arm.

5 Flip open the cable cover (arrow in step 1) on the brake lever, push the plain end of the inner cable through the brake lever and adjuster, then the outer cable. Finally, feed the inner cable through the cable pipe or noodle.

7 Slide the cable bellows onto the inner cable and thread the end into the cable clamp. Rotate the brake arms into an upright position and check that there is exactly 39mm of inner cable showing between the brake arms.

8 Tighten the cable clamp but not fully yet. Adjust the brake pads as explained on page 65, making sure that there is an equal gap between the pad and the rim on each side. The pad-to-rim gap should be about 2mm total.

9 Fully tighten the cable clamp. Then use the cable adjuster on the brake lever to check that the total pad-to-rim gap is around 2mm. Finally, adjust the tiny Phillips or socket head screws on the brake arms to equalize the pad-to-rim gap.

WHEN YOU NEED TO DO THIS JOB:
■ When upgrading from standard cantis.
■ The grease on the brake bosses has dried up.

TIME:
■ Two hours to remove old brakes, clean up pivots and fit both new brakes.

DIFFICULTY: ⚒⚒⚒
■ It can be tricky getting the brake arms as upright as possible, while keeping the 39mm between them. It sounds easy but it can take time.

BRAKE MODULATION

Brake modulators are found on quite a few recent bikes. Some modulators are built into the brake lever, as on the Shimano Servo Wave brake lever for vee brakes. Others are fitted to the brake arm, yet others are part of the brake cable on some children's bikes. It is said that by adjusting the modulator, you can choose exactly the amount of power that the brake will produce and the length of pull needed on the lever. However, the real reason for fitting modulators is to enable bike manufacturers to buy only one type of lever and use it with various types of brake. Probably the best thing to do is leave the modulator alone unless you have very definite reasons for fiddling with it.

Cantilever brakes: strip and adjustment

The most common type of cantilever brake is produced by Shimano. In this design, the main brake cable passes through a cable carrier. It then goes to one side of the caliper and is directly connected to one of the brake arms. The other arm is connected to the cable carrier by a link wire.

Link wire calipers need a bit of care in setting them up but they give better control over braking. They also make it possible to modulate the amount of braking, so it is easier to make a controlled stop.

The original design of cantilever brake was also adopted by Shimano, though it has not been made by them for some years. It is made in small numbers for touring bikes and cyclocross by Avid and other manufacturers. It depends on a straddle cable, which joins the brake arms and is then connected to the main brake cable by a metal yoke or cable carrier. When the main brake cable is pulled, the cable carrier moves upward and the straddle wire pulls the brake arms. However, unless the brake is set up very accurately it tends to pull one brake arm harder than the other.

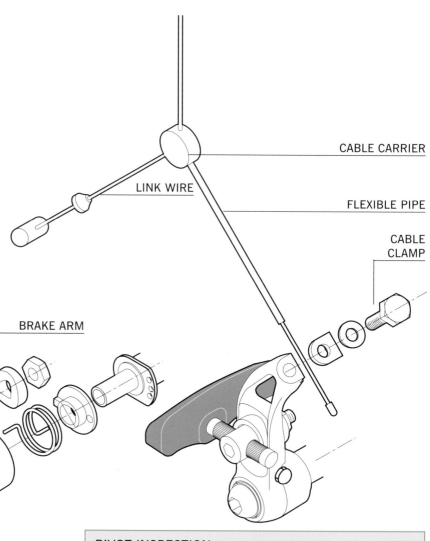

CABLE CARRIER

LINK WIRE

FLEXIBLE PIPE

CABLE CLAMP

BRAKE ARM

BRAKE PAD

PIVOT INSPECTION
When you strip down standard cantis or vee brakes, always inspect the frame pivots. If they are rusty, polish with emery cloth and reassemble with waterproof grease on the pivots. Check that the pivots are straight by measuring between their centers. If the distance is 80mm, they are probably OK. If not, or they look bent, get them looked at by a bike mechanic as you might have to get new pivots brazed on.

1 Screw in the cable adjuster to reduce the tension on the brake cable. If there is a straddle wire, unhook one end and lift it out of the yoke. On a link wire type of brake, undo the cable clamp with a Allen wrench and pull the cable away from the brake arm.

2 Undo the pivot bolt, freeing the brake arm and allowing you to pull it off the pivot boss. Try to hold the spring and washer in place on the pivot bolt or they could fly anywhere. Clean up all the parts ready for reassembly.

3 Once you have cleaned and greased the pivots, fit the spring into the middle hole on the pivot boss and fit the brake arm followed by the pivot bolt. Turn the adjuster with a wrench until each pad is 2mm from the rim, then lock by tightening the pivot bolt again. It is important to set pads an equal distance from the rim at this point. On standard cantis, you can fit the spring in the other holes in the pivot boss, if you want to increase or decrease the power of the spring, although the middle hole is nearly always right.

4 To make fine adjustments to the pad-to-rim distance, there is often a small screw at the base of the cantilever arm. Adjust by turning the screw clockwise to move the pad away from the rim and counter-clockwise to bring the pad closer to it.

5 Aim for a situation where the pads are equally spaced, 2mm from the rim. Sometimes the pads are also toed-in about 1mm, but this varies with the type of brake and brake pad. Full brake pad adjustment is covered on page 65.

WHEN YOU NEED TO DO THIS JOB:
■ Brakes feel stiff or jerky when you pull the brake lever and neither lubrication nor a new cable are any help.

TIME:
■ 30 minutes.

DIFFICULTY:
■ It is sometimes fiddly to fit the spring in the hole on the pivot and to adjust pad clearance.

Replacing cantilever cables

Though pretty rare now, the original type of cantilever brakes, using a triangular cable carrier and a short straddle wire, is still around. The brake cable is fitted to the cable carrier with a normal cable clamp, and the straddle wire sits in a channel at the back.

To set up a basic cantilever properly, first adjust the length of the straddle wire so that it roughly makes a right-angle with the brake arm when you lift it in the middle. Fit the straddle wire into the cable carrier next. Then try to gauge where the cable carrier should be fitted on the main brake cable. It must be high enough to pull the brakes on fully but not so high that it hits the outer cable or anything else that would prevent the brakes from coming on fully.

On both other types of cantilever brake, the main brake cable clamps directly to one of the brake arms, with a short link wire joining the cable carrier to the other one. Early designs have a cable carrier with a bolt running through it, or two separate slots for the cable. The wide slot is for adjusting the cable, the narrow one for when the brake is in use.

The latest link wire brakes have a cable carrier with a diagonal line running across it, or a round window for the nipple of the link wire.

The first step when fitting a new brake cable is to slide it into the cable carrier. Then slide the flexible hose onto the brake cable and fit the cable into the cable clamp on the brake arm. Set the length of the brake cable so that the end of the flexible hose touches both the cable carrier and the brake arm, then tighten the cable clamp. Now hook the link wire into the other brake arm and check that the link wire roughly aligns with the diagonal line running across the cable carrier, as in the picture in Step 7.

Next, adjust the spring tension with the small Phillips screws on the brake arms. Spring tension is correct when the cable carrier sits directly below the point where the inner cable emerges from the outer. Now fit the brake pads but do not worry if they touch the rim at this stage.

Reset the length of the main brake cable so there is a 2 to 3mm gap between the end of the flexible hose and the brake arm. When you have done so, the link wire should line up with the diagonal line across the cable carrier, as in the bottom picture in Step 7. Provided it does, center the brake pads using the Phillips screws again. Finally, make sure there is at least 20mm of free cable above the cable carrier.

On all types of cantilever brakes, the final stage is to adjust the pads properly – see page 64.

Link wire cantilevers

1 Screw in the cable adjuster and pull out the old cable. Check that the new nipple fits, grease it lightly and insert the nipple into the hole. Slide the outer cable over the inner and insert both into the adjuster.

2 On the early type, unhook the link wire from the brake arm next. Then, feed the new brake cable through the wider slot in the cable carrier and slide the flexible hose over the end of the cable.

Straddle wire cantilevers

1 Feed the brake cable into the cable clamp on the cable carrier and tighten lightly. Squeeze the brake pads against the rims and see if you can now lift the straddle cable into the channel on the back of the cable carrier. If it is a tight fit, lengthen the main brake cable slightly. If it is too loose, reduce the length of the cable a little. Tighten the cable clamp firmly.

2 With the brake off, the pads should now sit 2mm from the rim. If necessary, correct the clearance with the cable adjuster. For top braking power and control, the straddle wire should roughly form a right-angle with the brake arm. If it does not, loosen the cable clamp on the brake arm and adjust the length of the straddle wire until it does. Finally, check that there is enough free cable above the cable carrier for the brake to come on fully without interfering with the outer cable.

3 Set the length of the brake cable so that the flexible hose touches both the cable carrier and the brake arm. Hook the link wire back into the other brake arm and adjust the spring tension if necessary.

4 The spring tension is right when the cable carrier hangs directly below the end of the outer cable. The pads should be an equal distance from the wheel rim. Lengthen the brake cable if necessary.

5 Finally, check that there is enough free cable above the cable carrier to enable the brakes to come on fully. Then move the brake cable into the narrow slot in the cable carrier, the slot for normal braking.

CORRECT ANGLE FOR LINK AND STRADDLE WIRES

When setting up any standard cantilever brake, try to get something close to a right-angle between the link wire or straddle wire and the brake arm that it is attached to. In order to do this, you will have to experiment by lengthening or shortening the wire or the cable. When set up properly like this, all types of cantilever brake should feel smooth and powerful.

6 On the later types of link wire cantilever, the cable fits into the brake lever and the cable carrier in roughly the same way. Once you have centered the brake pads with the adjusters, the brake cable must be lengthened to leave a gap of 2mm to 3mm between the end of the flexible hose and the brake arm.

7 Again on the later types of link wire cantilevers, the wrong angle of the link wire shown in the left picture below will cause brake judder and make it difficult to control the amount of braking. In the picture on the right, the link wire lines up correctly with the diagonal line on the cable carrier. The brakes should therefore work nicely, forming roughly a right angle.

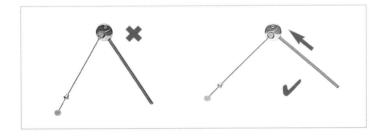

WHEN YOU NEED TO DO THIS JOB:
- Brakes tend to snatch or lock the wheel.
- The cable is frayed or broken.
- Lots of effort is needed to make emergency stops, suggesting the cable is sticking somewhere.

TIME:
- 10 minutes to fit a new cable to a straddle wire brake.
- 20 minutes for a link wire brake.

DIFFICULTY: 𝄢𝄢𝄢
- It is easy working on a straddle wire brake, but link wire brakes need careful adjustment to achieve a good balance between stopping power and delicate control.

SPECIAL TOOLS:
- A cable puller is very useful but not essential.
- Cable cutters.

Dual pivot and side pull brakes

All the moving parts of a side pull brake caliper fit onto the central pivot bolt. This creates a lot of friction, although the nylon washers, brass washers and even ball bearings sometimes fitted between the brake arms help to keep it down. When you strip a caliper, lay all the parts out in order to help you keep track. If you find any washers are damaged or missing, make sure you replace them.

If you find the brakes tend to stick, it may be possible to increase the spring pressure by reversing both nylon pads where the spring touches the brake arms. Brake levers are often spring-loaded as well, to make sure that the brakes release as soon as you let go of the brake lever.

You will probably find that the caliper constantly moves to one side, sometimes allowing the brake pad to rub against the rim. If you slip a heavy washer on the pivot bolt so that it sits in between the brake and the fork, you may find it easier to center the brakes and that they stay centered longer.

Campagnolo monoplanar calipers can be stripped in roughly the same way as a side pull caliper but don't strip dual pivot calipers. If they seem to be sticky or notchy, clean the whole caliper in degreaser, paying special attention to the pivots. Then re-lubricate with oil. On some dual pivots, you may be able to increase the spring tension by reversing a nylon pad, as on side pulls.

1 Pull off the cable end cap and undo the cable clamp. Now pull gently on the outer cable – with luck the inner will come out without fraying. Once the cable is free, the nipple may drop out of the cable anchor in the brake lever.

The latest Campagnolo brakes are dual pivot at the front and side pull at the back. They achieve a natural balance because the dual pivot brakes develop significantly more power, which is what you need at the front. Side pull brakes are weaker, which is better at the rear. They are both fitted with flats for an Allen wrench, to make it easier to center them when fitting.

2 Check how the brake is fixed to the forks next. Sometimes it is a self-locking nut or, more likely, a chromed socket-head sleeve bolt. Undo with a wrench or Allen wrench but be careful, it is sometimes hard to get replacements.

3 Pull the brake away from the forks. Then undo the dome nut and adjuster nut holding everything in place on the pivot bolt at the front of the caliper. Hook the ends of the spring off the brake arms, then pull the brake arms off.

4 Clean and reassemble, coating all points where friction occurs with light grease. Adjust the nuts on the pivot bolt for minimum friction between the arms without any sideways movement. Bolt the caliper back in place.

5 If one of the pads is close to or even touches the rim, loosen the fixing bolt, then use a thin wrench to hold the pivot bolt so that the pads are evenly spaced from the rim. Retighten the fixing bolt. You may find this part a bit difficult.

Dual pivot brakes

1 Slip the fixing bolt of the caliper into the mounting hole. Then fit the socket head sleeve bolt onto the long end of an Allen wrench and screw the sleeve bolt onto the end of the fixing bolt.

2 The end of the fixing bolt will not be visible inside the fork crown, so you may have to wiggle the Allen wrench a bit. Fit the wheel back in the frame, centering it carefully. Adjust the brake pads.

3 Then slacken off the fixing bolt and adjust the position of the caliper so that the gap between the pad and the rim is equal on both sides.

4 Tighten the fixing bolt for the last time and readjust the brake pads (see page 65). Finally, use the tiny screw on the Y brake arm to set the pad-to-rim distances exactly equal on both sides.

CENTRING A SINGLE-PIVOT CALIPER

If you have to keep on centering a caliper, only to find it keeps on moving to one side again, try this trick. Rest the end of a flat ended punch on the circular part of the return spring and hit the punch sharply with an engineer's hammer. Hit the same side of the return spring as the brake pad that is too close to the rim. This should solve the problem permanently, but if you cannot get the knack, go to a bike shop and get it done there.

TOE-IN ON SIDE PULLS AND DUAL PIVOTS

It is nearly always best to fit brake pads with about 1mm toe in – see page 65. There is no set way of doing this on a side pull brake although you can use an adjustable wrench to bend the brake arms. But before going that far, try fitting a shaped washer behind the pad holder, as used on MTB brakes and sometimes supplied with new brake pads. You will have to fiddle with the shaped washer until you find exactly the right position for it.

WHEN YOU NEED TO DO THIS JOB:

■ Brake action is still stiff after fitting a new cable.
■ Braking action feels rough and perhaps snatchy.

TIME:

■ Half-an-hour to strip, clean and reassemble. But maybe hours to center single pivot types.

DIFFICULTY: ✗✗✗✗

■ It can be difficult to refit the return spring and center the brake pads.

New cables for dual pivot and side pull brakes

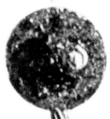

Brake cables are usually 1.5 or 1.6mm thick, substantially more than gear cables which are 1.1 or 1.2mm. They generally give a little when the brake lever is pulled, because the outer cable is wound in a spiral. Gear cables, by contrast, are non-compressible because the wires that make up the outer casing are arranged in a straight line.

The main division is between brake cables for a racer, which are fitted with a pear-shaped nipple, and those for pretty much every other sort of bike. These are drum-shaped. However, front brake cables are much shorter than rear ones. And mountain bike rear cables are much shorter than road bike ones.

Usually you can get away with just replacing the inner, but ask at the shop for one made from stainless steel. That way you get a cable that is strong, rust resistant and has natural anti-friction properties. Alternatively you can get cables treated with Teflon or some other anti-friction product.

But before you install either type, pump some oil or a synthetic lubricant into the outer cable so that it works smoothly for a long time.

However, some shops only stock a universal brake cable. This has a pear-shaped nipple at one end, a drum-shaped one at the other, and is long enough to act as the rear brake cable on a racing bike. You just cut off the nipple that you don't want, and then cut to length. If the nipple has been made slightly too big, clean it up with a file.

If you need an outer cable, you can make it yourself. Use the old one as a pattern and remember to fit a ferrule to both ends. However, it is probably better to buy a made-up one. These have ferrules built-in so that they keep the cable as straight as possible, and are cut to length. They are usually pre-lubricated as well. There are also top quality cables, sometimes with Kevlar or similar braided coverings, special anti-friction measures and often are sealed as well. This is particularly useful if you are running a bike cross country and want to keep the gears working.

When fitting new inner cables always complete the job by clamping a cable end to the cable. It'll prevent the cable from fraying again.

Dual pivots

1 When they get frayed, the inner cables tend to lose their strength and may become awkward to adjust.

Side pulls

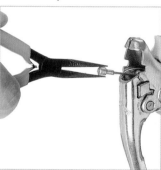

1 Peel back the rubber hood, if necessary, and pry out the plastic cover, if one is fitted. Open up the brake lever and push the nipple out of the nipple holder.

SPECIAL TOOLS
■ A cable puller or third h tool is desirable but not essential.

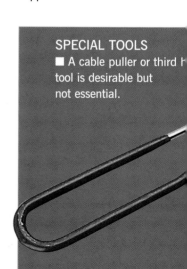

2 Cut the inner cable at a convenient spot and extract the remains of the inner cable with a pair of pliers.

3 Assuming the outer cable is OK, operate the quick release and fit the inner cable to the cable clamp.

4 The quick release can now be returned to its normal position and the brake tested for stopping power.

5 If needed, take up a little more of the inner cable through the cable clamp. Then cut off the spare part.

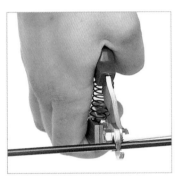

2 If the outer cable is damaged at all, you can use the old one as a guide to the length of the new one. Alternatively you can fit one that is already prepared.

3 Concealed cable brake levers have a guide hole at the back, and the brake cable goes through here and emerges by the inner curve of the handlebars.

4 Position the nipple in the nipple holder. Then, keeping the cable under slight tension, pass it through the cable adjuster and the cable clamp. Pull it as tight as you can.

5 Screw in the adjuster halfway, then hold the pads in contact with the rims. Tighten the cable clamp and adjust the pad-to-rim distance with the cable adjuster.

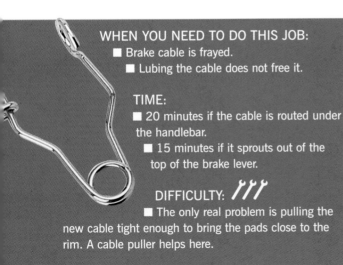

WHEN YOU NEED TO DO THIS JOB:
- ■ Brake cable is frayed.
  - ■ Lubing the cable does not free it.

TIME:
- ■ 20 minutes if the cable is routed under the handlebar.
  - ■ 15 minutes if it sprouts out of the top of the brake lever.

DIFFICULTY: 🔧🔧🔧
- ■ The only real problem is pulling the new cable tight enough to bring the pads close to the rim. A cable puller helps here.

If you're fitting a new brake cable to a combined gear and brake lever, pull the brake lever as far as you can. That will reveal the nipple at the start of the cable. It fits into the nipple holder in the same way as a normal brake lever. Pull the old cable out and thread a new one through the nipple holder, through the back of the brake lever and down to the brake. See page 90 for further details.

Cable disc brakes

An international standard disc brake.

D isc brakes are now fitted to a wide variety of bikes. Those in the affordable price range are often fitted with cable disc brakes, which are less responsive and heavier. However, the latest types are surprisingly effective. The more expensive bikes are fitted with hydraulic discs, which are powerful but very controllable and light in weight.

They can only be fitted to frames and forks equipped with disc brake mounts or tabs. Most types of caliper can be fitted to International Standard mounts, except for Hayes, which have their own fitting. As for the discs themselves, the International Standard six-hole fitting is very popular. However, some bikes are supplied with the Shimano Centre Lock system. Changing discs on these is simply a matter of removing the lock ring, swapping the disc and replacing the lock ring.

In wet and muddy conditions, rim brake pads just skid along the rim but do not grip. This is where discs really score, with powerful and consistent braking under all conditions, partly because the pads are larger and the caliper develops more power, but mainly because they are positioned away from the worst of the mud.

For instant braking, the gap between the pad and the disc is very small. So small that you can sometimes hear a light scraping noise when you spin the wheel. The small gap also means that when refitting wheels, after a puncture, for example, you must carefully slide the disc into position between the pads, before you fit the wheel to the frame.

The gap between the pad and the disc also makes it vital for the disc to run absolutely straight and true. Do not kick the disc, let it ground on a rock, or damage it in any other way. If the disc does go out of true, you will hear it rubbing on the pad and it must be replaced without delay.

As for maintenance, Fibrax says disc brake pads should be replaced every 1,200 to 1,600 miles (2,000 to 3,000km) or when they have worn down to 1mm in thickness, whichever comes first. Check in your bike handbook or with the seller for other makes. If the pads are not changed when specified, the steel backing will score the disc.

Whenever you fit new pads to cable disc brakes, or if you find that you have to pull the brake lever a long way to stop quickly, you must adjust the gap between the pad and the disc – see the box below. The only other maintenance job is to apply a little anti-seize grease to the caliper mounting pins every so often so they don't seize.

Shimano center lock disc brake mount.

Servicing cable

1 To remove a front wheel with a disc brake, turn the quick release lever to the open position. Then let the wheel drop out. If it seems to stick, undo the friction nut a few turns. When refitting, lift it carefully into place and tighten up the quick-release again.

5 Now shake the pad out of the holder. For health reasons, you must not inhale the dust but it must be cleaned off, so use a suitable brake cleaner to remove any dust inside the brake body or the pad holder. Check the thickness of the pad to see if it needs replacing.

Fitting new

1 When fitting new discs, make sure that the adaptor is clean and that the threads in the holes are clear.

ADJUSTING BRAKE PADS

Rest the bike on the saddle and handlebars. Locate the adjuster at the fork end of the brake arm. Use a 2.5mm Allen wrench to stop the central bolt from moving while you undo the 8mm lock nut around it about one turn. Turn the Allen wrench clockwise until the pads scrape the disc when you spin the wheel. Turn it half-a-turn counter-clockwise so that the pads scrape the disc very lightly. Hold the central bolt still with the Allen wrench while you tighten the lock nut. Operate the brakes a few times and spin the wheel. There should still be a very light scraping noise. Re-adjust the pads if they bind (scrape) on the disc, or there is complete silence, which indicates the clearance is too great.

disc brakes

2 To fit a new cable, hold the back of the cable clamp with a wrench while you loosen the cable clamp with an Allen wrench. You also have to do this when you have to strip down the caliper to free it or when you want to fit new brake pads.

3 When changing the brake pads, you next have to free the inner pad holder from the caliper body. So locate all three socket head fixing bolts and undo each one half-a-turn at a time. This careful method of working is to prevent any distortion of the parts.

4 When you have removed all three socket-head bolts, gently lever the pad holder away from the caliper body. The brake pad is held in place by a tiny spring, so pry it away with a small screwdriver. Be careful as the spring could fly in any direction.

6 Fit the new pads into the pad holder and disc brake body, holding them in place with the springs. However, the springs do not hold the pads in place very firmly and the pins on the pad holder are a tight fit in the holes in the caliper body, so be careful.

7 When properly fitted in place, the pad holder is a snug fit on the face of the disc brake body and there should be an even gap all the way around. Refit all three fixing bolts next, but only tighten them a quarter or a half-turn at a time to prevent distortion.

8 The disc brake body sits on three sprung pins. If you press it, the whole assembly should move sideways a little. If it seems to be stuck, strip it down and take care to fit it back together again evenly. Finally, refit the wheel and adjust brake pad clearance.

WHEN YOU NEED TO DO THIS JOB:
■ Every six months to clean out dust and check pad wear.
■ You hear squealing or grinding noises when you apply the brakes.

TIME:
■ Half-an-hour to strip, clean and reassemble a disc brake.

DIFFICULTY: ✏✏✏✏
■ Most of the parts are small and are all too easy to lose. Adjusting the pads can be tricky.

brake discs

2 The new disc usually comes with an anti-rust coating. Remove it with denatured alcohol and check the disc fits.

3 Coat the bolt threads with non-hardening thread lock compound. Line up the brake disc and fit the screws finger-tight.

4 Tighten all six screws evenly and progressively, working on opposite pairs of screws, and preferably using a torque wrench if the torque setting is known. You may be able to get this from the manufacturer or from the bike's handbook.

Bleeding hydraulic brakes

Hydraulic disc brakes

1 First, check that the fluid reservoir is horizontal. If necessary, loosen the lever clamp so you can adjust the position. Then open up the reservoir to check the level and refill as required.

2 Sometimes the reservoir has a screw top but here, the lid is held on by two screws. If you do not have a bike stand, get a friend to hold the bike upright. Now find the bleed nipple on the caliper.

3 Clean the area with a rag, then open the nipple a quarter-turn to check it opens easily. Fit a plastic tube onto the nipple and put the end of the pipe into a glass or metal container to catch the fluid.

4 Open the bleed nipple at least half a turn and gently pull the brake lever. Fluid plus air will squirt down the pipe into the container. Shut the nipple and repeat until the fluid comes out free of air.

5 Alternatively, the fluid reservoir is upside down on the brake lever. To bleed this type, first take an Allen wrench and adjust the position of the lever until upright.

6 Undo the screws that hold the lid on and remove it. Then bleed in the usual way. Finally, secure the lid again and return the brake lever to the normal position.

When working on hydraulic brakes, think of the hydraulics as the perfect brake cable. There is no stretching or binding and no friction, so the brake lever should always feel light but highly effective in action. If it does not, or the brakes seem to be losing their effectiveness, check for fluid leaks.

The best way to do this is to get a friend to pull the lever while you check the hoses and the area where the hoses are connected to the calipers. You will soon spot the leak if there is one.

On the other hand, if the lever feels spongy and the brakes do not pull you up hard, air could have gotten into the system.

If that has happened, when you pull the brake lever, the air just compresses and very little force reaches the pads. Once the air has been removed or bled out of the hydraulics, the pressure created by pulling the brake lever will once again push down the continuous column of fluid until it reaches the caliper. There it forces the pistons out of their bore in the caliper, and they press the pads against the disc.

As the pad wears, the piston moves out to compensate. So on most hydraulic discs, there is no adjustment for the pads. But they must be replaced before the friction material wears down to 1mm thickness. Keep an eye on the amount of wear because if you wear the pads down to the metal backplate, the resulting metal-to-metal contact will wreck the disc.

One method of bleeding the brakes is detailed here. But there are different procedures for the various makes, some requiring the use of a syringe, so you must always go by the manufacturer's instructions. Use the method given here only as a guide. The same applies when changing pads. Whatever the procedure, keep dirt, oil and other fluids away from the fluid reservoir. And be particularly careful when you are pouring fluid into the reservoir.

Bear in mind also that each maker specifies a particular type of hydraulic fluid. Some, like Shimano, use mineral oil, which must be kept away from the pads, discs and tires but is fairly harmless otherwise. Other makers specify an automotive brake fluid. There are various grades and you must only use the correct one, but they will all strip your paint and mark plastics if you spill it on them. They will also do you a lot of harm if you swallow the brake fluid or get it in your eye. Just in case, always wear protective glasses when working with these types of fluid.

During manufacture and normal use, a pattern of wear builds up on the surface of the disc. So when you fit new pads, they have to be broken in before they can generate anything like full braking power. Allow at least 50 miles of riding for this process and keep on applying the brakes lightly to help the process along.

Be very careful with the brakes when the wheels are out. If you operate the brake lever, the pistons could just pop out. They can also pop out by themselves if shaken. So if you have to move the bike with the wheels out, put a wooden block between the pads and tape it there to make sure it does not drop out.

Changing the brake pads

1 You can maybe get some idea of pad wear by peering through the window at the back of the caliper. But to get an accurate check, it is best to remove the pads after 500km and more frequently after that.

2 Take out the front wheel. Locate the end of the split pin (or maybe two) and bend them straight with heavy pliers. Then pull it right out. You may have to turn it a few times with the pliers to free it.

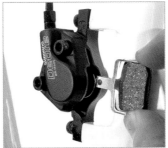

3 The pads should more or less fall out of the caliper. If they do not, push them out gently with a small screwdriver through the window in the back of the caliper. Do not inhale any of the dust.

4 There are two pads and sometimes a spring retainer as well. This will probably come out with the second pad. Check around the caliper for fluid leaks and wipe out the inside with a clean rag.

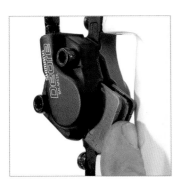

5 To refit old pads, sandwich the spring retainer, if there is one, between them. Then press them into place in the caliper. Check that they are in the right place through the window in the caliper.

6 As the pads wear, the pistons move out slightly. So if you are fitting new pads and finding it difficult, very gently lever the pistons back into the caliper so there is room for the thicker new pads.

7 The holes in the spring retainer and the pads must line up, so push a small screwdriver though to check that they do. Finally, fit the split pin and bend the ends over for safety. Always use a new split pin.

NEW BRAKE PADS

Looking at a new brake pad, it consists of a metal back plate plus a layer of friction material 3 or 4mm thick. The friction material is hard wearing, unless conditions are very muddy. Abrasive mud can accelerate the rate of wear enormously. If all the friction material gets worn away, the metal backplate will contact the disc and wreck it within a few miles.

There are many varieties of pad, including organic and metallic types. You will also find many different shapes and thicknesses of pad. When buying, take a sample to make sure that you get exactly the right type to replace the worn pads.

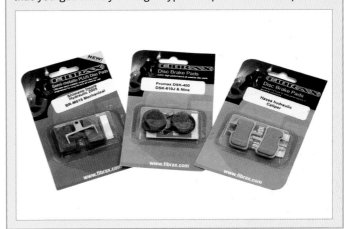

WHEN YOU NEED TO FIT NEW PADS:
■ When the friction material has worn down to a thickness of 1mm or less.
■ If the pads have been contaminated by oil or dirt.

TIME:
■ 30 minutes to fit new pads. Allow another 20 minutes for bleeding if necessary.

DIFFICULTY: Depends on the make.

Fitting new brake pads

Before changing pads, check the braking surface on the wheel rims. Light grooves in the braking surface are normal. On the other hand, if they go more than about 1.5mm deep you should have new rims fitted without delay as there is a danger of the wheel collapsing. But some rim walls now carry a groove, to act as a wear indicator. Replace the rim when the wear reaches the bottom of the groove.

If the rims seem to have worn out in months rather than years, chances are the brake pads do not suit the material that the rim is made of. If you fit the correct pads, it will improve the braking because they will have more "bite" on the braking surface.

Look also for pad material and dirt on the rims and check if they feel rubbery or slippery. If there is any sign, try cleaning the braking surface first with bike degreaser or, if that does not work, methylated spirit. Then scour the rims lightly with an abrasive pad. This will keep the new pads contamination free and give them a clean rim to bite on. And clean the rims and pads to prevent rapid wear after riding through mud.

Before starting work, check the instructions to see if toe-in is recommended. In some cases, pads are supplied with special spacers to set toe-in. By letting the front of the pad touch first, toe-in takes up the natural spring in the brake arms, preventing judder and noise when the brakes are used gently.

There may also be a particular way to fit the pads. This may be indicated by an arrow, which should be fitted so that it points in the direction of rotation of the wheel. Pads may also be marked left and right. But if the drain slots on the pad are arrow shaped, they should point in the opposite direction. Alternatively, fit the closed end (if there is one) of the pad holder at the front.

Worn cartridge pads are usually removed from the pad holder by undoing a short screw or bolt to release them. The new pads then slip in, but do not forget to retighten the screw.

Standard cantilevers

1 Slacken off the cable adjuster at the brake lever and then unhook the link or straddle wire from the brake arm. Loosen the pad clamp by undoing the nut behind the brake arm, holding the pad holder to stop it from moving.

BREAKING-IN PERIOD

Do not expect your brakes to generate top braking power with brand-new pads. The surface of most brake pads is slightly glazed and the braking surface of the wheel rim is never perfectly flat. So allow 10 or 20 miles (16 or 32km) of gentle riding to break the new pads in. You can help this process along by applying the brakes lightly when freewheeling downhill.

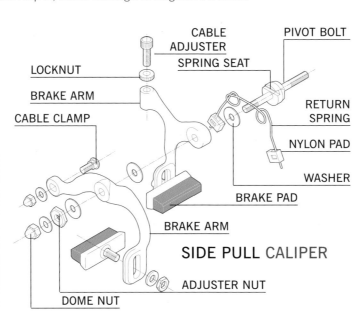

CABLE ADJUSTER
PIVOT BOLT
SPRING SEAT
LOCKNUT
BRAKE ARM
CABLE CLAMP
RETURN SPRING
NYLON PAD
WASHER
BRAKE PAD
BRAKE ARM
SIDE PULL CALIPER
ADJUSTER NUT
DOME NUT

WHEN YOU NEED TO DO THIS JOB:

■ Pads are worn down past the wear line or the slots have all worn away.

■ Pads are contaminated or are causing heavy wear to the braking surface.

TIME:

■ 20 minutes, including alignment of pads and readjustment of cable.

DIFFICULTY:

■ Not difficult, especially on road bikes.

Vee brakes

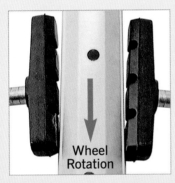

2 Pull the pad or the pad holder out of the clamp and check the condition. If there is a wear ridge either on the top or bottom, do not misalign the new pad in the same way. Take great care to keep the washers in the right order.

1 On some vee brakes, the pads are removed as on cantis. But on others, the pad fits in a slot as side pulls. If so, there will be washers and spacers to set the toe-in. But some have one shaped washer to adjust the toe-in.

Side pulls and dual pivots

1 Screw the cable adjuster in and operate the quick-release to give you enough room, then undo the brake pad fixing. Sometimes it is a socket-head bolt, sometimes a domed nut. Slip the pad out between brake and rim.

2 When fitting a new pad, turn the pad holder to one side if necessary, so you can squeeze it between the caliper and the rim. Leave a gap of about 2mm between the pad and the rim on each side, in case the wheels are slightly wavy.

BRAKE PAD ADJUSTMENT

Brake pad adjustment must be checked as in Steps 1 to 3 whenever you adjust the brakes, remove the brake pads or fit new ones. If brake pads are fitted parallel with the rim or – even worse – toe-out, it can cause judder or a squeak when the brakes are applied. On cantilevers and Vee brakes, this can be prevented by adjusting the position of the spacers and shaped washers that you should fit between the brake arm and pad holder.

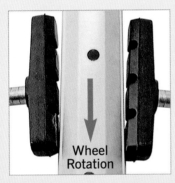

Wheel Rotation

1 Check that the pads are positioned correctly and tighten the pad securing nut a little. Fit the wedge-shaped washer so that there is a 1mm pad-to-rim gap at the front and a 2mm gap at the back. Use a piece of card to gauge this.

2 Now pull the brake lever gently and check that the top edge of the brake pad is between 1mm and 2mm below the top of the wheel rim. It is permissible to overlap the base of the rim a little but try to avoid this if at all possible.

3 Next, pull the brake lever again to see if the whole surface of the pad contacts the braking surface. If not, adjust the angle of the pad holder, check Steps 1 and 2 again and finally, tighten up the pad fixing nut.

MOLDED ONE-PIECE BRAKE PADS

Most cantilever brakes have an adjustable pad clamp. You fit the post through the clamp and can then adjust the pad in any direction. On the pads themselves, the wheel direction arrow and the wear line are usually molded into the pad material. The gap between pad and rim is set by moving the post toward or away from the rim. As the pad wears, you can move the post closer to keep the 1mm or 2mm clearance. Finally, check that the pad hits the rim squarely, at least 1mm below the top edge.

A combined brake and gear lever.

Brake levers

Mountain bike brake levers all follow roughly the same design. The handlebar clamp fits around the handlebar and is held in position by the clamp bolt. It is easy enough to alter the position of the brake lever, if you do not find it comfortable. But if the brake levers are integrated with trigger-type gear changers, this will limit where you can position the brake levers very substantially.

The main differences between budget and more expensive levers are the quality of the materials used and the provision of reach adjustment. Do not forget about this point as a comfortable hand position on the brake lever helps prevent you locking up the brakes on a loose surface. But people with really small hands should fit proper short-reach brake levers.

Hooded racing bike brake levers are all very similar to each other. So you can mix one make of brake lever with a different make of caliper without any problem. The main variation is that the cable springs out of the top of the lever on ancient types. On later designs, the brake cable comes out of the side, allowing you to tape it to the handlebars for a much tidier look.

On the other hand, STI, Ergopower and DoubleTap combined brake and gear levers are very different from each other. On STIs, there is a groove on the outside edge of the lever body down which you fit an Allen wrench to loosen or tighten them on the handlebar. With Ergopower and DoubleTap levers, the band-on fixing is in roughly the same position as a normal brake lever.

HANDLEBAR CLAMP BOLT

PIVOT

LEVER BLADE

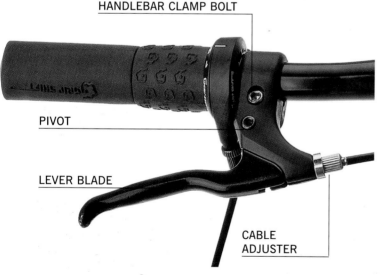

CABLE ADJUSTER

A twist grip for a Sturmey-Archer hub gear, next to the brake lever. Here the clamp bolt is underneath the brake lever.

VEE BRAKE DANGER

Vee brakes require special brake levers designed to be used with direct or linear-pull brakes. If cantilever brakes are used with Vee brake levers the brakes will come on hard the moment the lever is pulled. It will be difficult to modulate and will offer poor stopping power. Conversely, if Vee brakes are used with cantilever brake levers the brake will be spongy and the lever will travel back to the handlebar. If the pads do contact the rim, braking force will be excessive.

Road bikes

1 To reduce the effort needed for braking, lube the brake lever pivot in case it is sticky with old oil. Pull the brake lever next, so you can spray lube on the end of the cable – then work the lever so the lube spreads along it.

2 If the brake lever is loose or you want to adjust its position, remove the cable and, at the back of the hood, you will see the fixing screw. It may be tightened with a big screwdriver, but if it is an Allen wrench fitting, go for extra leverage.

3 To remove the brake lever without undoing the handlebar tape, loosen the fixing screw and pull the complete brake lever away from the handlebars. That is useful if you ever need to fit a new rubber lever hood.

4 The hood on a combined gear and brake lever has a button molded in, which engages with the other part of the lever to ensure a snug fit. Only lubricate in the same way as an ordinary brake lever if non-standard cables are fitted.

Mountain bikes and hybrids

1 Mountain bike and hybrid brake levers are exposed to wet conditions, so lube the pivots frequently. Pull the brake lever so that you can lube the cable as well. And give the cable adjuster a squirt of lube so it does not stick or corrode.

2 To adjust position or take off the brake lever, loosen the clamp bolt. Where the gear shifter is fitted to the brake lever, the fixing screw is usually tucked away under the shifter lever. Push it forward to get at the fixing screw.

3 On good-quality MTB brake levers, there is a small Phillips or Allen screw behind the cable adjuster. This allows you to alter the reach. With cantilevers, you should be able to do an emergency stop using the middle three fingers only.

4 On the other hand, if you have Vee brakes, you should be able to do an emergency stop using your forefinger and middle finger only. Be careful the first time you do this, as Vee brakes feel very powerful if you are not used to them.

COMBINED BRAKE LEVERS AND SHIFTERS ON MTBs
To remove the shifter, take off both cable adjusters and undo the Phillips screws that hold the indicator in place. Pull off and undo the hexagon socket-head screw holding the shifter to the brake lever. To refit, select the bottom gear on the shifter and line up the needle with the vertical line, then refit the socket-head screw.

WHEN YOU NEED TO DO THIS JOB:
■ Brakes feel heavy but not gritty, so the cables need lubricating.
■ The position of your hands when applying the brakes or resting on the brake levers is uncomfortable.

TIME:
■ 2 minutes to lube the levers and cables.
■ 5 minutes to tighten loose brake levers.
■ 15 minutes to remove both levers.

DIFFICULTY:
With racing bike brake levers, it can be difficult to reach the fixing screw at the back of the lever or refit the brake lever to the fixing band on the handlebars.

SPECIAL TOOLS:
■ Long workshop Allen wrenches or T-shaped Allen wrenches are extremely useful when working on road bike brake levers.

BMX brakes

SAFETY POINT

When a bike is being ridden on the road, including any BMX, it should have two independent brakes, both of them in working order.

However, riding BMXs without brakes is very popular on the streets. So we urge parents to check from time to time that the brakes have not been removed from any BMX bikes in their household, and to ground the rider until the brakes have been refitted.

BMXs are designed for maximum bike control at fairly slow speeds. The frames are built for strength rather than speed and the basic design does not vary a lot, although there are various different styles of riding. The most popular ones are race, street and freestyle. Only one size of frame is normally available, though the saddle adjusts up and down to cater for riders of varying height.

There is only one gear on these bikes, which means you can only vary the gearing by fitting a larger or smaller chainring. However, basic BMXs use a one-piece chainset, so you cannot change the gearing on these anyway. Higher up the price range, the chainsets are similar to normal cotterless ones and it is possible to change the chainring, see page 130.

Maybe the hardest part of a BMX to understand is the braking system. Most BMXs are fitted with compact U brakes front and back. However, many tricks involve spinning the handlebars, impossible without a special device called a rotor head. This features a back brake cable that splits into two near the brake lever. The cable adjusters screw into a loose plate at the top of the headset with the nipples located in the middle plate. A second pair of cables connects to the middle and lower plates but joins into one again before reaching the back brake. When you spin the handlebars, the stem and top plate revolve, but the bottom mounting plate stays still, so the cables do not get tangled up.

On the other hand, you can simply bypass the rotor head. The brakes then work much more efficiently, because the cables are shorter and they don't have the losses in the rotor to worry about.

Some BMX riding styles place a very heavy load on the frame and mechanical parts, so bear in mind that the manufacturer's guarantee probably only covers normal riding.

Adjusting rotor rear brakes

1 Screw in the cable adjuster on the frame as far as possible. Then loosen the straddle wire yoke and move it up the cable until it is about ½in from the frame and retighten. This will help to reduce the amount of pull needed to apply the brakes.

2 Release one end of the straddle wire and run it round the yoke. Refit the straddle cable to the brake arm, tension the straddle wire with pliers and then tighten the clamp bolt. There should be a right angle between the brake arm and the straddle cable.

3 Now check the cable assembly just below the handlebars. Make sure that the middle plates are free to move, and lubricate lightly. Adjust the brake cables so that both moving plates are an equal distance apart at their ends and level with the ground.

4 Test the tension on the top section of the rear brake cables. If they are slack, increase the tension using the cable adjuster near the brake lever and the adjusters on the top plate. Then test the back brake, using the cable adjuster on the frame if necessary.

Other BMX features

1 The front U brake is fitted with a cable pipe that fits into a socket on one of the brake arms. Check occasionally that the cable pipe still moves freely. When setting up the brakes, keep the straddle wire as short as possible, for maximum braking efficiency.

2 When front or rear pegs are fitted, you'll have to use a socket set with a 10in or 12in extension to tighten up or undo the wheel nuts. This is not the easiest task but if you get somebody else to steady the handlebars or the saddle, that will help a lot.

3 To check the chain tension, try lifting the chain at the mid-point of its bottom run. It is correct when you can lift it ½ inch. To adjust, undo the wheel nuts, move the wheel to the new position, check it is central and finally, tighten the wheel nuts a little at a time.

4 To prevent distortion of the clamp when adjusting the handlebar angle, undo one nut half a turn, then the diagonally opposite one the same amount. Undo the other two in a similar way and continue half a turn at a time. Reverse the procedure when tightening.

BMX PEDALS

If the frame or cage around the pedals gets bent or distorted, fit replacements immediately, or they can cause accident or injury.

As the pedals take a beating every time a BMX is dropped, and that can be quite often, fit good-quality replacements as they will take the punishment better.

4

GEAR SYSTEMS

Types of gears

Nearly all bikes are fitted with either derailleur or hub gears. Derailleur systems have a front mech to shift the chain between two or three chainrings and a rear mech with up to ten sprockets. Hub gears have fewer speeds and need occasional workshop maintenance.

NINE-SPEED MOUNTAIN BIKE REAR MECH
These mechs have a long chain cage to allow for a very wide range of gears, and are controlled by a handlebar mounted gear shifter. They can also be used on hybrid and touring bikes, which need very low gears for hill climbing and load carrying.

REAR
MECH

TEN-SPEED RACING BIKE REAR MECH
Sports and racing rear mechs for use with double chainsets (see left) have a short chain cage for low weight and a better gear change. Rear mechs for use with triple chainsets (see above) have a medium length chain cage to allow for a wider range of gears. Both types are controlled by combined brake and gear levers.

ECONOMY REAR MECH
These are made of steel, not alloy, usually with a bolt-on hanger for use on budget frames not fitted with a gear hanger. Short cage models are also available.

HUB GEARS

With seven, eight or nine speeds, these are modern designs that bear little resemblance to the classic hub gear. They are fitted to comfort and city bikes but the back wheel is much more difficult to remove from the frame. They are available with various types of brakes.

HUB GEAR

THREE-SPEED HUB GEAR

Mainly for utility bikes. These hub gears need occasional adjustment to the cable tension, but the latest versions do not even need oiling. Controlled by a click shifter, usually on the handlebars, they can be combined with a coaster brake, a hub brake or a roller brake.

FRONT MECH

MOUNTAIN BIKE AND HYBRID FRONT MECH

MTB front mechs have a deep, heavy duty chain cage so they can cope with triple chainrings and big differences in chainring size. This particular type has a very rigid chain cage mounted at the top of the mech for a lighter, better change. Separate top pull, bottom pull and combined models are all available.

ROAD BIKE FRONT MECH

Road front mechs are fitted with a light chain cage, with separate models for double and triple chainrings. But this type is specially made for a compact chainset, with a carefully shaped inner plate. Most types bolt on to the down tube with a clamp but high-grade road frames have a special brazed-on fitting for bolting the front mech to.

Rear mech: care and inspection

All rear derailleur mechanisms (rear mechs) need frequent lubrication and occasional servicing to keep them working well, so give the rear mech a few shots of aerosol lube every other time you oil the chain. And spend a few minutes cleaning it when the dirt starts to build up, or the gears stop working accurately.

Shimano and the latest Campag rear mechs are fitted with a top jockey wheel that moves a little from side-to-side. This allows the chain cage to run slightly out of line with the sprockets, so the indexing will work even if the adjustment is not quite right.

If your rear mech throws the chain off the sprockets, it needs the limit screws adjusted. But if you hear a continuous metallic rattling sound in most of the gears, the indexing needs correcting – in which case see the next page. If the jockey wheels are badly worn, they need replacing rather than stripping and greasing.

If you just cannot get the gears to work right, remember that Campagnolo gears on the one hand, and Shimano and SRAM on the other, are spaced differently. So it is just possible that someone has fitted a Shimano rear mech with a Campag cassette, or the other way around.

1 If you have to clean the chain due to a buildup of dirt, the rear mech will need cleaning as well. Give it a squirt of aerosol lube or grease solvent and wipe it thoroughly with a cloth. Then lube the main pivots and top pivot bolt.

2 Pay particular attention to the jockey wheels because they pick up hard-packed dirt from the chain. Soften the dirt with solvent and scrape off with a small screwdriver. Wipe, and then lightly spray lube into the center of both jockey wheels.

4 The jockey wheels wear out more quickly than any other part. So pull the chain cage forward to free the bottom jockey from the chain, then test for movement by trying to wiggle it. Check also that the jockey wheel turns freely. If it does not, strip and grease.

5 Pull the chain away from the upper jockey wheel and do the same check. On many rear mechs, the upper jockey wheel moves sideways a bit, so it is a definite wobble that indicates that it needs renewing. If it just moves sideways, that's intended by the makers.

On most road bikes and some MTBs, the gear cables run under the bottom bracket. But they can get damaged easily, so check in case of problems, especially with the front mech. If the cable has a sleeve to reduce friction, make sure you transfer it when fitting a new cable.

WHEN YOU NEED TO DO THIS JOB:
- Steps 1, 2 and 3 – every time you clean the chain.
- Steps 4, 5 and 6 – every time you give the chain a thorough clean. It is also worth going through 4, 5 and 6 when checking over a second-hand bike.

TIME:
- 1 minute to lube the rear mech when you do the chain. 5 minutes to check wear and crash damage.

DIFFICULTY:
- Quite easy, but you are liable to get your hands pretty dirty. Consider wearing latex gloves.

3 The cable should instantly transmit each movement of the gear lever. To make sure it does work like this, lubricate the inner cable, then operate the gear lever a few times so that the lube works its way right down the outer cable.

6 Hanging down beside the back wheel, rear mechs often get damaged when a bike falls over or is in a crash. To check for damage, clamp the bike in a workstand or get somebody to hold it upright. Then position yourself behind the back wheel, your eye level with the hub. You should be able to see if the gear looks out of line with the frame. If you suspect it is, check the gear hanger for cracks or chips in the paint – a sure indication that it is bent. It is also worth checking that the chain cage looks straight. If it is, the top and bottom jockey wheels will line up exactly with the sprockets. If the chain cage is out of line, the rear mech may be damaged or just worn out.

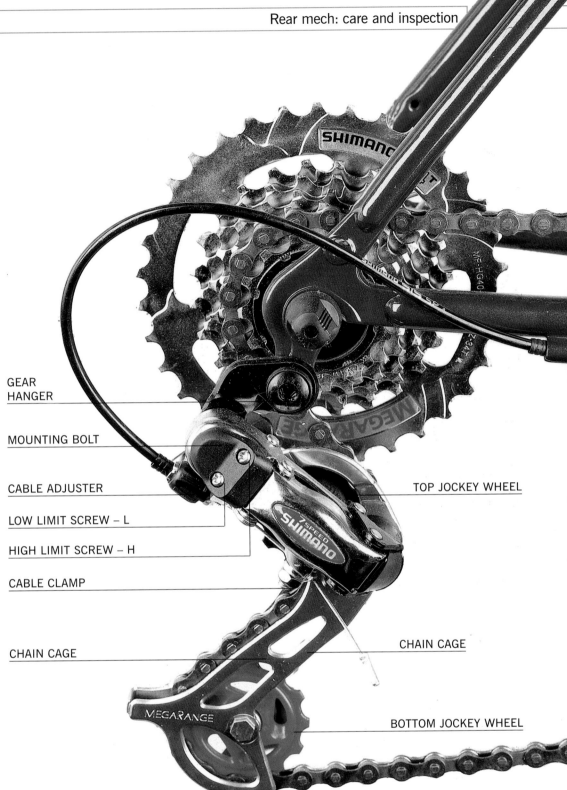

GEAR HANGER

MOUNTING BOLT

CABLE ADJUSTER

LOW LIMIT SCREW – L

HIGH LIMIT SCREW – H

CABLE CLAMP

CHAIN CAGE

TOP JOCKEY WHEEL

CHAIN CAGE

BOTTOM JOCKEY WHEEL

EXTRA LOW GEARING

Shimano Megarange and some other wide-range rear mechs can cope with any size bottom sprocket right up to 34 teeth. They can do this because the rear mech is mounted slightly further back than usual, and has a bottom jockey wheel with 13 or more teeth. The extra large jockey wheel has to be used to cope with the extra long chain. Some Megarange gears use the Low Normal design. If this applies, go to page 78 for special instructions on adjustment.

Rear mech adjustment

The first step when you are adjusting any rear mech is to make sure that the inner cable is free of friction as it moves in the outer cable. This applies when fitting a new cable, or a new rear mech or reusing the existing parts. The most likely cause of any friction is the short length of outer cable that connects to the rear mech. So, to avoid problems, some experts fit a new one every time they fit a new inner cable.

You then adjust the high and low limit screws, which control the movement of the chain cage from side to side. If you ever find that the chain has jumped off the sprockets and gotten jammed in the spokes, the limit screws probably need adjusting. The same applies if the chain jams between the top sprocket and the frame.

On mountain bikes and hybrids, you select the gears with either a rotary changer built into the handlebar grip or a trigger-type changer. But nearly all modern sports bikes and racers have combined brake and gear levers (pages 90–91). Older road bikes have indexed levers on the down tube.

For an indexed rear mech to work, the gear changer has to move the cable exactly the same amount for each gear change. But this set amount can only be transmitted accurately to the rear mech if the cable is under a lot of tension. If the cable stretches or the outer cable compresses, reducing the tension, the indexing stops working well.

You will probably notice the noise of the chain running slightly out of line when this happens. To increase the cable tension again, give the cable adjuster one half-turn counter-clockwise. If that does not work, go through the procedure below to re-adjust the indexing. But if you still cannot get the gears to change smoothly and precisely, fit a new inner and outer gear cable (pages 80–81), then repeat the adjustment procedure.

Adjusting the indexing

To see how the indexing is working, give the bike a road test. First check that the chain runs silently in top gear on the biggest chainring. If it makes a rattling noise, turn the cable adjuster (large arrow) – not the H and L limit screws (small arrows) – half a turn counter-clockwise if the chain is trying to jump off the top sprocket. On the other hand, if it is trying to climb onto the second sprocket, give the cable adjuster half a turn clockwise. Keep on with the road testing, changing up and down through the gears and adjusting the cable tension, until the bike runs silently in top.

Next, change down to the next to top or second gear with the gear lever and turn the cable adjuster one quarter-turn counter-clockwise at a time, until you hear a metallic clattering sound as the chain tries to climb onto the third sprocket. Then turn the adjuster clockwise until the clattering noise stops, but absolutely no further than that. Road test again to make sure that the gear changes are quick and accurate. But when you are checking out the gear change up onto the biggest sprockets, change down to a smaller chainring.

Be very careful when changing down into bottom gear the first few times as you might "overshift" the chain off the biggest sprocket and into the spokes. If you cannot get the gears to shift properly, lubricate the outer cable again. Better still, fit a completely new inner and outer cable. Also check the adjustment of the B screw, see page 83.

REMEMBER, AT THE BACK WHEEL:
The smaller the sprocket, the higher the gear. So adjust the screw marked H for High.
The larger the sprocket, the lower the gear. So adjust the screw marked L for Low.
BUT AT THE CHAINWHEEL:
The larger the chainring, the higher the gear. So adjust the screw marked H for High.
The smaller the chainring, the lower the gear. So adjust the screw marked L for Low.

Rear mech setup

1 Check that the inner cable is not weakened or frayed anywhere. And make sure that the outer cable is not kinked or damaged, especially the short cable down near the rear mech. Then spray some aerosol lube down each section of outer cable. Do not forget to check the cable guide under the bottom bracket. Now lift the back wheel and select top gear, turning the pedals slowly so that the chain jumps down onto the smallest sprocket

2 Undo the cable clamp to free the gear cable, if necessary. Then pull the rear mech backward to make it easier for you to see the position of the jockey wheels. On index gears, a vertical line through the middle of both jockey wheels should line up with the OUTSIDE edge of the smallest sprocket. To move the jockey wheels to the right, turn the H for high limit screw counter-clockwise. To move the jockey wheels to the left, turn it clockwise.

3 Make sure that the gear lever is still in top gear position. Then screw the cable adjuster in most of the way and fit the gear cable, pulling it as tight as possible with pliers before you tighten the cable clamp. Using the gear lever, change down slowly until the rear mech is in bottom gear. The jockey wheels should line up with the MIDDLE of the bottom sprocket. If they are to the right of that point, or the rear mech will not change down to bottom, turn the L for low limit screw counter-clockwise. Turn the limit screw clockwise if the chain cage is to the left of the largest sprocket

4 If you have trouble finding the H (high) and L (low) limit screws, they are usually on the top or back of the rear mech. But on budget Shimano and nearly all Campagnolo gears, they are on the side, near the cable clamp. If the limit screws are not labeled H and L, you will have to use trial and error to sort out which one is which.

FOR 10 SPEED CAMPAGNOLO ONLY
Zero the Ergopower control button by operating it at least 10 times, and move the chain onto the smallest sprocket and the largest chainring. Find the screw on the chain cage and tighten it clockwise. Then adjust the position of the rear mech with the low limit screw so that the top jockey wheel is below the centerline of the smallest sprocket. Fit the gear cable and tension it. Place the rear mech on the fourth sprocket from the top and turn the cable adjuster one way or the other until the top jockey wheel is perfectly aligned with it. Then, if necessary, adjust the limit screw so that the chain climbs onto the largest sprocket, without touching the spokes. Finally, do a test ride to check the adjustment, adjusting the screw on the chain cage if it touches the sprockets at any point.

FOR 9 or 10 SPEED SHIMANO (not Low Normal)
Set up as in Steps 1 to 4 but then select the second smallest sprocket. Take up the slack in the gear lever and turn the cranks. If the gear changes up to the third smallest sprocket, tighten the cable adjuster clockwise until it returns to second. But if there is no noise at all, turn the cable adjuster counter-clockwise until it makes a slight noise. Then, to check the best setting, take up the slack in the lever again. The rear mech should make a slight noise but not change down onto the third sprocket. Finally, check that there is no noise in all the gears.

WHEN YOU NEED TO DO THIS JOB:
- Rear mech is noisy.
- Gears will not change smoothly and accurately.
- Chain jumps off into spokes or jams between sprocket and frame.

TIME:
- 30 minutes from fitting new mech to completing adjustment of indexed rear mech.
- 5 minutes to fine-tune the indexing, including test ride.

DIFFICULTY:
- Basic adjustment is straightforward, but getting the indexing working perfectly can take patience.

Shimano Low Normal

Shimano Low Normal rear derailleur gears work the other way around from normal. So when the tension on the gear cable is released, they move toward bottom gear and not top gear like other rear mechs. There are no road rear mechs that are Low Normal, but the old XTR and some other mountain bike rear mechs were. As for current production, the 2007 Deore LX and XTR give you a choice of either Low or High Normal, as do various Nexus groupsets.

The advantage of Low Normal is that theoretically, it's more difficult to get a rear mech to climb up onto a bigger sprocket than to drop down onto a smaller one. With Low Normal, the climb up to the larger sprockets is spring-aided, while the drop down to the smaller ones is purely manual. So the limit screws are adjusted in the reverse order, and then the indexing is adjusted at the bottom end of the cassette rather than the top.

Shimano Low Normal

1 The rear mech is attached to the bike in the usual way. It works in reverse to normal, so the chain cage has to be positioned under the MIDDLE of the biggest or bottom sprocket. Check that the low limit screw (L) is set correctly by making sure that the chain runs silently.

2 Move the rear mech by hand into top gear, setting the high limit screw (H) so that the chain cage is under the OUTSIDE of the top or smallest sprocket.

3 Return the rear mech to bottom gear. Operate the gear shifter at least 10 times, to put the gear selector in bottom gear. Then connect the gear cable to the rear mech, ensuring that it's securely held by the cable clamp.

4 If necessary, adjust the B screw so that the chain cage is as close to the sprockets as possible but doesn't interfere with them. This will only be necessary in extreme circumstances, see page 83.

5 Check again that the rear mech is in bottom gear, on the largest sprocket. Then change to second gear, the sprocket next to the largest one. Take up the play in the gear shifter and turn the crank.

6 If it changes to third gear, turn the cable adjuster CLOCKWISE until it returns to second. But if no noise is heard at all, turn the cable adjuster COUNTER-CLOCKWISE, until the rear mech touches third gear and a slight noise is heard.

7 The best setting is achieved when the cable adjuster is turned CLOCKWISE until a noise occurs but without changing gear, then turned COUNTER-CLOCKWISE between 90° and 180°. Check that there is no noise in any of the gears.

WHEN YOU NEED TO DO THIS JOB: (applies to Low Normal and SRAM)

■ Fitting a new rear mech.
■ Indexing isn't working.

TIME:
■ 30 minutes for fitting a rear mech.
■ 10 minutes if the indexing needs looking at.

DIFFICULTY: ✗✗✗
■ Either job is not difficult but each step has to be gone through methodically.

SRAM rear mech

SRAM gear adjustment

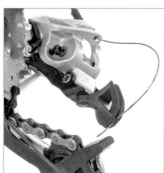

SRAM rear mechs work on a different principle from the others. Roughly speaking if you move the gear cable by 1mm, the rear mech also moves by 1mm. This is known as the 1:1 actuation ratio, as opposed to the 1:2 ratio used on other makes. Therefore the gear cable doesn't need to be adjusted so accurately and there is no need for the top jockey pulley to move from side-to-side. The practical effect is that SRAM rear mechs shouldn't need so much maintenance as the other types, because the indexing works more reliably.

X.7, X.8, X.9 are all basically the same as X.0 but they use progressively more expensive materials. However, the Force and Rival rear mechs for the road take the principle one stage further. They have Exact Actuation, which means that exactly 3mm of cable is required to make each change from top gear to bottom gear.

The only SRAM design that doesn't comply with these design principles is the MRX, which is completely Shimano-compatible.

1 Set the high limit screw so that the chain cage is positioned under the OUTBOARD EDGE of the top or smallest sprocket. Then move the rear mech to bottom gear with your hand. Set the low limit screw so that the chain cage is under the MIDDLE of the bottom or biggest sprocket.

2 Set the correct length of the chain if necessary. The chain is taken around the big chainring and the biggest sprocket, plus two links, but leaving out the rear mech. Connect the cable. Set the gear shifter to top gear, then the cable goes through the cable adjuster, around the cable guide and connects to the cable clamp. Use a pair of pliers to pull it tight.

The SRAM Force road rear mech, which differs from the mountain bike rear mechs in detail. But it's set up using the same method, even though it looks very different from the various members of the X series.

SRAM/Gripshift gear changers
Gripshift rotational shifters are made by SRAM. Their ESP shifters only work with SRAM gears also made to the ESP design. Non-ESP Gripshift designs work well with other rear mechs including Shimano. The latest "half pipe" shifters have a bigger grip for easier gear changing, plus a better internal mechanism.

Normally, Gripshift shifters need no maintenance. If one becomes stiff to operate, fit a new inner and outer cable. Then check that the plastic washer between the handlebar grip and shifter moves freely. If neither of those things reduces the amount of effort needed to shift the gears, flip off the cable cover or open the escape hatch and spread a match head size bead of Jonnisnot lubricant around the cable track and another around the ratchet. Do not use any other lubricants or degreasers because they might swell the plastic.

3 Adjust the B screw if necessary, see page 83, although it probably isn't. Test the rear mech by turning the pedals and changing up and down several times. Put it into top gear and move the gear shifter one notch.

4 If it doesn't go into second, turn the cable adjuster COUNTER-CLOCKWISE half a turn, and then again if necessary. If the rear mech moves beyond second gear, turn the cable adjuster CLOCKWISE. Check by repeating this process. Then test the rear mech by running up and down through the gears, making sure that it changes swiftly but silently.

5 The SRAM mountain bike rear mech, correctly set up and ready to go. This is the X.0 but the same method applies to almost all the current SRAM mountain bike and road rear mechs.

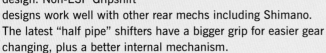

Fitting new gear cables

A ll inner cables look very similar but that can be misleading. So when buying, specify whether you have indexed gears or not. The high quality cables for indexed gears are stiffer than normal ones and both inners and outers are often specially treated to reduce friction. That means it is OK to use indexed cables on ordinary gears, but not the other way around. If you use non-indexed cables on indexed gears, it will affect the gear change and you will have to adjust them more often.

When fitting new inner cables, check the outers for kinks and breaks as well. On indexed gears, it's best to use ready-made outers with metal ferrules rather than making complete cables up yourself. Anyway, special outer cable is made for indexed gears. This has separate wires running the length of the cable, held together by a plastic cover. This kind of outer cable does not compress when the inner is fully tensioned, so it does not affect the way the indexing works.

Many cable clamps are designed so that the inner cable wraps around the cable clamp slightly. There is usually a shallow groove to fit the cable into, but you should make a mental note of the old cable path before removing the old inner cable, just in case. If the gears do not work well after fitting a new cable, you may have fitted it on the wrong side of the cable clamp.

Lubricate inner and outer cables with silicon, mineral oil and synthetic lubricants or white chain wax.

MTB and hybrid

1 Some handlebar shifters have a partly hidden cable recess. Look for it by moving the lever forward, then tracing the path of the cable around the lever. If you screw the cable adjuster right in, the nipple may pop out of the recess.

2 On underbar set-ups, the best way to get at the inner cable is to take the bottom cover off. In most cases, it is held in place by two or three tiny Phillips screws.

7 When the end of the cable emerges from the cable adjuster, feed the end into the outer cable and keep pushing it through until it pops out the other end. Then pull it tight, carefully seating the end of the outer in the cable adjuster.

CABLE SEALS

The length of outer cable between the frame and the rear mech can get filled with dirt and water and this has a major effect on the performance of the rear mech. Fit a new outer cable every time you fit a new inner and fit a cable seal as well to prevent the gear change from deteriorating again.

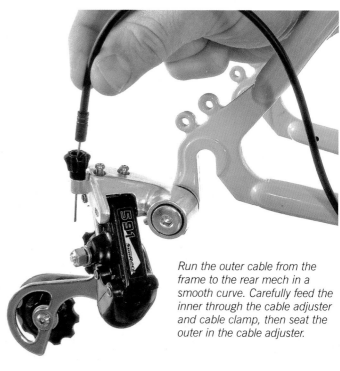

Run the outer cable from the frame to the rear mech in a smooth curve. Carefully feed the inner through the cable adjuster and cable clamp, then seat the outer in the cable adjuster.

3 With the cover out of the way, check that the inside is not choked with old grease. If so, wipe it all away. Then give the inside a short spray of aerosol lube. Do not overdo it.

4 You also have to remove the cover to change the inner cable. Then pull the outer cable out of the adjuster and push the inner cable toward the shifter, freeing the nipple.

5 On some other designs, including rotary shifters, access to the inner cable is by a screw-in plug. Unscrew the plug and spray lube in there, or pull out the old cable.

6 When fitting a new inner cable, you may find it easier to work from underneath, as here. Hold the cable between finger and thumb and gradually feed it into the changer.

Sports bike gear cables

1 Move the lever to top gear position and separate the old inner cable from the rear mech. Then pull it out of the outer cable and the cable guides, if fitted. Push the nipple up and out of the recess, using pliers if necessary.

2 With down tube shifters, check that the guides under the bottom bracket are not damaged or blocked. Carefully uncoil the new cable to prevent any kinks and, if you are reusing the old outer cable, make sure it is OK.

3 Check that the gear lever is in top and that the chain is on the top sprocket. Feed the new inner cable through the nipple recess in the lever, slide it into the cable guides and thread it through the cable stop down by the rear mech.

4 Feed the inner cable into the outer and take it in a smooth curve down to the cable adjuster on the rear mech. Check which side of the cable clamp the cable should run, pull it tight with pliers and tighten up the cable clamp bolt.

WHEN YOU NEED TO DO THIS JOB:
■ If the cables are frayed or sticky, leading to a heavy gear change.
■ When there is a mystery fault with the indexing and lube does not help.

TIME:
■ 30 minutes to fit a rear mech cable, less to fit a front mech cable.

DIFFICULTY:
■ Easy to fit new cables on a racing bike with down tube shifters, but handlebar and twist grip shifters are very fiddly.

TOOLS:
■ A cable cutter is desirable.

READY-MADE CABLES
Once the cable from the frame to the rear mech has started to deteriorate, there is no point in trying to clean it out again with thin wire or aerosol lube. Replace with a short length of outer cable made for this job and sold individually. No need to buy a complete cable set.

Rear mech: removal and refitting

There are three different ways in which the rear mech is fitted to a frame. On good-quality bikes, the mounting bolt is screwed straight into a threaded hanger that hangs down from the rear drop-out.

Be careful to keep the bolt straight as you screw it in. If it goes in at an angle and you force it, that could strip the thread in the hanger. If you do this on a steel frame, you will have to get it tapped out by a professional bike mechanic. It is also worth getting the threads tapped out after a respray, in case the threads are choked with paint. On the other hand, if it is an alloy frame, you just fit a new gear hanger – see the box opposite.

A similar method is shown on page 75 and is usually found on leisure and hybrid bikes. Here a small extension plate is bolted onto the gear hanger and the mech itself is fitted to the rear end of the extension. This places the rear mech further back than usual, which allows much larger sprockets to be fitted. To remove the rear mech, undo the socket-headed bolt as if it were the mounting bolt.

The final way of fixing the rear mech to the frame is shown on page 84. This method is used on budget bikes, which do not have a built-in gear hanger. Instead, a separate steel gear hanger is bolted to the rear end, with an oval nut on the inside, shaped so that it fits into the drop-out. On budget hybrids, the bolt-on bracket is extended like the extension plate described above.

To remove a rear mech fitted using a bolt-on bracket, first remove the back wheel. Then remove the bottom jockey wheel or break the chain. Finally, you loosen the fixing bolt at the rear of the bracket and pull the mech forward, away from the frame. When refitting, make sure the oval nut fits into the slot for the wheel in the drop-out. As you tighten the bolt, stop the oval nut from turning by holding it with a wrench on the flats. There is no need to overtighten because the bracket is held in place by the wheel nuts as well as the fixing bolt.

Whatever the method of fixing, lightly coat the thread of the mounting bolt with anti-seize grease. And if you are fitting a new rear mech, bear in mind it is always best to fit a new chain as well. Set the correct chain length as explained on page 117.

Finally, set the B screw adjustment as explained on the opposite page. This ensures that the jockey wheels and sprockets do not touch when you go down into bottom gear.

1 This shows the way to remove a rear mech by breaking the chain. Hold the mech with one hand while you undo the pivot bolt with a long Allen wrench as it may be tight.

2 If you intend to refit the mech, take the opportunity to do a quick strip down and clean – see pages 84–85. Always clean the jockey wheels, then lube with waterproof grease.

5 Fit the gear cable now, tensioning the inner before you do up the cable clamp. Snip any spare inner cable off close to the clamp and fit a cable cap to stop it fraying.

6 Turn the pedals slowly and change gears one by one down to bottom gear. Adjust the low limit screw if the chain does not jump onto the largest sprocket or run there silently.

Fine-tuning index gears

1 If the indexing is having an off-day, increase or decrease the cable tension by turning the cable adjuster a quarter-turn. Experiment to find out which way is best.

2 Racing bikes with STI and Ergopower combined gear changers usually have a thumb adjuster on the down tube so you can alter cable tension when riding along.

3 When fitting a rear mech to the frame, it is easier to screw the top pivot bolt into the gear hanger if you steady it by tucking your forefinger behind the gear hanger.

4 Now fit the chain – see pages 114–117. Then adjust the throw by turning the high limit screw until the jockey wheels align with the outer edge of the top sprocket.

DAMAGED GEAR HANGERS

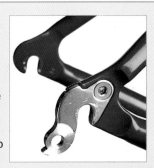

Hanging off the side of the frame, the rear mech and gear hanger often get damaged when a bike falls over. To prevent this from happening, you can replace the standard top pivot bolt with a breakaway bolt. This provides a weak link that snaps off to stop the mech from getting damaged. For an easy way to straighten the hanger on a steel frame, see page 27. Other materials are less forgiving and so frames are often fitted with a replaceable gear hanger, retained by a short socket head bolt. However, each frame needs a different hanger, so ask for a spare when you buy a new bike.

7 Check that the outer cable is arranged in smooth, large radius curves. Then go through the final indexing adjustment on page 76 and give the bike a road test.

WHEN YOU NEED TO DO THIS JOB:
■ The old rear mech is worn out.
■ A rear mech needs stripping down completely.

TIME:
■ 30 minutes to fit a new rear mech, plus another 30 minutes to adjust and test gear change

DIFFICULTY:
■ Care is needed when screwing the pivot bolt into the gear hanger. Otherwise it is easier than overhauling a rear mech.

SPECIAL TOOLS:
■ None.

THE B SCREW ADJUSTER

As well as the two limit screws, nearly all rear mechs have a third adjuster. It's usually known as the B screw but it's also referred to as the chain adjuster. You do not normally need to touch it.

But if you fit a large bottom sprocket, 28 teeth or more, the top jockey wheel sometimes touches the sprocket and interferes with the gear change. If this happens, select the smallest chainwheel and sprocket, then adjust the B screw to give the smallest possible gap between the jockey wheel and sprocket. Increase the gap slightly if bottom gear does not run smoothly.

On SUNTOUR MTB mechs, you set the gap at 6–8mm but on their road mechs, you adjust the B screw so that the main plates are parallel with the chainstay.

Rear mech: overhaul

There is no set period of time, or number of miles, after which you should strip down and clean a rear mech. The kind of mountain biker who cannot keep away from muddy tracks might need to do it once a month, or even sooner. On the other hand, many riders leave the gears untouched for years. However that is leaving it too long. Over that sort of time, the jockey wheels will probably have started to seize up and the gear change will have deteriorated, all without you noticing. To prevent this from happening, you should inspect the rear mech occasionally, maybe when you are cleaning the chain. If it looks as if the teeth on the jockey wheels are starting to wear down, it's time to strip and clean the rear mech.

Most gears can be broken down into more parts than shown in the diagram. But you do not need to go any further than separating the chain cage plates and the jockey wheels. Jockey wheels sometimes have deeper washers on one side than the other, so make a note of which side they fit. Any remaining parts, like the springs and the high and low limit screws, can usually be cleaned with solvent, while they are still in place.

That leaves the question of how badly worn the rear mech is. To check while the mech is still on the bike, hold the bottom of the chain cage with two fingers and see how far you can move it without forcing it. If it moves more than 10mm, investigate further.

This is done by stripping the rear mech and gripping it above and below the two main pivots. Then see if you can feel any movement or play between the top part of the gear and the bottom part. The movement you are trying to detect is from front to back. Do not confuse this with the normal sideways movement. If you can feel more than the slightest amount of play, fit a new mech as shown on pages 76–77.

The easiest way of removing the rear mech from the frame is to undo the jockey wheel bolts, which frees the mech from the chain. Then just undo the top mounting bolt. Use this method whenever possible because it saves having to break the chain. Nevertheless, if you cannot undo the jockey wheel bolts, and they are sometimes almost impossible to budge, you will have to split the chain, as shown on pages 114–115.

Clean and dry all the parts thoroughly before reassembly but remember that the Shimano and the latest Campagnolo top jockey wheels are designed to move from side to side a little. So if the pulley is marked "Centron" or has a metal bush molded into it, or in the case of Campag is marked upper, it is the top jockey wheel. Half fill the center of both jockey wheels with waterproof grease, before putting the washers in place. And use anti-seize grease on the jockey wheel bolts to make sure it is easy to undo them in the future.

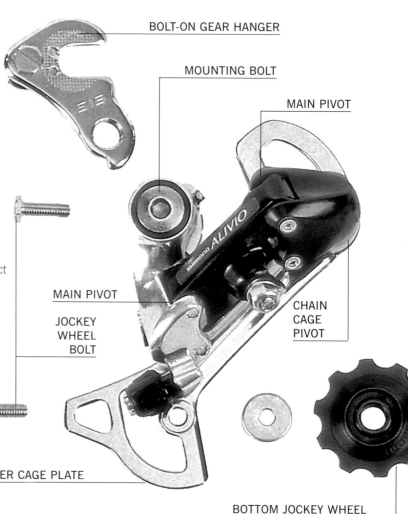

BOLT-ON GEAR HANGER

MOUNTING BOLT

MAIN PIVOT

MAIN PIVOT

JOCKEY WHEEL BOLT

CHAIN CAGE PIVOT

OUTER CAGE PLATE

BOTTOM JOCKEY WHEEL

Rear mech details

Campagnolo

Shimano

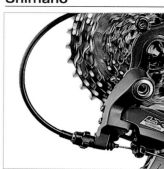

Campag only make gears for road bikes, mainly with Ergopower combined brake and gear levers. They can only be used with Campag cassettes because of the spacing of the sprockets. Campag also makes gears for Miche.

Shimano makes gears for MTBs, racers and utilities. But most Shimano rear mechs can be used with other Shimano components. They can also be used with most SUNTOUR bits and non-ESP Gripshift changers.

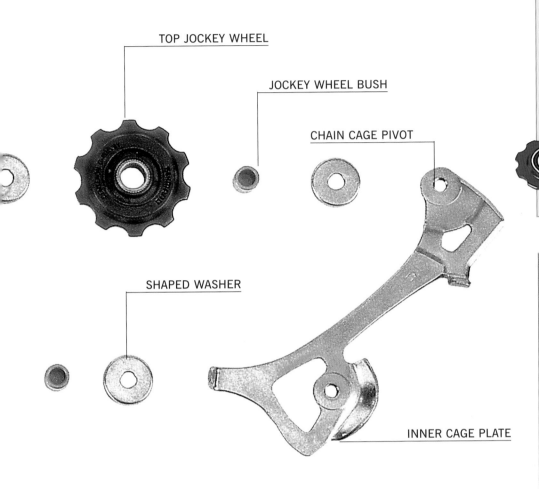

TOP JOCKEY WHEEL

JOCKEY WHEEL BUSH

CHAIN CAGE PIVOT

SHAPED WASHER

INNER CAGE PLATE

SEALED JOCKEY WHEELS

If the jockey wheels are worn, you have a choice between using spares from the maker or fitting sealed jockey wheels with proper ball bearings from another supplier. These will last longer and need less maintenance, though they are around twice the price.

WHEN YOU NEED TO DO THIS JOB:

■ Poor gear changing indicates rear mech needs cleaning.

■ Inspection reveals jockey wheels are worn.

TIME:

■ About 1 hour to remove, thoroughly clean and refit a rear mech.

DIFFICULTY:

■ It is sometimes hard to reassemble the jockey wheels correctly. Try making a drawing as you take the chain cage apart so you do not mix up the various washers and bushes.

SPECIAL TOOLS:

■ It is very important to have a well-fitting wrench or Allen wrench to undo the jockey wheel bolts.

SRAM

SRAM rear mechs are now made of metal but earlier designs were mostly plastic. They are very different from any other design, so should only be used with other SRAM parts. ESP rear mechs can only be used with ESP changers.

Sun Race

Sun Race is a budget alternative to Shimano. They are adjusted in the same way and you can use Sun Race with any Shimano-compatible components. So far, all Sun Race rear mechs are steel but alloy ones are on the way.

SUNTOUR

SUNTOUR is back in the market with new Swing Arm designs. A limited number of their rear mechs are adjusted as Shimano and can be used with Shimano cassettes and changers.

Front mech fitting and adjustment

There's an ever-bigger gap between front derailleur mechanisms for mountain bikes and for road bikes. Front mechs for mountain bikes have heavy-duty chain cages, with an extra-deep rear plate. This allows for the big range of chainwheel sizes that they have to cope with, typically 42/32/22 or 48/38/28.

They are often convertible between top pull and bottom pull, although the former is generally more popular. With top pull, the cable is routed along the top tube and stays clear of dirt and mud. It's also much less likely to get damaged. Those mountain bikes with bottom pull are nearly all elderly, if not actually old.

On the other hand, most road front mechs are much lighter. The chain cage in particular is narrower and lighter, and works by means of bottom pull. However, triple chainsets demand a compromise set-up, with bigger chain cages but a lighter build so far as the actual mechanism is concerned.

Compact chainsets have given rise to some differences. Shimano front mechs can cope with both standard and compact chainsets, but Campag requires a special one for theirs. However, the big problem with front mechs in general is coping with the different sizes of down tube. Shims are supplied with most front mechs with a band-on fitting, to fit tubes up to 31.8mm wide. However, there is a braze-on type of road front mech as well. This normally covers up to 31.8mm, but there is now a screw-on frame adaptor that makes it possible to cover larger sizes too.

Do not try to make a mountain bike type of front mech fit a road bike, or vice versa.

A modern Shimano mountain bike front mech, which is convertible between top and bottom pull.

1 When fitting a new front mech or tuning up an old one, position the outer plate of the chain cage between 1mm and 3mm above the teeth of the outer chainring. The red tab on a new mech is to help you get this right.

2 Arrange the outer plate of the chain cage exactly in line with the chainrings, then tighten the clamp around the seat tube. The chain should be fitted at this point but has been left out here to make it easier to see what is going on.

3 Fit the chain onto the inner chainring and adjust the low limit screw of the front mech so that the inner plate of the chain cage is about 0.5mm clear of the chain. Spin the cranks to check that the chain does not touch the chain cage.

4 Next, lift the chain up onto the big chainring and operate the front changer with your fingers. Then adjust the high limit screw of the front mech so that the outer plate of the chain cage is also 0.5mm clear of the outer edge of the chain.

5 Fit the cable at this point, checking that the inner cable moves freely and that the outer is not kinked. Make sure also that it is seated correctly in the cable stops. Lube the inner cable and the mech.

6 Feed the inner cable between the chain stays and tension it with one hand and tighten the cable clamp with the other. Now check that the front mech changes from ring to ring without delay.

7 On an indexed front mech, road test the bike to check if the indexing is working well. The big test is the jump from the middle to the biggest chainring, with the chain on the second biggest sprocket. If that change does not go through quickly and accurately, increase the cable tension by turning the cable adjuster half a turn at a time until you get an instant change with one click of the shifter. If you find the chain rubs on the chain cage in some of the gears, try making small adjustments to the high and low limit screws. But when you use the biggest chainring with one of the biggest sprockets, or the other way around, the chain nearly always rubs lightly on the chain cage. To stop the noise, "trim" the chain cage left or right a fraction using the gear changer as you ride.

WHEN YOU NEED TO DO THIS JOB:
■ If the chain jumps off when you are changing from one chainring to another.

TIME:
■ 10 minutes to adjust or remove the front mech.
■ Another 10 minutes to check adjustment with a test ride.

DIFFICULTY:
Much easier than dealing with the rear mech.

FRONT MECH ADJUSTER SCREWS
Sometimes the limit screws on front mechs are marked H = high = the biggest chainring, and L = low = the smallest chainring.

This is similar to a rear mech, but the letters are often so small or so hidden that it is very hard to read them. To identify which screw is which, just give the outer one an experimental half-turn and make a note of which direction the chain cage moves.

Front mechs: continued

If you're out on your bike and find the chain rubs on the chain cage when you select a top or bottom gear, adjust the position of the chain cage slightly using the gear shifter. This is known as "trimming" the front mech. However, you can only do this with certain front changers. Shimano shifters usually have a "ghost" half-shift to allow for this problem.

Braze-on road front mech

1 To fit a braze-on front mech without breaking the chain, remove the nut and bolt from the chain cage, as shown. Pull the cage plates apart and fit the front mech over the chain. Replace the nut and bolt. Then slide the front mech up or down the bracket until there is no more than a 1mm to 3 mm gap between cage and chainring. Tighten the bolt.

2 Unlike a band-on front mech, you do not have to align the chain cage with the chainring, unless something is bent. So with the chain on the smallest chainring, set the low limit screw. Then fit the cable and lift the chain onto the outer ring. Adjust the high limit screw and road test. Adjust the limit screws to minimize the amount of trimming needed.

Fitting and removal

1 To remove a front mech without breaking the chain, loosen the cable clamp and pull the inner and outer cable away. Undo the clamp bolt to release the clip around the frame and then move the front mech back along the chain to improve the access.

2 Turn the front mech upside down so you can get at the back of the chain cage. Remove the nut and bolt holding the chain cage together and pull the plates apart. Slip the front mech off the chain. Reverse this process to fit a new front mech.

Cable routes

A pair of dual-pull front changers, showing the different routes that the cable can take.

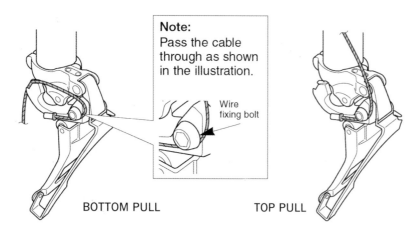

Note:
Pass the cable through as shown in the illustration.

Wire fixing bolt

BOTTOM PULL   TOP PULL

BOTTOM BRACKET FRONT MECH
To save assembly time, some bike manufacturers fit the front mech on a bracket that is held in place by the sealed bottom bracket cartridge. This is not a problem, apart from the fact that you cannot adjust the position of the front mech at all. If you ever want to fit a larger or smaller chainring, consider replacing this type with a conventional band-on front mech.

Gear shifters

Mountain bikes are fitted with index gears that are controlled by shifters mounted on the handlebars. Avoid dismantling the shifter gears because they are almost impossible to put back together again. However, you can do the necessary lubrication by external spraying, or by removing the gear change indicator and spraying internally.

As for road bikes, most modern bikes have gear shifters that are combined with brake levers. These are covered on the next page. A few older bikes still have gear shifters controlled by levers on the down tube.

Most of them are friction changers, and when setting them up check first that the right-hand lever moves smoothly. If it doesn't, loosen the central screw slightly. If it feels loose, tighten the center screw very slightly. Set the limit screws next, using the same method as outlined in rear mech adjustment, except that the H limit screw must be adjusted so that the chain cage is directly below the center line of the top sprocket.

Fit the cable and then road test the bike. When changing gear, move the lever a little until you feel and hear the chain jump to the next sprocket. Adjust the position of the lever slightly if the gear makes any noise as you pedal.

In top gear, the chain should run almost silently. If there is a slight but regular metallic clacking or coughing noise, try adjusting the high limit screw one eighth-turn counter-clockwise. If that makes the noise worse, turn the high limit screw clockwise a little until the noise goes away.

Now change down carefully, one gear at a time, until you get to bottom gear. Turn the low limit screw clockwise if there is a clacking or coughing noise. If that makes the noise worse or the chain jumps down onto the next sprocket, adjust the low limit screw counter-clockwise one quarter-turn at a time until the chain runs silently on bottom gear.

If in doubt about any of this, check the chain cage from behind to see if it has moved too far to the left, or too far to the right, and then adjust the limit screws as required.

If the gears run quietly at first but get noisier, or they keep jumping to a higher gear, tighten the center screw of the lever very slightly. But if the top jockey wheel seems to get tangled up with the bottom sprocket, adjust the B screw as explained on page 83.

There are also a few road bikes around with down tube levers that are indexed, or where you have a choice between indexed and friction. They must not be stripped down, but should be given an occasional shot of lube to keep them working properly. Point the aerosol can at the edge of the changer and work the lever so that it penetrates into the mechanism.

See the next spread for combined brake and gear levers.

FRICTION SHIFTER

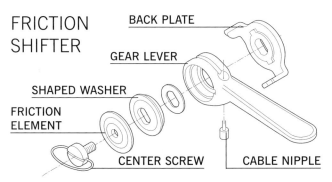

BACK PLATE

GEAR LEVER

SHAPED WASHER

FRICTION ELEMENT

CENTER SCREW

CABLE NIPPLE

1 On simple trigger shifters, maintenance consists of an occasional spray with aerosol lube, then a wipe over. Try to direct the spray at the cable nipple, then operate the gear lever a few times to spread the lube around.

2 Rapidfire Plus levers have a separate lever for up and down shifts. Do not strip them down because they are spring loaded. To lube, remove the rubber cap over the nipple, if fitted, and squirt aerosol lube into the nipple recess.

3 Later Shimano changers all have a nipple recess accessible by removing a Phillips screw head. This reveals the nipple, allowing you to lube the cable by introducing an aerosol. You can also lube the gear change indicator.

4 Rotary changers do not often require lubricating. However, when they do, open up the cable port and spread a match-head size bead of lubricant around the cable track and another round the ratchet. Do not over-lubricate.

5 On sports bikes with indexed down tube levers, aim one shot of aerosol lube at the outside edge of the central housing. When you apply the lube there, it is more likely to find its way into the ratchet mechanism, where it's needed.

6 Most down tube shifters screw into bosses fixed to the frame, though a few have a band-on fixing. To remove, undo the central screw and pull off. To refit, make sure you locate the square cut-out on the back plate correctly.

Combined brake and gear levers

There are now three firms that make combined brake and gear levers – Shimano, Campagnolo and SRAM. Shimano was the first with a system called STI, and it remains the only system which has the gear cable coming out of the side of the lever. Campag followed with Ergopower, which has both cables concealed. And instead of using the brake lever to change down as Shimano does, they have the big gear lever to change down with and a button or small lever to change up.

SRAM approaches it differently, using a gear lever that is completely separate from the brake lever to change both up and down. A short sweep of the lever changes up, while a longer sweep changes down.

Fitting the Shimano lever is a matter of finding the groove on the outside of the hood, when the brake lever is in the normal position. Reach down the groove with a 5mm Allen wrench and loosen the clamp, position the lever and tighten the clamp. On Ergopower, the Allen wrench–fitting clamp bolt is inside the lever, in exactly the same place as an old fashioned brake lever. SRAM is reached in the same way as Campag but the clamp bolt is slightly easier to access. Try to fit them in such a way that a smooth transition is achieved between the handlebar and the tops of the levers.

When fitting the gear cables, all three systems require that they be put in top gear first. So with Shimano, you operate the gear lever until you get top gear. As for Campag, you operate the button or lever until you get top. And for SRAM, you give the gear lever at least 10 short taps. Each one also has a slightly different position that the gear cable emerges from.

So far as the brake cable is concerned, all three are quite simple. You open up the brake lever as far as you can, and that reveals the brake nipple. The nipple can be removed with fingers or a pair of pliers, and a new one threaded in.

When fitting and servicing these systems, bear in mind that the performance of the cable is the main factor. Only use top quality inner and outer cables, either the maker's own brand or a branded alternative. These cables are pre-lubricated, so you don't need any oil or grease unless they dry out in use. Then lube them with a wax chain lubricant or similar.

Keep the cables free of dirt and grit but never attempt to strip the levers down. They are strictly manufacturer service only, although the experience is that they very seldom fail.

STI combined levers

1 STI levers have the gear cables emerging from the sides. The large lever is the brake lever while the gear lever is mounted behind it.

2 To remove an old brake cable, pull the lever right back and draw out the cable. The gear change mechanism moves with the brake lever.

WHEN YOU NEED TO DO THIS JOB:
■ When fitting new combined brake and gear levers.
■ If the gear changing or braking has gotten worse and will not respond to tweaking, indicating new cables are required.
TIME:
■ Allow a couple of hours in case you have to sort out problems with the outer cable as well as the inners.

DIFFICULTY: *////*
It is not difficult just to fit the inner cable. But if the outers also need work, it starts to get a little difficult.

3 The new brake cable is threaded through the nipple holder. It takes a bit of finding to push the cable out the back of the lever and down.

4 To change the gear cable, select top gear. Then tie the brake lever back to the handlebars. You can also see the groove for the lever clamp.

5 Extract the tiny rubber bung, revealing the gear cable nipple. If the cable shuttle isn't visible, select top gear with the small gear lever.

6 Pull out the nipple and cable with your fingers, or dig it out with a small screwdriver. Replace the gear cable by reversing the process.

Ergopower levers

1 An Ergopower lever, showing the gear lever, with the small lever on the other side. See page 90 for changing the brake cable.

2 Put the rear mech into top gear. The Campag gear mechanism is in the body of the lever, so it is longer than the Shimano one.

3 Fold the rubber hood back over the front of the lever. It has to be lifted off the small lever so that the bare body is revealed.

4 Working on the opposite side, dig out the gear nipple with a small screwewdriver and pull the old cable out. Reverse the process to replace.

DoubleTap levers

1 A DoubleTap lever, with all the gear change functions concentrated in the one gear lever. It's smoother in appearance than the others.

2 The brake cable emerges from the nipple holder. Pull out the broken one and replace with new, threading it through the nipple holder.

3 To get at the gear cable, fold the rubber hood back. Then push the broken cable from the other end to get it clear of the housing or shuttle.

4 The gear cable emerges on the inside of the lever. Reverse the process to replace it, then fold back the rubber hood to normalize everything.

CHAPTER

5

HUB GEARS, BRAKES AND DYNAMOS

NEWARK PUBLIC LIBRARY
121 HIGH STREET
NEWARK, NEW YORK 14513

Hub gears: an introduction

Hub gears have always been very popular in Holland, Germany and other countries where the tradition of cycling to work and for convenience has always been very strong. Now that countries like the USA and Britain are catching up, hub gears are returning to popularity there as well. However, they are making no inroads in countries like France and Italy, where even the utility bikes are equipped with derailleur gears.

There are three main manufacturers of hub gears. Sturmey-Archer is the best known name but it has recently added an eight speed hub to its traditional three, four and five speed. Shimano has three, seven and eight speeds. And SRAM has seven, eight and nine speeds in addition to its traditional Torpedo three speed. Sturmey and Torpedo three speeds are largely unaltered for most of the last 100 years but the multi-speed hub gears are new designs.

Inside all hub gears are a lot of carefully made parts that are the most complex designs found on a bicycle. They have more in common with the automatic gearbox of a car than anything else. Fortunately, these internal parts seldom go wrong but when they do, the simplest thing is to fit a new hub. You should never try to strip down a hub gear as it is unlikely you will ever get it together again without the proper tools and knowledge. Just limit yourself to removing the back wheel and replacing the gear cable.

When a hub gear goes out of adjustment, fix it without delay. Riding it incorrectly adjusted damages a hub gear and eventually reduces it to scrap.

Once a bike has a hub gear, it's easy for bike makers to add a hub brake and a hub dynamo as well. It is impossible to cover all the combinations but representative designs have been selected for coverage. Maintenance is easy apart from removing the back wheel, so punctures are repaired with the wheel in place if possible.

Sturmey-Archer three & five speeds

The most common problem on a Sturmey-Archer is finding that you can only pedal in one gear. Somehow you're in between or in neutral when the gear lever is in a different position. Another big fault is slipping in the gears – there is a coughing noise, the pedals jerk around but then everything goes back to normal for a while. It often happens when you are pedaling hard to go uphill, when a sudden free movement of the pedal can be downright dangerous. These and most other faults are caused by incorrect adjustment of the gear cable, a broken cable or a broken control chain.

Adjustment and replacement of the gear cable are covered here. New cables are supplied with both inner and outer, as you can't separate them. If the chain runs over a pulley, check that it revolves freely. And if the outer cable is held in position with a cable clamp, it must be repositioned if it proves impossible to adjust the gears.

If the control chain needs replacing, it screws out of the hub and a new one just screws in. But to avoid problems, check the adjustment of the control rod and chain.

Older Sturmey-Archer hub gears with a metal or black plastic oil port need a few drops of light oil, about once every two weeks if the bike is used frequently. But if there's no oil port, it follows that it doesn't need oil. However, the grease in the hub should be replaced at the same time as the hub is serviced.

Wheel bearings are the cup and cone type, which are adjusted in the usual way but you'll probably need an especially thin spanner. Adjust on the opposite side from the chain.

Something that closely resembles a traditional click-type gear lever is available but there are new types of gear shifters such as a rotary changer as well.

New cable and adjustment

1 On modern bikes, the control chain and cable are concealed by a plastic shroud. Pull it off and check if the control chain is stiff or broken. Screw in a new one if necessary.

2 Put the gear shifter into top gear and unscrew the outer cable from the back. Fit the new cable, clamp it in exactly the same place and bring the adjuster up to the knurled nut.

Remove back wheel

1 On hub gear bikes, the gear cable connects with the back axle, so the first step is to put it into gear. Then undo the knurled wheel on the gear cable one quarter-turn, then undo the adjuster about twelve turns to release the cable.

2 Slacken both wheel nuts with a wrench, then undo them the rest of the way with your fingers. To prevent the axle from turning, special washers fit around the axle and into the frame. Place the wheel nuts and washers to one side.

3 Push the axle forward with your thumbs, but try to hold the wheel as it drops away to stop it from bouncing around. Now support the frame with one hand while you lift the chain off the sprocket and put the wheel to one side.

4 When refitting, replace the shaped axle washers. Then tighten the wheel nuts lightly, pulling the wheel back so that it is centered, with about 12mm of play in the chain. Tighten the wheel nuts, giving each side a turn at a time.

WHEN YOU NEED TO DO THIS JOB:
■ Cable is broken.
■ Control chain is stiff or broken.
■ Gears will not engage. Or they slip (steps 3 and 4).

TIME:
■ 15 minutes to fit new cable.
■ 2 minutes for step 3.

DIFFICULTY:
■ It is easy to fit a new cable but adjusting the gears can be awkward.

TOOLS:
Special cone wrench.

FIVE SPEED HUB GEARS

The Sturmey-Archer five speed is very similar to the three speed, except for some details. Adjustment is similar to the three speed, including putting it into second gear and pedaling a few times. Then instead of lining up the shoulder on the control rod, you line up the little notch on the control rod with the end of the axle. The little notch is either painted red or blue. The five speed is more fiddly than the three speed, and is more likely to go out of adjustment.

3 Sometimes the chain simply turns the corner but modern bikes have a pulley to reduce the effort. Select N or 2 on the gear shifter, pedal a few times and look at the end of the axle.

4 Adjust the cable so that the control rod is level with the end of the axle (see diagram). Tighten the knurled nut up to the adjuster. Change up to third, then back to second, turning the pedals. Check the adjustment and do a test ride to make sure that you can get all three gears.

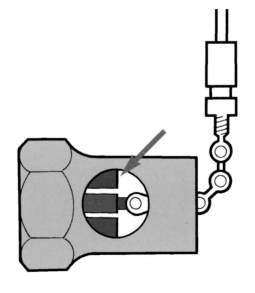

Most types of Sturmey-Archer hub gears don't have a pulley at the end of the axle. Instead there is a large nut with an inspection hole. Put the gear shifter in second gear, then look down through the inspection hole toward the end of the axle. Adjust the cable until the shoulder of the control rod is level with the end of the axle.

The European Bike of the Year 2007 was fitted with a Sturmey-Archer eight speed hub gear.

Back wheel out

WHEN YOU NEED TO DO THIS JOB:
■ If the gears go out of adjustment.
■ You have to take the back wheel out for a puncture.

TIME:
■ 5 minutes to readjust the gears.
■ 15 minutes the first time you take the back wheel out.

DIFFICULTY:
🔧 To adjust the gears.
🔧🔧🔧 To remove the back wheel.

SPECIAL TOOLS:
■ None.

1 The cable adjuster is a keyhole fitting in the frame. Turn it to one side and line it up to remove it.

2 Undo the hub nuts with a pair of 15mm ring wrenches. Be careful that you don't bend the disc brake.

Sturmey-Archer eight speeds

The eight speed is a new design that is quite distinct from older Sturmey-Archer types. It is a modular design, so it definitely should not be taken apart but anyway, service problems usually arise outside the hub. Happily, it requires no maintenance, only the replenishment of grease when the hub is stripped for servicing.

   The gear shifter is a rotary device, with a very clear indicator. Most of the gears are 13% up or down on the previous one, with 28% difference for the top and bottom gear. Hence the range of gears is much wider than previous Sturmey-Archer designs. It's often fitted with a hub brake as well, although these pictures show a hub gear with a disc brake.

On the Sturmey-Archer rotary shifter, remove the Allen screw at the bottom to lubricate the mechanism or change the gear cable.

Basic adjustment

1 The rotary gear shifter, with fourth gear selected as this is the gear that is used for adjusting the hub gear.

2 Incorrect adjustment as the yellow arrow doesn't match up with the yellow patch that is flanked by the red stripes.

3 Make the adjustment at the cable adjuster below the chain stay. Check and re-adjust if necessary.

4 Correct adjustment, with the yellow arrow aligning with the yellow patch flanked by the red stripes.

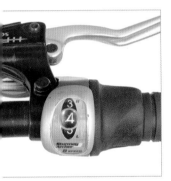

3 Each side there is a lock washer that fits in the frame, to stop the axle from turning around in the drop-outs.

4 Free the gear cable by grasping it and pulling backward, then forward to free the screw-on nipple.

5 To put the wheel back in the frame, the nipple is replaced, then the cable is dragged back into its groove.

6 The chain is tensioned by pulling the wheel backward until there is about ½ inch play in the chain.

Shimano Inter and Nexus hub gears

Inter-3, Inter-7 and Nexus Inter-8 are the three Shimano hub gears that are currently in production. But there used to be a four speed and a seven speed hub of slightly different design, which was very widely used and is featured here as typical of what Shimano does.

Generally speaking, these hub gears don't need anything in the way of routine lubrication. But if a hub brake is fitted and they start making a noise, get the hub topped up with fresh grease by a dealer. There's a hole for this purpose on the outside of the brake unit.

For the Inter-3, Inter-7 and Nexus 8 speed, replacing the cable is a matter of setting the Revo-shift gear shifter into first gear. Then undo the screw holding the cover of the Revo-shift in place and strip out the old cable. Pass the new cable through the hole in the winder unit into the cable adjuster and take up the slack. Insert the inner cable into the groove in the cable guide so that the nipple fits into the recess in the winder unit.

Cut the new outer cable to the same length as the old one, using it as a pattern. Feed the inner cable into the outer cable and fit the center of the fixing bolt exactly 101mm (127mm for Inter-7 and Nexus eight speed) from the end of the outer cable. Then take it around to the pulley. The flats on the fixing bolt will fit into the hole in the pulley. Secure the outer cable in the outer cable holder by way of the slot. Alternatively, fit the outer cable in the outer cable holder and use a 2mm Allen wrench in the hole to turn the pulley. Fit the fixing bolt into the hole in the pulley.

With Inter-7 and Nexus hub gears, check the cable adjustment by looking in the window down by the chainstay, if the bike is on its wheels. But if it's upside down, there's another window too. Put the bike into fourth gear and try to see either the red lines in the case of Inter-7 or the yellow lines in the case of Nexus eight speed. Wind the cable adjuster in or out until the two lines exactly coincide. Change to first gear and then back to fourth to check. The Inter-7 or the Nexus eight speed is now correctly adjusted.

Removing the back wheel

1 Put the bike in first gear, where the gear cable is as slack as possible.

2 Remove the shroud covering the gear change and the chain guard. Pull the gear cable out of the outer cable holder and hook it out of the hole in the pulley.

3 Undo the hub nuts and take them off.

New cable and adjustment

1 When fitting a new cable or adusting the gears on an older type of Shimano hub gear, select fourth gear on the gear shifter with the rotary changer.

2 Remove the old cable by undoing the three tiny Phillips screws holding the cover onto the gear shifter. The screws fit from underneath.

3 Working from the top, lift off the cover and pry the nipple out with a screwdriver. Cut the cable at a convenient point and pull it out.

4 Undo the grub screw down at the hub and pull out the remaining part of the old inner cable. To fit the new cable, start at the gear shifter.

5 Thread the new inner cable around the three rollers in the gear shifter and feed the end through the cable adjuster and the outer cable.

6 Push the inner cable into the outer cable and out by the rear drop-out. Take the cable through the outer casing holder and tighten the cable clamp.

7 Tighten the grub screw to keep the inner cable under tension and check that fouth gear is still selected. Then screw the cable adjuster in or out until the two red lines line up. Ignore the yellow marks. Road test to check that the gear changes go through easily and the hub gear is silent, apart from when changing gear.

4 Remove the friction washers.

5 Take out the back wheel. Refitting the wheel requires reversing the process, taking into account the instructions on fitting a new cable in the main text.

WHEN YOU NEED TO DO THIS JOB:
- Back wheel must be removed.
- New cable is needed.
- Hub gear has gone out of adjustment.

TIME:
- 5 minutes to remove the back wheel.
- 30 minutes to replace the cable.
- 5 minutes to adjust the gear.

DIFFICULTY:
- All jobs are fairly easy; fitting a new cable takes time.

SPECIAL TOOLS:
- None.

Removing the

SRAM and Torpedo

SRAM, or Torpedo as they used to be known, probably makes the greatest variety of hub gears. There are two three speed hubs, a five, a seven and now a nine. The original Torpedo hub gear came out in 1903 and has been largely unchanged since that time. It's used on countless bikes in northern Europe, and is even now a vital part of the Brompton folding bike. It differs from the Sturmey-Archer because it'll always give you drive. It's impossible to get stuck between gears.

To adjust the gears, first put the bike into third gear and turn the pedals a few times. You then push the cable onto the control chain so that it's taut, without any play. It's a ratchet device, so you just push it on as far as you reasonably can. To check, select first gear and turn the pedals. If the control chain is not tight enough, you can take up the slack by screwing the cable adjuster counter-clockwise. And if it's too tight, you can screw the cable adjuster clockwise. Then give the bike a test ride. Disconnect the cable for taking the wheel out by pushing the chrome tag.

i-MOTION 3 is similar but instead of a control chain, it's got a control cable. This allows all the control stuff to be kept inside of the chainstay. P5 and S7 have five and seven gears respectively. They introduced the Clickbox, through which the cable selected the gears. Clickbox installation is dealer-only but it can be removed from the hub by turning the knurled bolt on the end that holds it in place. Wheel removal is then fairly straightforward, requiring you to disconnect the brake and release the retaining washers.

Putting back the wheel is the reverse, but re-installing the Clickbox entails pushing it onto the stop on the axle. Check that the guide of the locating sleeve engages with the slot on the housing. Finally, tighten the knurled bolt at the end of the Clickbox.

i-MOTION 9 is the latest SRAM design, which replaces the Clickbox with a connecting tube. In addition to making the largest number of gears for the moment, apart from Rohloff, they have made it compact and easy to remove the back wheel.

1 Typical of the bikes that fit the i-MOTION 9 gear, it comes fully protected. Pull off the plastic shroud around the gear mechanism.

3 Undo the wheel nuts and take off the friction washers that prevent the axle from turning in the frame. You'll need a screwdriver to pry them off.

An old type of three speed combined with a back pedal or coaster brake.

5 It's an easy connection to undo. And you place the circular part of the joint in the hole in the control cable to put it together again.

wheel

Adjusting i-MOTION 9

2 Take off the rest of the chainguard, both the upper and lower parts. It's all done without using any tools, just by hand pressure alone.

1 Drop down from seventh gear to sixth gear, as that is the one for carrying out adjustment of the gears.

2 Use the adjuster on the control tube or the gear shifter to line up the red and yellow marks.

3 One adjustment window can be seen beside the seat stay and another from underneath the bike.

4 The control cable is inside of the chainstay and under it. Turn the thickened part of the control cable to free the connection from the hub.

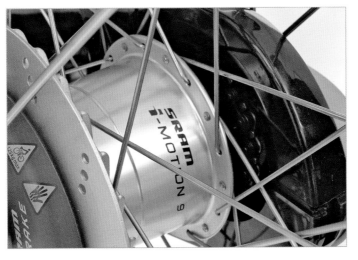

The latest SRAM product is a nine speed hub gear, with a completely different approach to installation in the frame. A quick release control tube connects the gear to the cable, and is fitted out of harm's way inside of the chainstay.

Torpedo hub gears

6 Slip the chain off the sprocket and take the wheel away. Reassembly is the reverse process, but the chainguard does need patience.

1 Check that the control chain flexes easily and that it's pushed fully home. Select H or 3 position on the gear shifter. Also known as the SRAM, which has a plastic pulley instead of a hub nut.

2 The cable comes in one piece, with a plastic ratchet that clicks onto the control chain. Overall length of the inner cable is adjusted with an Allen wrench so it just reaches the control chain.

3 Bring the end of the control chain and the ratchet together, then push them together with finger pressure only. Check that the cable feels taut but not under pressure as that'll put the adjustment out.

Hub brakes

There are three types of hub brake – conventional brake, roller brake and coaster brake. The conventional brake has brake shoes and operates like a simplified car brake. Sooner or later the shoes will wear out but in practice, they last almost indefinitely.

Then there is the roller brake, which has a brake shoe that completely lines the brake housing. There are five rollers in contact with the brake shoe and when you apply the brake, a set of cams comes into action. They come into contact with the rollers, which ride up on the cams and force the brake shoe against the inside surface of the brake housing.

It sounds like a complicated system but in practice it works well. Furthermore, the latest ones are grease-filled, so the service life of the brake shoes is virtually unlimited. The only adjustment is to the cable but it does need occasional greasing. But because they are totally enclosed and generate a lot of heat due to their efficient braking, a cooling disc is usually included in the design. Don't confuse a roller brake with a cooling disc with a disc brake.

Finally there is the coaster or back-pedal brake. This is operated by simply back pedalling, which brings the brake shoes into contact with the braking surface onto the inside of the hub. Again the service life is unlimited and they need neither a brake lever nor adjustment.

All these designs are virtually waterproof, maintaining their braking power in virtually all conditions. Furthermore, the hub bearings are dustproof and waterproof as well. If you have to replace the cable, hub brakes are generally fitted with a cable 2mm in diameter.

Adjust a conventional hub brake by turning the aduster counter-clockwise until it locks the brake, then the other way until the hub brake revolves without binding or touching at all. Alternatively, adjust the knurled adjuster until there is 2cm of free play in the brake lever, before the brake bites.

This is a SRAM coaster brake, combined with a three speed hub gear. Normally these need no maintenance but after much use the brake might need re-adjusting. Take up the free play in the adjuster until the brake locks, then back off approximately 90°.

Shimano roller brake

1 To remove the wheel, first disconnect the Nexus brake by flipping the cable end.

2 This has a dynamo as well, so disconnect that and loosen the hub nuts.

3 The wheel is free, apart from the brake reaction arm which is yanked out. When refitting make sure the reaction arm locates correctly.

4 Apply some heat-resisting grease to the inside of a Nexus brake occasionally.

Refitting the wheel to the bike involves reversing the process, taking care to locate the brake reaction arm and to reconnect the hub dynamo.

Removing a back wheel

1 Disconnect the brake cable from the operating lever of the hub brake.

2 Unscrew the brake cable from its fitting and the gear cable, if one is fitted.

3 Unship the chain and look out for any other parts that have to come off.

4 Undo both of the hub nuts with a ring wrench, before removing the wheel.

5 Take off the mudguard stays, if necessary, and pull off the lock washers.

6 The wheel is now ready to come out, in this case it is pulled out backward.

7 Take the wheel out and free the chain. Reverse the process to fit it back in.

A SRAM nine speed hub gear combined with an i-brake, which is a re-packaged conventional hub brake.

Hub dynamos for sporting applications either come ready-built in a wheel by Shimano, or in a SRAM version with a quick release hub.

Hub dynamos

Hub dynamos are manufactured by the trio of Sturmey-Archer, Shimano and SRAM. Sturmey's Dynohub is fairly traditional but it's fitted with sealed cartridge bearings and is available in 2.4 and 3 watt versions. It can be supplied on its own but usually comes with a hub brake.

Shimano makes a similar device but it generally looks better. It's available separately or in conjunction with a hub brake, or in various complete wheels. There are road and mountain bike versions with quick release and bolt-on hubs, plus a disc brake option as well.

SRAM's hub dynamo is much the same as the other two, down to an output of 2.4 or 3 watts. It can also be supplied as a stand-alone quick-release front hub.

Usually, hub dynamos are connected to front and rear lights made by the firm of Bausch and Muller or Basta. Modern hub dynamos are normally wired with a twin cable, unlike the bottle-type dynamo. This is usually fitted with a single wire and an earth return. But some bike manufacturers have used clever systems where the mudguards carry the current by means of a printed circuit, only using wires for the connection at both ends.

One of the drawbacks of dynamo lighting is that it stops when the bike comes to a halt. However, Bausch and Muller make lights fitted with a condenser so that the electrical energy is stored for when the bike stops, keeping the lights going.

The picture sequence shows a Sturmey-Archer Dynohub being removed but the Shimano and the SRAM come off and go back on in a similar way.

Removing a wheel

1 Undo the connnections for the Sturmey-Archer Dynohub at the terminal block. They are down by the fork, so they're out of the way but awkward to disconnect.

2 If any sort of brake is fitted, disconnect the controls as well. Then undo the hub nuts, preferably with a ring wrench. Remove any parts that are fitted under the hub nut.

3 The Dynohub has a special axle washer, which anchors it to the frame. It probably has to be levered off with a large screwdriver, thereby freeing the whole wheel.

4 When the wheel comes off, you have to pull the brake reaction arm out of the fitting on the frame. It's awkward to replace when putting the wheel back in the frame.

A typical Bausch and Muller front light, with integrated reflector. These lights are unlike previous generations of bike lights because with a decent input and halogen lamps, they are good enough to see with and not just act as a marker.

The Shimano hub dynamo only differs from the Sturmey-Archer and the SRAM in detail. But the Shimano terminal block is much easier to access.

This is a single-sided shifter, with all of the control functions concentrated in one hand. The hub gear part of the system is controlled by the thumb shifter, with the gear ranges indicated by means of "pictograms." On the same hand is a rotary gear shifter, which is indexed in the normal way.

SRAM DualDrive

The control cable enters the hub gear by means of a Clickbox, which fits on the end of the axle. It's the same as some modern SRAM hub gears. When the back wheel has to be removed, put the derailleur gear into top gear and the hub gear into Uphill. Push the Clickbox button down and pull it off the axle. Then unscrew the control rod and take the wheel off.

To fit a new cable to the hub gear, follow the same steps apart from unscrewing the control rod. Snap open the Clickbox and use a 4mm Allen wrench to undo the cable clamp. Then remove the escape hatch on the outside of the gear shifter and pull out the old cable. Feed in the new one from the gear shifter end, pulling it tight. Replace the escape hatch and pull the cable through until you reach the Clickbox again. Position the cable in the cable clamp and tighten the Allen screw.

Trim the cable and put back the cover of the Clickbox. Re-install the Clickbox on the axle and place the gear shifter in the flat or level position. Turn the cable adjuster until the marks in the window of the gear shifter are in exact alignment.

The derailleur part of the system consists of a normal SRAM rear mech, which is adjusted in the same way as any other, see page 79. As for fitting a new cable, it is also very similar apart from the gear shifter. You open the shifter by undoing the screw and then pulling open the cable change sleeve.

ADJUSTER WINDOW

DualDrive consists of a hub gear equipped with a freehub, on which is mounted either an eight or nine speed cassette. The hub gear is controlled by means of a cable which fits on the end of the axle in a Clickbox.

CHAPTER

DRIVE SYSTEM

CHAINRING
BOLT

Drive system: components

The drive line is a very complicated part of the bike, with lots of subtle differences. It is worth taking a minute to figure out exactly what you've got.

If you've got a bike with derailleur gears, you certainly have a ³⁄₃₂in chain. But if you're moving toward replacement, both nine and ten speeds have a specific chain. Hub gears, on the other hand, use a ⅛in chain, which is wider and more reliable, while single speed bikes can use either a ⅛in or a ³⁄₃₂in. Generally speaking the more expensive the bike, the more likely it is to have a ³⁄₃₂in chain.

So far as multiple freewheels are concerned, eight speeds or more are bound to have cassette-type sprockets. But the real reason for having them is to make the hub stronger. Before cassettes, it was common for rear axles to give up under the strain.

Pedals are really dependent on what kind of bike you have. Rubber pedals of various kinds are fitted to city bikes, and sometimes to trekking bikes as well. Clips and toe-straps fit onto mountain bikes and road bikes for riders who choose to wear ordinary shoes. On the other hand, the various clipless styles require a special shoe to go with them, and so are more specialized. Nevertheless, the Shimano pedal system is based on shoes that can be used for long-distance walking as well. Other systems tend to be for racing-only as walking in them is very difficult.

Finally, in the next chapter there is a choice between sealed bottom brackets and cup and axle bottom brackets. Most modern bikes are fitted with a sealed bottom bracket, as it is convenient for the bike assembler and also substantially more waterproof.

CHAINRING

CRANK

PIN

Four-bolt chainsets are very popular on mountain bikes. In theory five-bolt chainsets are better but it is really just a matter of styling. This chainset is medium-price, and offers a choice of either square taper or Power Spline fitting.

1 This is a ³⁄₃₂in chain, fitted to all derailleur systems. However, six, seven and eight speed gears need one chain, while nine and ten speeds have their own types.

2 Some single speed or hub gear bikes have a ⅛in chain, with a joining link that is pried apart. A ³⁄₃₂in chain won't work as it is too narrow to fit the sprockets.

3 A cassette-style sprocket cluster fits onto a free hub. It is lighter than the other type, and the hub is much stronger, which was the reason for the switch in the first place.

4 The other type of sprocket cluster screws onto a separate body, which in turn screws onto the hub. It is too wide for more than seven speeds and much heavier.

5 Hub gears have the one sprocket, but it can be changed to allow changes of gearing. They are usually fitted with ⅛ chains for cheapness and reliability.

6 Single speed bikes are usually fitted with fixed gears, which means that the rider has to pedal at all times. But kids' and BMX bikes are fitted with freewheels.

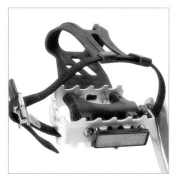

7 These pedals are fitted with toe clips and straps, which are a simple way of improving the connection between the pedal and the foot, improving power transfer.

8 Pedals also come in a clipless style. This type is far more efficient at transferring power from the foot to the chainwheel, and is more comfortable in the long run.

9 Sealed bottom brackets have swept the market in the last ten years, thanks to their water resistance and convenience. They are covered in the next chapter.

10 Ordinary bottom brackets are still around in vast numbers and will be for many years They are mostly neglected and many are badly made.

11 Recently, external bearings have started to appear. They replace the sealed bottom bracket, spacing the bearings farther apart for more rigidity and a longer life.

12 Cotter pins are a rarity now, but the one-piece chainset and bottom bracket is much more common on kids' bikes, BMX bikes and very cheap adult bikes.

Drive system: care and inspection

It's either the build-up of oily dirt on the chain, sprockets and chainring or the absence of oil altogether that causes most wear in the drive system. Keep the chain clean, replace it often, and the drive system will last thousands of miles before anything more needs replacing.

You can test the chain for wear by pulling a link away from the chainring. If you can move it more than ⅛in, you need to carry out the checks on this page. Roughly speaking you need to replace the chain every 1,500 miles, but that is only the roughest possible guide. A mountain bike used across country may need a chain replaced every 500 miles, while a chain in an oil bath needs replacing every 2,500 miles. It all depends on the way it is used.

Next, take a look at the sprocket or sprockets. If the chain hasn't been changed for thousands of miles, a new chain won't run successfully on the sprockets but will fluff or cough every time it goes around. On the other hand, if the chain has been replaced regularly the sprockets will last four or five chains.

The same thing applies to the chainrings. They are usually made of aluminium alloy, which is soft at first but picks up a harder layer as it's used. First of all check that they are properly fixed to the cranks. Then look for wear. Eventually the chainrings become blunted or hooked. And though they will continue to drive a chain, they will cause a new chain to wear out fast, or an old chain to work very inefficiently.

As for the chainset, check first for creaks and grinding sounds, which can usually be cured by greasing the crank bolt and/or the pedals. At the same time, see if you can detect any movement when you hold one crank still and attempt to move the other. If there's movement in a crank, tighten the crank bolts as hard as you can and check again after a quick ride around the block. Then every 100 miles, until you can tighten them no more.

Then check for wear in the bottom bracket bearings. Slip the chain off and see if you can feel movement in both cranks. If it's a cup and axle bottom bracket, you can try to adjust it out. But if it's a sealed bottom bracket, it's worn out and must be replaced. Check also for noise in the bearings, or excessive tightness. Again this indicates the bottom bracket needs stripping down or replacing, depending on whether it is a cup and axle bearing or a sealed one. If the bottom bracket bearings need replacing, fit a sealed bottom bracket if you haven't already done so. It'll cost a little more but it's one of the most effective upgrades you can do.

Finally, test the chainrings for run-out, as it is all too easy to bend the rings. All these operations on the chainset and bottom bracket are described in the next chapter.

1 As chains wear they also stretch. So if the chain can be lifted off the chainring more than ⅛in, it needs further investigation. See more about this topic on the next page.

2 Check that the chainring bolts are tight, and that the smallest ring is also firmly located. The sleeve nut at the back may turn, so use a special slotted screwdriver

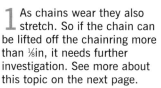
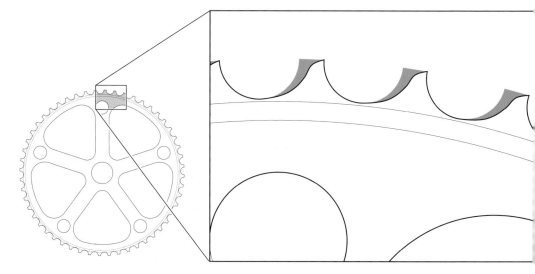

3 Look closely at the chainring for wear. If the outline of the teeth has clearly been blunted it's time to fit new chainrings. By the time the teeth have become even slightly hooked, as shown here, the chainring is very badly worn. Until the chain, sprockets and chainrings have all been replaced you may put in a lot of effort but you'll waste a lot of it due to inefficiency in the drive system.

CHAINLINE AND GEAR SELECTION

You get minimum wear when the chain runs in a straight line. But derailleur gears work by making the chain run out of line, so the best thing is to set up a bike so that a line through the middle of the chainrings hits the middle of the sprocket cluster. Check the chainline by eye and if it seems to be out, ask a professional mechanic to check whether the wrong length of bottom bracket axle, the rear hub or misalignment of the frame is putting things out.

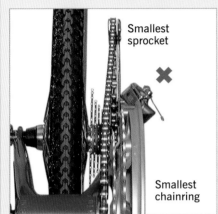

Smallest sprocket

Smallest chainring

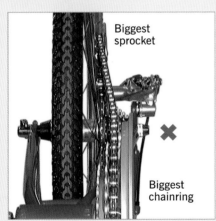

Biggest sprocket

Biggest chainring

Avoid selecting gears where the chain has to bend in a noticeable curve as the chain will wear very fast, as shown on the left. You will also waste a lot of energy with maximum crossover, because of the extra friction created in the chain. If you use these extreme gears by mistake, change gear again as soon as you can.

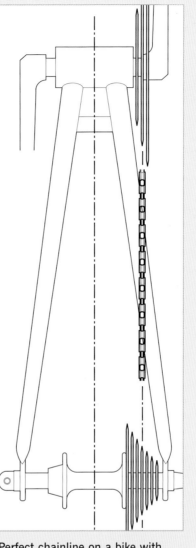

Perfect chainline on a bike with 21 speeds – seven sprockets and three chainrings.

4 Test for movement by holding one crank while attempting to wiggle the other. Tighten the crank bolt hard if you feel movement. But grease the bolt heads if you hear a noise, then tighten hard again.

5 Slip the chain off. Then hold both cranks near the pedal and turn. If you detect movement, or hear noise, or it feels rough, then the bottom bracket needs greasing or possibly changing.

6 Using the chainstay as a fixed point, turn the crank so that you can see if the gap between the frame and the chainring varies. If it does, try to straighten the chainring, otherwise replace.

WHEN YOU NEED TO DO THIS JOB:
■ Every few months on a bike in regular use.
■ When you're overhauling a neglected bike.

TIME:
■ 10 minutes for a complete inspection.

DIFFICULTY:
■ The hardest part is figuring out which part of the chainset is causing problems.

TOOLS:
■ Allen wrenches and slotted screwdriver.

Chain: clean and check

Most bikes are fitted with derailleur gears, so they're automatically fitted with ³⁄₃₂in chains. Bikes with six, seven or eight speed gears all work perfectly well with a standard ³⁄₃₂in chain, but nine and ten speed must be fitted with one that is specially made. The nine speed chain is narrower than the standard ³⁄₃₂in, while the ten speed is narrower still. Campagnolo supplies its own tool for working on its ten speed chains.

However, if you've got a bike with a hub gear, or a single speed machine, chances are it's a ⅛in chain. Unlike ³⁄₃₂in chains, these are joined with a spring link. If you plan to change the chainring or the sprocket to change the gearing, they must also be ⅛in.

Regular chain cleaning has been covered already, complete with instructions on how to use a chain cleaning machine. But sometimes a more thorough job is needed. In that case, apply some solvent cleaner with a toothbrush and give everything a good scrub. This is particularly true for the jockey wheels and the chainring, both of which get covered with a mixture of dirt and grease. A C-shaped brush is useful as well for dealing with really impacted dirt, down between the sprockets.

If you tend to lose the chain off the chainring frequently, particularly if the tension arm on the rear mech goes back almost horizontally, try chopping a link out of the chain. That may make all the difference.

Firms like Shimano and Campagnolo make chains that are particularly suited to their own gear systems and chainsets. However, Shimano alone makes chains that are so tightly riveted that they must be replaced with a new pin each time.

On the other hand, Wippermann, SRAM and Taya make chains that suit all makes of gears and sprockets, including Shimano and Campagnolo. What is more they tend to be cheaper and are at least as good. In addition, they incorporate special joining links instead of the elaborate arrangements of both Shimano and Campag.

Wippermann chains in 8-, 9- and 10-speed.

What chain?

If you do not know which type of chain is fitted, clean the side plates and check the brand name. Sedis, Wippermann, SRAM and Taya are the most common brands of standard chain. The rivets can easily be pushed out to shorten the chain using almost any chain tool.

Shimano chains are marked UG, HG or IG. Unlike other chains, the rivet heads are slightly larger than the hole in the side plate. So when a rivet is pushed out, the rivet hole becomes enlarged. That means special joining rivets must be used to join the chain again.

CHAIN CLEANING FLUIDS

Chain cleaning machines are often sold with a bottle of cleaning fluid as a special offer. But once that bottle is finished, any standard degreaser, normally used with a brush, should work fine in the machine and probably cost a lot less. However, you must dispose of these solvents in the trash, preferably pouring them onto a wad of newspaper so that they are absorbed. Do not ever pour them down a sink or road drain where they may leak into the ground water and contaminate the environment. You could use a more environmentally friendly citrus alternative but the residue still has to be disposed of carefully as it will be contaminated with the hydrocarbons used in chain lubricants.

Easy chain cleaning

1 If your chain is caked in mud, hose it clean first. But if it is just covered in oily dirt, remove the worst of the mess with a cloth. Take care to clean the back of the chain as well.

2 Use the edge of a cloth and a screwdriver or a special C-shaped brush to scrape out the dirt between the sprockets. Also wipe the teeth of the chainrings with the cloth.

3 The cloth will not reach between the chain rollers, so spray with solvent and scrub with an old toothbrush next. Then flush away with an old sponge and plenty of water.

4 When the chain is clean, dry with a rag. Then spray with aerosol lube to drive out the water. Next day, complete job with chain lube, preferably either wax- or teflon-based.

Checking chain wear

1 Measuring the length of a known number of chain links is a more reliable method of gauging wear than the lifting off method. Use a steel ruler as they are easy to read, positioning the zero of the ruler on the center of a rivet.

2 Count out twelve links of chain. Twelve links of new chain will measure 12in to the center of the rivet. A badly worn chain, one that is ready for the trash, will have stretched out to 12⅛in.

3 The easiest and most straightforward way to assess the condition of a chain is to use a Wippermann or Park Tool gauge. Just fit the hooks at each end in the space between the links, 20 links apart. If the chain is in good shape, the tool will form a triangle, with a gap between tool and chain. If it is worn out, the tool will lie flat along the top of the chain.

WHEN YOU NEED TO DO THIS JOB:
- Every month when the bike is in daily use.
- When the chain is visibly dirty.
- After a ride through mud or heavy rain.

TIME:
- 15 minutes to clean a dirty chain; another 15 minutes to clean your hands. Consider using disposable latex gloves, available at auto parts suppliers.

DIFFICULTY:
- No special problems.

TOOLS:
- Chain cleaner machine, old toothbrush, lots of cloths, newspaper or old carpet to absorb any drips.

Chain: remove and replace

When you are faced with a really dirty or rusty chain, it is usually best to fit a new one. But if you want to bring an old chain back into use, try soaking it in paraffin or diesel oil, until it is clean and flexible again. Either way, you have to take the chain off the bike, so first identify the type of chain you are dealing with – see page 112.

Once you know that, you can pick the correct method of removal and refitting. If you are dealing with a Shimano chain, you will need a replacement rivet to rejoin the chain. You cannot use the old one. There might be a spare one concealed in the chain tool but if not, you will have to get one from a bike shop before you can do this job. These have a long stalk that has to be broken off with pliers to complete the job. Unfortunately there are several different types, so take your bike or the chain to the shop with you, so that they can identify the one you need.

When you are choosing which rivet to push out, make sure you don't pick one of these replacement rivets. If you do, it will weaken the side plates and the chain will probably break at some time in the future. If you are dealing with a super narrow nine or ten speed chain, you may find that it takes a lot of force to push the rivets out, so only use a top quality chain tool.

Other types of chain don't require a joining rivet, you just replace the rivet that you've pushed out. But on recent bikes you may not have to remove a rivet at all. They may have a chain with a PowerLink or a Connex or a similar joining link, which can be split without a chain tool, see the next page. However, some ten speed chains are joined with a special link that cannot be reused.

HANDLE

REPLACEMENT RIVET

Shimano Chain Tool

Standard chain

1 Wind the punch out and position the chain on the forward or front guides. This is a standard chain tool or cutter but Shimano chain tools function just as well. You just have to adjust the support screw so that it presses on the back of the chain, to give it some support.

2 Make sure the chain is seated securely on the guides. Next, wind the punch in until the pointed end hits the dimple in the center of the rivet. Check that the punch is exactly centered, then screw it in just under six full turns. It will be stiff at first but become easier after the first half turn.

Shimano HG and IG chain

1 Select a silver rivet – never a black-headed one – to push out. Fit the chain onto the guides furthest from the punch and adjust the support screw so that it firmly supports the back of the chain plate.

2 Check that the punch is centered, and then start pushing the rivet out. You will probably be surprised at how much force is needed. Drive the rivet right out, undo the chain tool and separate the two halves.

WHEN YOU NEED TO DO THIS JOB:
■ The chain is badly worn.
■ The chain is rusty.

TIME:
■ Allow 20 minutes the first time you split the chain as you will need to take your time and check each stage carefully.

DIFFICULTY: ✔✔✔✔
■ You will have to use a lot of force to push out the rivet, which makes this job a bit nerve wracking until you're used to it.

TOOLS:
■ Standard or Shimano chain tool.
■ Hefty pliers and small file.

UPPORT SCREW

GUIDES

PUNCH

3 That forces the rivet out but not all the way. Then flex the chain to separate it. If it's still tight, push the rivet out a bit further but not right out. Leave a short length of rivet inside the chain plate so you can snap the chain back together. To rejoin, carefully push the rivet back into place.

SHIMANO STRENGTH

Always press a Shimano joining rivet back in from the direction in which you pressed it out in the first place. And select a rivet to push out by following the diagram. That way you will preserve the original strength of the chain.

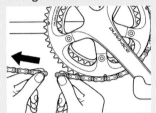

The chain must be cut here, so that the rivet selected for punching out is a leading rivet.

Direction of travel

LEADING

TRAILING

INNER LINK

OUTER LINK

SPECIAL SHIMANO REPLACEMENT RIVET

Prying open the master link on ⅛ inch chain

1 Utility bikes fitted with ⅛in chains often have a chainguard to protect the chain from dirt. It is nearly always easier to take the chain off if you remove the chainguard first.

2 Turn the cranks until you spot the master link. Lift the tail of the spring clip off the head of the rivet with a screwdriver. Take care or it will fly across the garage as you do so.

3 With the spring clip out of the way, dislodge the loose side plate by flexing the chain. Then pull out the rivet part of the spring or master link as well.

4 Rejoin the chain by reversing the process for taking it off. The closed end of the spring clip must point in the direction in which the chain moves.

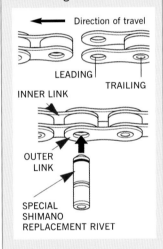

3 To rejoin the chain, push the new rivet into both holes in the side plate so that the tip is just visible. Slide the chain into the chain tool, then screw in the punch until it hits the center of the new rivet.

4 Wind the new rivet in until the groove in the replacement rivet emerges on the other side of the chain. Snap off the part that sticks out. If it does not break off cleanly, smooth the end with a file.

STIFF LITTLE LINKS

If you hear a regular cough or feel a regular jump through the pedals, one of the chain links is probably stiff. You can sometimes loosen up a stiff link by flexing the chain backward and forward with your thumbs, on either side of the rivet. But if the rivet sticks out farther on one side than the other, fit the chain tool with the punch touching the rivet that sticks out. Then push the rivet in a tiny fraction by turning the handle about sixty degrees.

Fitting a new chain

With a new chain, you get around 114 links; all of them may be needed if your bike has a very large chainring or sprocket. But normally, you have to shorten a new chain and that means you have to gauge the correct length.

This is important because the chain tensioning mechanism on a rear mech can only cope with a certain amount of slack. It normally has to deal with the difference between the chain running on the big chainring and big sprocket, and the small chainring and the small sprocket. Additional links of chain can be too much for it, causing the chain to jump off the chainring occasionally and slowing down the gear change.

The easiest way to decide chain length is to run the new chain around the big chainring and the biggest sprocket, then add two more links. Or, select the biggest chainring and the smallest sprocket. Then set the chain length so that the chain cage points roughly 90° to the ground.

But if the bike has a bottom sprocket with 26 teeth or more, it is probably best to fit the chain on the biggest chainring and sprocket, then shorten the chain so that the chain cage points at 40° or 45° to the ground. On bikes with rear suspension, you have to find the point in the suspension travel where the chain is tightest. This is best done by using your weight to compress the suspension and watching the rear mech swing forward. Note where it swings farthest forward and set the length of the new chain so that the chain cage is 45° to the ground at that point.

If you have a bike where the chain jumps off a lot or the chain cage on the rear mech swings right back in bottom gear, you can try removing one or two links to see if that improves things.

Normally, you should replace a Shimano IG chain with an IG, and an HG with an HG. But if you're in any doubt, the lockring of the cassette is normally marked with the type of chain preferred.

POWERLINK, CONNEX AND SIMILAR JOINING LINKS

Breaking a chain with a chain tool creates a weak link, even if it is done very carefully. To get around this, many new chains can be joined up without a chain tool, although you still need one if the chain has to be shortened.

To separate a SRAM PowerLink or similar, find the special joining link. Then push the two neighboring links in toward the joining link. When you feel the joining link give way slightly, the link has separated and you can take it apart.

Wippermann chains have Connex joining links and work the same way, except that the holes in the side plates are slightly curved. KMC MissingLink II works similarly, except that when you have assembled it, you pedal forward. An audible click indicates that it has come together. But the KMC Snap-On link works differently, as you flex it with your thumbs to break it apart. To rejoin it, you fit the sideplate with two fixed rivets, add the loose sideplate, and flex again. With some ten speed chains, a special joining link is required each time the chain is parted. Join the chain by doing the operations in reverse.

1 A SRAM PowerLink, conveniently positioned for taking the chain apart.

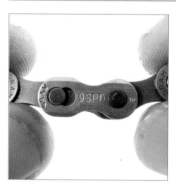

2 Pick up the link in your fingers, ready to press the inner links toward the center.

3 The joining link has now clicked, so it is now ready to be taken apart.

4 One sideplate goes with one link, and the other with the second link. Rejoin by reversing.

Setting correct chain length

1 To fit a new chain, select bottom gear on the rear mech and the big chainring on the front mech. Thread the new chain through the chain cage, then around the biggest sprocket and chainring.

2 Bring the two ends of the chain together – it is usually easiest on the bottom run. Then count the number of links to see how far they overlap with the rear mech chain cage at roughly 45° to the ground.

3 Shorten the chain by the number of overlapping links that you counted. Don't push the rivet right out – leave enough in the chain plate so that you can snap the other end into place. Don't join the chain yet.

4 Lift the chain onto the biggest chainring and biggest sprocket. If all seems to be well, push the chain rivet in the rest of the way. Check that the link is not tight, then road test to act as a check.

5 An alternative way of gauging chain length is to fit the chain to the largest chain wheel but the smallest sprocket. Bring the ends together and overlap until the chain cage points at a right angle to the floor. Count the number of overlapping rivets as before, shorten the chain and then rejoin it. Check and road test, making sure you can get all the gears.

BIKES WITH ONLY ONE SPROCKET

This category includes bikes with hub gears, single freewheels and fixed wheels. You usually adjust the chain tension on these by moving the back wheel. So when fitting a new chain, position the wheel in the middle of the slot in the rear drop-out. Then remove the spring link – see page 115 – and wrap the chain around the chainwheel and sprocket. Pull the chain tight and grip the link where the ends overlap with two fingers. Remove the surplus chain with a chain tool and join the ends with the spring link. Finally, move the back wheel backward or forward until there is about ½in of slack in the middle of the bottom run when you lift it with your finger.

FIXED WHEEL

When riding a fixed wheel, you have to pedal all the time. This is an interesting change from being able to freewheel. But you can only ride a fixed wheel bike safely by fitting wheels with special track hubs. The fixed sprocket screws onto the larger thread on the hub. The lock ring has a left-hand thread and screws onto the smaller one. Alternatively, some riders use an adaptor that fits onto the hub. The sprockets are splined onto the adaptor, which makes it a little easier to swap them around.

Cassettes: fitting and removal

Cassettes are now the most common form of sprocket cluster, available in seven, eight, nine or ten speed versions. They fit onto a freehub, a hub with the freewheel body built-in. If you ever have to grease a freehub, use the manufacturer's own brand because any other kind can interfere with the freewheel mechanism.

If you find you don't have a high enough or a low enough gear, you can change the sprockets or fit a completely new cassette. It's more common to change a whole cassette along with the chain, as that way you avoid problems with compatibility. When fitting a ten speed cassette to a nine speed hub, you have to fit a narrow spacer behind the cassette.

Shimano, SRAM and other cassettes all have spacing that fits Shimano gears. Campagnolo is the only exception, with their own unique spacing for Campag gears. However, if you are fitting Wippermann, SRAM, Taya or KMC chains, they fit either spacing.

There is no need to change the freewheel body every time you change the cassette. But after a while – perhaps after two or three new cassettes – the freewheel body will show signs of wear and it'll have to be changed. It fits in one of two ways. One involves a large Allen wrench fixing, while the other is unique to Campag and involves a hexagon screw. It's not a stock part, so chances are your bike shop will need to order the new component.

To remove a Shimano freewheel body, first remove the locknut and cone at the non-chain side of the hub and pull out the axle. Then remove the large Allen fixing at the chain side, freeing the freewheel.

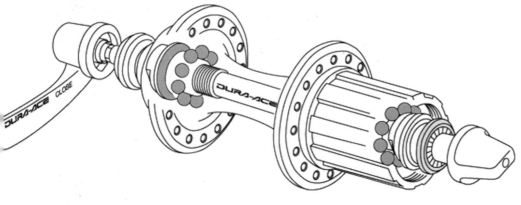

A freehub showing the axle bearings spaced as far apart as possible, supporting the axle over its full length. With the axle supported in this way, breakages are unknown.

When fitting a ten speed cassette onto a nine speed freehub, you must fit a thin spacer. It fits into the cut-outs on the freehub and is held in position by the cassette.

CAMPAG LOCKRINGS

Unfortunately you need a special wrench to undo a Campagnolo lockring, although the only difference from Shimano is the number of cut-outs around the center of the lockring.

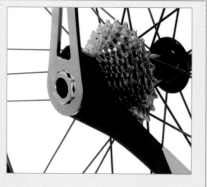

SEPARATE TOOLS

You can undo a lockring using a chain whip, a separate tool that engages the lockring, and an adjustable wrench. But the Pedro's tools, as shown in the main pictures, are better.

Removing a cassette

1 This is a Shimano cassette, but more or less all makes are removed in the same way.

2 One tool holds the sprockets, the other prepares to undo the lockring.

3 The lockring is undone in the usual direction. Unscrew until you hear three or four clicks.

4 It takes a lot of force to undo the lockring at first, but then it becomes easier.

5 Take the cassette off as a unit, otherwise the sprockets will fall everywhere.

6 With the sprockets removed, the freehub body is left alone on the hub.

WHEN YOU NEED TO DO THIS JOB:
■ New sprockets may be needed if you have not fitted a new chain for thousands of miles.
■ Different size sprockets may be needed if you go climbing mountains.
■ The freehub body may need cleaning with solvent or replacing if it will not freewheel smoothly.

TIME:
■ 10 minutes to remove sprockets.
■ 10 minutes to strip out hub axle, if necessary.
■ 5 minutes to remove freehub body.
■ 30 minutes to put everything back together again.

DIFFICULTY:
■ One of the most difficult jobs you are likely to encounter on a bike. Removing the lockring is hardest, so your tools must be in good condition. The hub must be reassembled with great care.

TOOLS:
■ Correct lockring tool.
■ Chain whip or cogwrench.
■ Large adjustable wrench.
■ 10mm Allen wrench, preferably a long one.

Campag freehub body

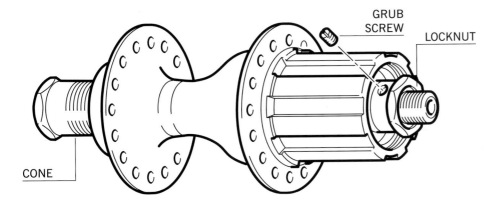

GRUB SCREW

LOCKNUT

CONE

You can remove a Campag freehub body by undoing the grub screw or hexagon socket screw, then removing the locknut that holds it in place.

Blocks: fitting and removal

Sprockets are the toothed wheels fitted to the back wheel that the chain runs on. The sprockets make up a multiple freewheel or cluster, which is either a block or a cassette. The difference between these is that the block is an old design, with the sprockets individually screwed onto a large body that in turn is screwed onto the hub, while a cassette is the modern design, with a freewheel body that is part of the hub. For five, six or seven speeds, a block works satisfactorily. But for eight speeds or more the rear axle needs the extra support that a cassette provides if it is to resist breakages.

Blocks can be changed, if the gears are the wrong size, by changing the individual sprockets. However, you'll have to find a specialist supplier because blocks are becoming difficult to source. You change the sprockets by holding them stationary with one chain whip while unscrewing them with another. Fitting a compact chainset might be a better idea, because it'll alter the whole gear range, not just one or two gears.

A block is taken off with a simple tool that fits into cut-outs around the axle hole. However, make sure you've got the correct block remover because there are several different types.

Screw-on multiple freewheel

A block has several different size threads that the individual sprockets screw onto. And around the center of the axle hole is a series of cut-outs or ridges into which the block remover fits. Modern blocks have a tooth profile that assists the chain in moving from sprocket to sprocket, along with ramps on the side.

WHEN YOU NEED TO DO THIS JOB:
■ Sprocket teeth are worn.
■ Freewheel is noisy and feels gritty.

TIME:
■ Allow 10 minutes to remove a screw-on freewheel as it is best to take your time.

DIFFICULTY:
■ Be careful – it is easy to damage the cut-outs.

SPECIAL TOOLS:
■ Only attempt this job if you have the correct freewheel remover for the type of block and it is completely undamaged.

Removing a screw-on freewheel

1 Undo the hub nut or the friction nut on the quick release. Then fit the remover into the cut-outs in the block center. Carefully check that it fits perfectly. If it does not, you could wreck both the block remover and the cut-outs.

2 Once you are satisfied that everything is OK, refit the hub nut or friction nut. Turn it to finger tightness so that it holds the freewheel remover in place. If you have a firmly mounted workshop vice, clamp the remover tightly in the jaws.

3 With the wheel in the vice, turn the rim an inch or so counter-clockwise. Alternatively, use an adjustable wrench to turn the remover about an inch counter-clockwise. Loosen the hub nut a little, then unscrew the cluster a bit more.

4 Keep loosening the hub nut and the cluster bit by bit until it will unscrew by hand. When refitting, spread anti-seize grease on the threads and be careful – the thread is very fine and it is all too easy to cross-thread it.

Single speed

Single speed bikes fall into two categories. First of all there are freewheels, which are fitted to BMX bikes, children's bikes and a small number of adult bikes. In most cases these require a screw-on rear hub that is very similar to the fitting for a screw-on block.

Then there are fixed wheels, which are fitted to track bikes for racing and a few road bikes. In this case the rear hub has to be specially threaded, with one normal thread for the fixed wheel and a separate smaller thread for the lockring. The thread for the lockring is a left-hand thread so that when the rider pushes back to slow the bike down, the fixed wheel does not unscrew. Most fixed wheels are ⅛in wide but some are ³⁄₃₂in, although most will take a ³⁄₃₂in chain if necessary. And most hubs have a fixed wheel on each side so that if they are used on the road, you can have a choice of sprockets, depending on whether you want a high gear or a low one. For the road, 46 x 17 or 18 is commonly used but for the track, it's more like 48 x 13 or 14.

Miche makes a sprocket system where an adaptor is first screwed onto the fixed wheel fitting. Then the sprocket slips onto the adaptor and the whole thing is locked into position with a lockring. This allows easy changes to the sprocket, requiring just one tool.

Finally, there are rear hubs with one fixed and one freewheel. They are growing in popularity because they allow the rider to choose either to pedal downhill, or to freewheel down.

Chain tension is achieved by pulling the wheel back in the drop-outs, or by a chain tension device if that is not possible, or by means of an eccentric bottom bracket.

REMOVING SINGLE SPROCKETS

If a BMX-type freewheel with a four peg fitting is fitted, remove with a suitable tool.

If not, place a flat ended punch in the recess and hit it with a fairly heavy hammer. Two or three heavy blows should be enough. If the punch shows signs of cutting into the freewheel, try a different blunt edged tool.

Removing a screw-on sprocket

1 This is a fixed and free hub, where one side is threaded for fixed wheel and the opposite side for a freewheel.

2 To fit a freewheel, you just screw it onto the threads. They are very similar to the ones for a block.

3 For a fixed wheel, you screw the fixed wheel on in the normal way, then the lockring, which has a left-hand thread.

4 To remove a fixed wheel, a chain whip is wrapped around the sprocket and it unscrews counter-clockwise.

5 The Miche system requires an adaptor, followed by the sprocket and finally the lockring to hold things together.

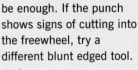

A chain tensioning device, which allows a single speed to be fitted to a modern frame with only one position for the back wheel. But track frames have a horizontal rear opening drop-out, which allows the chain to be tensioned by carefully positioning the back wheel.

Pedals: removal and refitting

When they are doing the budget for a bike, makers often leave the choice of pedals for last, when all the money has been spent. As a result, lots of bikes leave the factory fitted with the cheapest possible pedals. They are often made of plastic, not metal, and don't have proper bearings.

This is not good because you will never be able to pedal efficiently with pedals that do not rotate freely or are broken. And if the bearings suddenly seize or the cage suddenly falls apart completely, you can easily be thrown into the road. To prevent problems, replace the pedals right away if you suspect they are unsafe.

Even when decent bearings are fitted, they are often given only a quick dab of grease at the factory and this soon gets washed away. This makes it worth stripping and greasing the pedals as a precaution, even if your bike is new or only a few months old.

DUST CAP

WASHER

BEARINGS

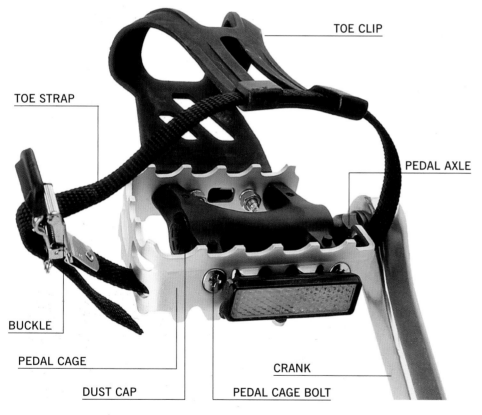

TOE CLIP

TOE STRAP

PEDAL AXLE

BUCKLE

PEDAL CAGE

DUST CAP

PEDAL CAGE BOLT

CRANK

BEARINGS

RUBBER SEAL

AXLE

1 To remove the pedal on the chain side, fit a narrow 15mm or 17mm wrench onto the flats on the pedal axle. A proper pedal wrench as in the picture is the best tool for the job. Undo in the normal, counter-clockwise direction.

2 You may find it difficult to shift the pedal. Try spraying the axle end with aerosol lube from both sides. Leave for a while and try again. If that does not work, turn the crank until the wrench is roughly parallel with the floor.

3 Hold the saddle and handlebars and put your foot onto the end of the wrench – be careful, as it will probably move suddenly. If that doesn't work, use a length of tube to extend the wrench and try again.

GETTING STARTED WITH PEDALS

The weight of the pedal often makes it awkward when you are trying to get the pedal thread to start screwing into the thread in the end of the crank. So use both hands, holding the weight of the pedal with one hand while you turn the axle to screw it in with the other. Vary the angle of the pedal axle to the crank a little at a time until the pedal thread engages the thread in the crank.

4 Now for the left-hand pedal: this is very unusual because it has a left-hand thread, designed to stop it from unscrewing as you ride along. You therefore undo a left-hand pedal by turning it clockwise – the opposite way from normal.

5 To make it easier to remove the pedals next time, coat the thread on the axle with anti-seize grease. If you do not have any anti-seize grease, use some ordinary heavy oil. This is particularly important if the cranks are made of alloy.

LOOK FOR THE HEXAGON SOCKET

Nearly all pedals have flats for a wrench on the axle. But some pedals also have a hexagon socket formed in the end of the axle – easily spotted if you look at the back of the cranks. If you are working on pedals with a hexagon socket, it is usually easier to undo the pedals with a long workshop Allen wrench than with a wrench.

LEFT- AND RIGHT-HAND PEDALS

Pedals are nearly always marked L for Left and R for Right, on the wrench flats by the crank end of the axle. There is a small chance of you coming across ones marked G for Gauche meaning Left and D for Droite meaning Right.
NOTE:
Left-hand pedal: unscrew clockwise.
Right-hand pedal: unscrew counter-clockwise.

REVERSE DIRECTION WHEN REFITTING.

WHEN YOU NEED TO DO THIS JOB:
■ If you are fitting new pedals.
■ When stripping and greasing pedals.

TIME:
■ 5 minutes.

DIFFICULTY:
■ The most trying part is remembering about the left-hand thread on the left-hand pedal.

TOOLS:
■ Long narrow wrench or purpose-made pedal wrench, or long Allen wrench.

Pedals: strip, grease and reassemble

Pedals take quite a beating from the elements, so it's not surprising that they need stripping down and regreasing occasionally. There are two kinds of pedal covered here – one with separate bearings, and one with a single ball bearing that is fixed in the pedal body. However, pedals may look differnt from the ones in the pictures but chances are they will follow one of these patterns. Even rubber pedals, as fitted to some city bikes, follow one of these designs.

Nevertheless, when stripping down a pedal, take care to avoid damaging any rubber parts and to put them back, without twisting, in the groove or wherever they came from. When the seal fits into the pedal cage around the inner bearing, it is sometimes best to stick it in place with ordinary clear glue. This makes assembly easier and prevents the seal from falling out in the future.

The other way to combat water is to coat the bearings with plenty of water-resistant grease. Once you have assembled and greased the pedal bearings properly, they should not need attention again for many miles. Do not worry if you find the axle or cones are slightly pitted. They will still run smoothly despite a certain amount of damage.

It is sometimes difficult to refit the dust cap as they usually have a very fine thread. But if it is missing, the pedal bearings will fill with water. See if the dust cap from an old pedal will fit as they sometimes do. If not, try covering the open end of the pedal with adhesive tape.

When reassembling, adjust the bearings so that the pedals turn smoothly – see pages 152–153 for how it is done with hubs. But take extra care with the locknut. If it is not tight enough, the bearings could fall apart, the pedal will then disintegrate and maybe leave you sprawled out in the road.

You will also find that smooth-turning pedals help you develop a good pedaling technique. There is no one pedaling style but as a guide, your foot should be positioned roughly horizontal at the top of the pedal stroke. You then apply as much power as you comfortably can on the down stroke, which is when you put most of the power in. Some people keep the heel slightly below the horizontal, others keep it slightly above. But these variations can be figured out by experimenting.

On the upstroke, most riders find it best to lift the heel slightly, to offer minimum resistance to the other foot that is making the power stroke.

Single ball bearing

1 If you cannot get access to the pedal bearings, take off the pedal cage.

2 Undo the dust cover, which protects the bearing and keeps out the water.

3 This reveals the locknut and washer, which controls the pre-load on the bearing.

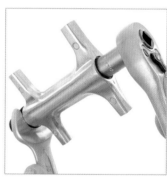

4 Remove the locknut by holding with an open-ended wrench and a socket.

5 The pedal shaft can now be removed, leaving a single bearing in the pedal.

6 Clean with WD-40, then grease the pedal shaft and bearing and reassemble.

Separate bearings

1 Some pedals have a cage that can be separated from the pedal body. The cage certainly makes it awkward to work on pedals, so strip it off whenever possible. It may be easier if you use a vice.

2 Dust caps with domed centers are easy to pry out. But sometimes they are flush and you have to use a tiny screwdriver. Unscrew metal dust caps with pliers or grips with wide-opening jaws.

3 Where there is a separate pedal cage, use either a socket wrench or a ring wrench to undo the locknut. On many types, only a socket will reach far enough into the pedal to loosen it.

4 Once you have removed the locknut, take out the lock washer next. Sometimes this is difficult if there's a tag that fits into a groove in the axle. Tip the pedal down to shake it off if necessary.

5 While unscrewing the cone, hold the axle in the pedal body with your index finger, or you will get showered with greasy ball bearings. Or hold the axle in a vice by the wrench flats.

6 Catch all the loose bearings in an empty can or on a piece of newspaper. Some will not drop out, so scrape them out with a pen top or similar tool. Clean and inspect all the minor parts but do not worry about minor pits in the bearing surfaces.

7 To reassemble, stick the ball bearings into the inner bearing with grease, then lower the axle in. Holding the axle, turn the pedal up the other way, stick the outer bearings in, and refit cone, washer and locknut.

WHEN YOU NEED TO DO THIS JOB:
■ With new pedals, in case they are not properly greased.
■ If the pedal bearings feel rough and gritty.
■ When the pedal bearings are loose.

TIME:
■ 20 minutes per pedal, if you have a vice.
■ 30 minutes per pedal if not.

DIFFICULTY:
■ There can be problems getting to the outer bearing if you cannot remove the cage from the body. Otherwise stripping the pedal bearings is very good practice for greasing and adjusting other bearings. Do not overfill with grease.

TOOLS:
■ Vice, wide-opening pliers or slip-jointed gland pliers.

General-purpose cycling shoes, suitable for commuting as well as leisure use. The main difference is that the Shimano shoe has instep straps while the other doesn't. Instep straps take on a lot of the strain of pedalling and are easily adjustable, so most riders consider them to be worthwhile.

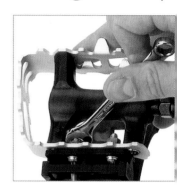

1 There are nearly always circular holes in the pedal cage for the toe clip bolts. If not, toe clips are usually supplied with a backing plate to overcome this problem. But when buying, remember that pedals with built-in toe clip fixings look much neater.

Toe clips, straps and clipless pedals

Riders are sometimes put off using toe clips because they look unsafe. However, experience shows that although it takes a little while getting used to them, clips and straps are a safety feature. On a bike with toe clips, your foot cannot slip off the pedal and cause a sudden swerve or loss of control, but that is exactly what can happen without toe clips. If you fall off with your feet in toe clips, you seem to instinctively pull your foot out before you hit the ground.

The other advantage of toe clips is that they help you position the ball of your foot over the axle of the pedal. This makes it easier to flex your ankle at the top of the stroke, and directs all the power of your legs into the pedal.

Seldom do you need to tighten the toe straps. Most of the time, they just steady the toe clip – you only pull them tight when a major effort is needed, such as going up a steep hill. You can even buy short toe clips without straps, if you feel a "halfway house" would help you get accustomed to using them.

When buying toe clips, check that you get the right size for your foot and pedal combination. As for the pedals, go for ones with proper toe clip mounting holes and, preferably, a tag at the back of the cage to help you pick up the toe clip more easily when you are starting off from rest.

But once you have tried clipless pedals, you'll realize why they are so popular, as far as serious cyclists are concerned. Of the many shoe and pedal combinations, this page deals with Shimano SPD because they are the favorite type for general use. In particular, they are easy to walk in for a reasonable distance. However, you must change the cleats when they are showing signs of wear. You must also optimize the spring tension and the position of the foot on the pedal. This is done by fitting different cleats that allow the foot to adopt a more or less extreme angle, known as "float."

There is also Shimano SPD-R. It also has a two hole fixing but along the shoe, as opposed to the basic SPD, which is two holes across the shoe. In addition there is the Shimano SPD-SL, plus Look, Time and many other pedal makers who tend to go with one or other of the 3 hole fixings for really serious cycling or racing.

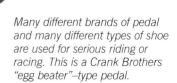

Many different brands of pedal and many different types of shoe are used for serious riding or racing. This is a Crank Brothers "egg beater"–type pedal.

Clipless pedals

2 Some road bikes are fitted with lightweight platform pedals. These are sometimes made of resin, sometimes alloy. Fit the special toe clips using the countersunk screws that come with the pedal. No nuts are required, because the holes are threaded.

3 To fit nylon or leather toe straps, feed the strap through the slots cut out of the sides of the pedal cage. If it is too tight, pull the toe strap through with pliers. On most quality pedals, there is a tag on the pedal cage to stop the strap from rubbing against the crank.

1 Many general-purpose shoes can be used with toe clips. But for clipless pedals, the sole may be ready to accept cleats, or the protective strip must be removed.

2 Inside the shoe is a loose insole or sockliner. Take the sockliner out and get your fingers behind the cleat holes. Then position the cleat itself and the cleat adaptor.

4 Pull the toe strap tight and position the buckle just outside the pedal cage. Leave enough slack between the buckle and the cage to keep the pedal from cutting into the strap too much – this is where they tend to break eventually.

5 The buckles are not intended to hold the toe strap firmly. Just pass the end under the knurled roller, then through the cut-out in the sprung part. Tighten the toe strap, when necessary, by giving the free end a jerk.

3 Holding the cleat holes, position the cleat mounting bolts and tighten firmly in the middle of the adjustment to start with. Waterproof with the sticker provided.

4 Fit the pedal to the crank. Then adjust the position of the cleat so that the ball of the foot is right over the pedal axle. If necessary adjust the cleats and tighten again.

6 Fitting reflectors to the back of the pedals is particularly effective. They are almost unmissable to drivers and other road users because the twinkling light from the reflectors is constantly on the move. Most reflectors have a simple two-bolt fixing, similar to toe clips.

5 With Shimano pedals and some other brands, you also have to adjust the tension of the spring. This makes it more or less hard to pull the foot out.

6 Try out the pedals before going out on the road. You press the pedal down and forward for getting in and twist the foot for coming out.

7

CHAPTER

CHAINSETS AND BEARINGS

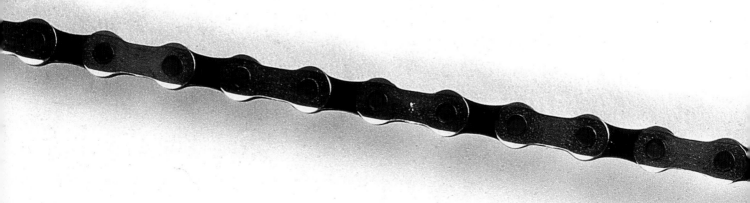

Chainrings

Alloy cotterless chainsets are fitted to nearly all modern bikes, with replaceable chainrings in most cases. Older chainrings can be bolted to the crank spider in any position but newer ones fit in only one position.

The first thing that determines where they fit is the large pin, which prevents the chain from dropping into the gap between the crank and the chainring. Many chainrings are pinned and ramped as well. What this means is that there are pick-up pins that help the chain climb from one chainring to another, while ramps are specially profiled chainring teeth that also lead from one chainring to another. Before unbolting the chainrings, make a sketch of the fitting marks and how they relate to each other and the cranks.

Mountain bikes usually have a four-bolt fixing while road bikes have five, although it's more a matter of style than anything else. But the bolt circle diameter or BCD determines whether or not a chainring fits a crank. The BCD is the diameter of a circle joining all the fixing bolts. For example, the BCD of most mountain bikes is 94mm but for Shimano road bikes is 130mm, while Campagnolo uses 135mm. On a road bike the smallest possible chainring that can fit is a 38 or 39 tooth, unless a triple chainset is used, these have chainrings of 52 x 39 x 30 or similar. However, all manufacturers are making compact chainsets for road bikes now, both racing-style bikes and straight bar hybrids. These have a large chainring of 48 or 50 teeth and a small one of 34 teeth, with a BCD of 110mm.

When a chain and a chainring have been used together for some time, or the chainring has worn out, you have to replace both at the same time, and probably the sprockets as well – see pages 116–120. But it may possibly be cheaper to replace the chainring than the complete chainset. If you cannot obtain the original rings, you may be able to get suitable replacements from the French firm TA. They specialize in chainrings and can supply almost any combination of BCD and number of fixings.

Removing chainrings

1 Nearly all chainrings are bolted to the crank spider with chrome or alloy socket head bolts. Undo the first bolt half-a-turn, then the next one half-a-turn, continuing until all of the fixing bolts are loose enough to undo by hand.

2 The socket-head bolt shown fits into a sleeve nut that extends through all three chainrings plus the crank spider. Pull off the outer ring by pulling gently on opposite sides – it is a tight fit to prevent unwanted movement.

Many chainsets have only four spider arms, the fifth bolt screwing into a threaded boss on the crank. To keep the bottom bracket axle short, the cranks are low profile (S-shaped). And on triples, the smallest chainring is bolted into place with a second ring of bolts.

TORQUE WRENCH

Bike and component makers now say that you should always use a torque wrench when fitting a nut or bolt. Torque wrenches measure the amount of force being applied to a nut or bolt via a standard socket wrench. The sockets fit on the torque wrench in the usual way but the 3/8in size is best for bikes. A certain amount of force is set down for each individual nut and bolt on a list in the maker's handbook. When tightened to the force specified, nuts and bolts should never break or come loose. The attraction for manufacturers is that if they are faced with a warranty claim, they can reject it unless the claimant can show that a torque wrench was used when working on the item.

3 Check for spacers or washers between the chainrings, then lift the outer ring away for cleaning or straightening. The other rings usually remain in place until you draw the sleeve nuts out of the holes in the cranks.

4 In some cases, the small inner ring is bolted in place with a separate ring of bolts. Undo them all and the inner ring will come off. You may find that the smallest ring is made of steel so that it does not wear too quickly.

A compact chainset, with a BCD of 110mm. This allows you to have a road chainset with a 48 big ring and a 34 small ring, although you may be able to go smaller still. These are now becoming popular and may soon outsell the 52 or 53 x 39, which is standard for racing bikes.

WHEN YOU NEED TO DO THIS JOB:
■ Chainrings are worn or bent.
■ You want to change the gearing.

TIME:
■ 20 minutes for chainrings.

DIFFICULTY: ///
■ Changing a chainring requires care to prevent bending or distortion.

SPECIAL TOOLS:
■ Sold at bike shops, a special slotted screwdriver sometimes makes it easier to remove, or tighten, the chainring bolts.

BOLT CIRCLE DIAMETER (BCD)
When you want to change the overall gearing on a bike, or the whole transmission is badly worn, you will have to change the chainrings. In that case, you need to know what the bolt circle diameter (or pitch circle diameter) of the chainring is. So just unbolt the existing ones and measure the distance D, then check the table.

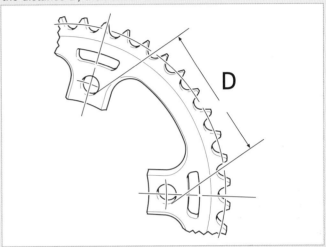

D (mm)	BCD (mm)
34.1	58
43.5	74
50.6	86
55.3	94
67.7	110
71.7	122
76.5	130
79.4	135
84.7	144

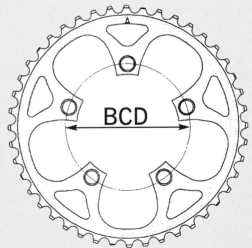

The bolt circle diameter is the diameter of the circle joining the centers of all the fixing holes. When ordering, you will also have to specify four bolts or five.

Square taper and other cranks

Stronglight uses the square taper design, as do better known makes like Shimano and Campagnolo.

One of the changes in the last few years is the appearance of a great variety of bottom bracket axle designs, and the way in which the chainset is attached to them. However, the square taper design is, for the moment, easily the most popular.

The extractor tool required to remove the cranks is a narrow one that fits the small end of the axle. Some extractors are fixed, so they require a smear of grease to help the extractor turn, but most have a floating tip. This makes it much easier to extract the crank.

When refitting, reverse the process for removal, assembling the crank and axle with a very thin film of grease where they touch. That means apply a little grease to the square taper, then wipe it off. That will be enough to prevent corrosion and make it easier to take the crank off later. In addition, put some grease under the crank bolt and washer to help stop creaks and groans.

Tap the cranks into place with a soft mallet, or a hammer with a piece of wood to cushion it. Then tighten the crank bolts as much as you can. The extractor tool usually has a socket wrench on it for this job, but you can get more leverage with a socket and ratchet from a ⅜in set, if it fits.

Tighten up the cranks after a ride around the block and then every 100 miles or so until they stop breaking in. Do not ride a bike with loose cranks, as the hard steel axle easily damages the soft alloy crank. If you do damage the crank in this way you can buy just the left-hand crank, which is a lot cheaper than a complete chainset.

This covers square taper cranks but the methods shown can also be applied to Power Spline, ISIS and Octalink cranks.

CRANK LENGTHS FOR NORMAL CYCLING	
Under 5 foot 10 inches	170mm
5 foot 10 inches to 6 foot	172.5mm
Over 6 foot	175mm
Go for slightly shorter cranks if you have creaky knees. But bear in mind that most riders find 170mm cranks work fine.	

Removing extractor cranks

1 Remove the dust cap, if fitted. Some require a wrench with two pins to take them off, while others have an Allen wrench fitting or just pry off.

2 Get the extractor ready by unscrewing it all the way until the end is fully retracted. This type has a floating tip, so it doesn't need grease.

Removing one-key-release

1 Wind the crank fixing bolt in an counter-clockwise direction with a long 6mm or 8mm Allen wrench. Stop the cranks from moving with your other hand. You will need to use a lot of force to do this.

2 Pull the crank a little to finally detach it from the axle. In this case, an Octalink bottom bracket axle is fitted but you are more likely to find a bottom bracket with a square taper axle for the cranks.

Some bikes are fitted with steel cranks that fit on a square taper axle. They are handled in exactly the same way as the much more common alloy cranks.

WHEN YOU NEED TO DO THIS JOB:

■ Bottom bracket needs checking.

TIME:
■ 15 minutes to remove a pair of cranks the first time.

DIFFICULTY: ✹✹✹
■ It's nerve-racking the first time you take off a pair of cranks, but from then on it's easy.

TOOLS:
■ Crank extractor with undamaged threads, socket wrench.

3 Make sure that you get the extractor threaded in right, then tighten it up. If it goes in crooked, take it out and try again until you get it right.

4 Tighten up the extractor until it forces the crank off. It will need a lot of effort at first but then it becomes easier as it comes off the taper.

5 Undo the extractor and pull the crank right off, then take the other crank off. Reassembly involves simply reversing the process.

cranks

3 Gather the protective outer cap, crank fixing bolt and narrow washer together so that you don't lose them. The washer sits in the recess in the crank, so you may have to pick it out with your fingernail.

4 Check that the bottom bracket is running silently and smoothly. If all is well, carefully clean all the old grease off the minor parts. Re-grease the fixing bolt and washer with good quality grease.

5 Locate the crank on the end of the axle, slip the washer in the crank recess and fit the crank fixing bolt. Tighten the crank bolt with a torque wrench to the specified figure, or as tight as you can.

6 Check that the outer cap ring is tight using a pin wrench. Take great care to fit the cranks exactly 180° opposite each other on Octalink chainsets as it's all too easy to assemble the cranks in the wrong way.

Sealed bottom brackets and cranks

Sealed or cartridge bottom brackets come in a variety of shapes but they all fit in much the same way. So although this picture sequence shows a Shimano Octalink cartridge bottom bracket, it might just as easily show a square taper, a Power Spline, or an ISIS. It doesn't matter what shape the axle is, the method of working is identical.

Except, that is, for the very early Shimano cartridge units. These have a collar that screws in from the chain side to lock the unit in position, which is the reverse of the later types. However, there are fewer and fewer of these around, the majority having been replaced by a modern unit of some kind.

You can get a sealed bottom bracket at any cycle shop, but will need to specify the make and type of chainset. That said, the bearings will probably be 68mm wide, with an axle of either 108mm for a double chainset or 113mm for a triple. The big exception is an Italian bottom bracket, which will probably have 73mm bearings and be 118mm wide.

It's impossible to say how long a sealed bottom bracket will last. A cheap one could only last a couple of thousand miles, while a Royce bottom bracket will cost you plenty but last indefinitely. It's best to check whether the ball bearings are smooth and silent or are starting to feel rough every six hundred miles or so.

Whether refitting an old bottom bracket or fitting a new one, it's best to clean up the bracket area and check that the cartridge bottom bracket will go in with the threads running free. If need be, get a pair of old bearing cups and run them in and out, until the threads are clear.

When fitting a square taper chainset, put a very thin film of grease on the tapers, then wipe off. This will leave enough grease to prevent corrosion, without stopping the chainset from being fully tightened. But when fitting Power Spline, ISIS and Octalink, use plenty of grease on the splines and take care that you fit the cranks 180° apart. There's nothing more annoying than having to do it again because you have fitted the cranks one or two splines out. Finally, tighten the crank bolts, then tighten again after a ride around the block.

The square taper and the Power Spline require a narrow type of extractor, while the ISIS and the Octalink need a wide type. If you're buying one, get an extractor that fits both, with an extension piece that converts one to the other.

SQUARE TAPER
Square taper is the standard design of bottom bracket, and has stood the test of time for 50 years. It's used by Stronglight, Campag, Shimano, Truvativ and countless others. However, the square taper design is likely to be replaced at last by the other types of axle and the outboard bearing designs over the next few years.

POWER SPLINE
Power Spline is a Truvativ design, with 12 splines instead of a square taper. It forms a stiffer joint and a stronger axle than the square taper, but doesn't cost as much to machine as the ISIS bottom bracket. So far it's not used much but as Truvativ chainsets are selling well, chances are it will become more popular.

ISIS
The ISIS bottom bracket, which was the American answer to Octalink. It's 25 percent stiffer than a square taper and twice as strong. However, it's a very complicated design, so stick to the same brand of bottom bracket as the chainset – then you won't have problems with slight differences due to machining tolerances.

Removing an Octalink bottom bracket

1 Here is an Octalink bottom bracket, ready to come out. You will need a bottom bracket adaptor and ratchet.

2 Place the adaptor in the non-chain side, holding it there with your fingers in case it slips or worse.

3 This is the same as the previous picture, and we are turning the locking collar *COUNTER-CLOCKWISE* to take it off.

4 With the locking collar out of the way, you can switch to the other side. Put the adaptor in the chainside.

5 Screw the chainside collar *CLOCKWISE* (left-hand thread) to take it out. There are no loose ball bearings to get lost.

6 When the chainside collar has been freed, take the complete sealed unit out of the bottom bracket.

7 Getting ready to replace the cartridge bottom bracket. Clean up the bracket area and clear the threads if necessary.

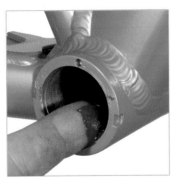

8 To ease the way in, put some grease on the threads. Put the chain side in first, screwing it *COUNTER-CLOCKWISE*.

9 Grease the splines, crank stops and crank bolts, then fit the cranks 180° apart. Tighten them as much as you can.

WHEN YOU NEED TO DO THIS JOB:
■ When a cartridge bottom bracket is worn out.
■ If a cup and axle bottom bracket is worn out.

TIME:
■ An hour the first time, down to about 30 minutes when you're really well practiced.

DIFFICULTY:
■ You have to keep your wits about you, especially refitting the cranks.

TOOLS:
■ Extractor, bottom bracket adaptor.

FAG SEALED UNITS

Giant bearing manufacturer FAG produces units under its own name and under various other names as well, such as Campagnolo. The axle and bearings are made of steel, but the collars are made of resin. You can fit and remove a FAG bracket with a large pair of grips, but various special tools make the job much easier.

Bottom bracket and bearing cup tool for FAG sealed units.

Cup and axle bottom brackets

This is the old design of bottom bracket. It's still in use on the very cheapest bikes, and there's a backlog of millions of old bikes that have them. But when a bottom bracket needs replacing, you should take the opportunity to fit a sealed unit, see the previous page.

The adjustable cup is normally threaded, so it unscrews counter-clockwise. But the chain side fixed cup is left-hand thread, so it unscrews clockwise.

The main problem with cup and axle bottom brackets is water penetration. When that happens, the movement of the bearings churns the grease and water into a sticky but non-lubricating mess. If you're lucky, the bottom bracket will develop a squeak or a groan, telling you that it's time to take a look.

Alternatively, if there's no squeak but the bottom bracket feels rough it's also time to strip it down and have a look. Finally, if all seems well but if the bike is used regularly and a couple years or so has elapsed since you stripped it down, then once again it's time to have a look.

If the parts of the bottom bracket all look fine, then they can go back. But final adjustment is easier if you fit the chainside crank first, but not the non-chainside yet. Then screw the adjustable cup in or out until you can only feel a very slight movement at the end of the crank. If you tighten the lockring at this point it will pull the adjustable cup out slightly. This is often enough to make up for the way the adjustable cup turns when you tighten the lockring. However, if you don't get it right the first time and the bearing is either too loose or too tight, repeat the process until you have the slightest amount of play at the end of the crank. Finally, fit the other crank and tighten both crank bolts up as much as you can. Ride around the block and then tighten them again.

On the other hand, if the bearing tracks in the cups or on the axle have developed a series of pits or worn patches, or the bearing tracks are very deep, it's time to fit a replacement. That means a sealed bottom bracket, replacing the whole thing with one that's effectively waterproof.

You may find that you have a bottom bracket with the bearings in a cage. Don't worry about this as it simply speeds up assembly, although separate ball bearings are better. And pack the bearing cups with waterproof grease, preferably PTFE-based, not a cheap automotive type.

All the items you need to replace a cup and axle bottom bracket.

LOST YOUR BEARINGS ?
Look out for these basic faults when you are deciding whether to refit the old parts, or to fit a new cartridge bottom bracket. On the left-hand bearing cup above, the chrome has flaked off and the bearing track is covered in tiny pits. The right-hand cup is heavily worn and in some areas, the surface of the metal has been worn away. On the axles, the upper one has many small pits while on the lower one, the hardened surface is worn through and the soft metal underneath is crumbling fast.

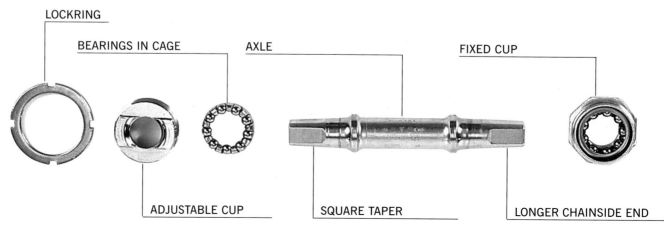

LOCKRING

BEARINGS IN CAGE   AXLE   FIXED CUP

ADJUSTABLE CUP   SQUARE TAPER   LONGER CHAINSIDE END

Removing a cup and axle bracket

WHEN YOU NEED TO DO THIS JOB:
■ If a cup and axle bottom bracket needs adjustment or is worn out.

TIME:
■ An hour the first time, down to about 30 minutes when you're really well practiced.

DIFFICULTY:
■ You have to keep your wits about you, especially refitting the cranks.

TOOLS:
■ Large wrench, hammer and punch or large pair of grips.

1 After removing the cranks, work on the non-chain side. The lockring should be removed with a C-wrench. Alternatively, use a suitable punch on the cutouts to tap the lockring counter-clockwise.

2 As you tap the lockring, it may drag the adjustable bearing cup with it, or you may need to get a pin wrench. After a few turns you should be able to undo the bearing cup using just your fingers.

3 The bearings inside are probably loose, so be careful to catch them as you free the adjustable cup. Wipe the cup but only reuse it if it's free of pitting and the surface isn't discolored.

4 Take out the axle and wipe it free of grease and dirt. If the bearing tracks are not pitted, it can go back. But if it's showing signs of wear, fit a sealed bottom bracket instead.

5 Remove the fixed cup, remembering that this is a left-hand thread so you undo it *clockwise*. Replace the bearings or the sealed bottom bracket by reversing the steps.

6 If all is well, half fill the cups with waterproof grease and add 11 ball bearings. Only the grease stops them from falling out, so use a pen top to press them into the grease.

Alternative tools for the job are a massive pair of grips . . .

. . . just a couple of thin screws and a screwdriver . . .

. . . and a large adjustable wrench for the fixed cup.

Shimano outboard bearings and chainsets

Removing a Shimano chainset

Shimano was among the first to move on from improving the bottom bracket bearings to looking at the bottom bracket design as a whole. They came to the conclusion that the entire system needed a redesign.

The biggest single improvement they came up with was to improve the spacing of the bearings from 48.3mm to 87.5mm. This was done by fitting the bearings outboard, rather then inboard, but still using the same bracket shell in the frame. They also incorporated a much thicker bracket axle than was standard, which was at the same time significantly lighter because it was hollow. Finally, the axle was driven at high pressure into the right-hand crank. As a result, the left-hand crank was the only place where it could flex. And the left-hand crank joint is designed to be as stiff as possible anyway.

Refitting Hollowtech II cranks to a frame that has been prepared for them is easy. But for those frames not already prepared, a tap must be run through the threads of the bottom bracket and it must be faced. That is to say, both faces of the bottom bracket must be made parallel to each other and perfectly flat, otherwise there's a strong possibility of the bottom bracket running out of true. This is a job for a well-equipped cycle shop, not for home.

The left-hand crank showing the plastic cap and the original fixings. A different arrangement was adopted in the later design.

WHEN YOU NEED TO DO THIS JOB:

■ To fit a new Hollowtech II bottom bracket.
■ When a Hollowtech II bottom bracket has worn out.

TIME:
■ About 20 minutes to remove the chainset and bottom bracket.

DIFFICULTY: ⫻
■ This design is much easier to work on than the old one, as it doesn't require a lot of force to extract the crank.

TOOLS:
■ The Shimano tool for undoing the bottom bracket cups is essential. A torque wrench is very desirable.

1 A Shimano chainset, ready to be taken off. It's a Deore LX model.

2 Unscrew the plastic plug with the correct tool, or on some designs by careful use of a large plain screwdriver.

3 Undo the pair of bolts that hold the non-chain side crank onto the axle.

4 Take away the bolts and the piece of plastic that fits in the gap in the cranks.

5 The crank can now be removed, leaving the external bearing exposed.

7 Unscrew each bearing using the correct tool . . .

8 . . . turning in the opposite direction to the tighten markings on the bearing.

6 Using a mallet tap the end of the crank axle and withdraw the chainset and axle from the bearings.

9 Remove the bearing, complete with the spacer and the plastic sleeve.

10 When refitting the chainset, this tiny pin fits into the gap in the splines.

11 Use a torque wrench to tighten the bolts to no more than 11ft/lb. If you don't have a torque wrench this means firm but not too tight.

Shimano updated

As explained on the previous page, Shimano pioneered outboard bearings in the mass market. But there were problems, particularly as there were no shoulders on the axle. As a result there was nothing to stop the bearings from being smashed if the bike were dropped on them.

So Shimano made a second attempt at developing the technology. The Hollowtech II system that produced lightweight hollow cranks was retained – indeed, the new system is lighter than the old one – and the right-hand crank permanently fixed to the bottom bracket axle was retained as well. But the new system allows adjustment of the bottom bracket bearings. This is achieved with an adjustable collar that's effectively part of the left-hand crank.

The new chainset looks the part and is distinctly high end, with a titanium and carbon fiber middle ring. However, this design is expected to spread downward to the cheaper groupsets and onto the road as well in the next few years.

The new chainset looks a lot more finished than the earlier one, particularly around the left-hand crank. There, the new attachment system is a vast improvement on the earlier one.

Removal, re-fitting and adjustment

1 To remove use the special tool TL-FC35, undo the crank arm cap by unscrewing in a clockwise direction (cap has a left-hand thread).

2 Ensure the crank arm threads are clean then screw in the tool in a counter-clockwise direction, tightening as far as it will go.

3 Check that the tool is correctly engaged – failure to do so could result in the crank arm threads being stripped during removal.

4 Using an 8mm Allen wrench, which passes through the tool, unscrew counter-clockwise – this action will pull the crank arm off the axle. It will be tight.

5 Remove the tool from the crank arm, then loosen the adjustment nut retaining bolt using a 2.5mm Allen wrench. Ensure that the adjustment nut is threaded back into the crank arm in readiness for re-fitting of the crank arm at a later stage.

6 To re-attach ensure that the splines on the axle align with the crank arm then insert the crank bolt and tighten clockwise (45–55Nm). Re-fit the crank arm cap, tightening counter-clockwise with tool TL-FC35. Now adjust the bearings.

7 Use tool TL-FC17 to unscrew the adjustment nut on the back of the crank arm to remove play between the crank arm and bottom bracket, and to pre-load the bearings. Re-tighten the retaining bolt using a 2.5mm Allen wrench.

Special tools for the updated Shimano chainset are adapter TL-FC35 for the removal of the crank arm cap and extraction of crank arm, and adapter TL-FC17 to adjust the adjustment nut for bearing clearance.

Truvativ GXP bearings and chainsets

Truvativ chainsets are selling really well at the moment, but only a few of their more expensive chainsets have GXP external bearings. It's far more common for Truvativ chainsets to have a square taper or a Power Spline bottom bracket, and they're covered on page 134.

GXP bearings require that the frame be prepared for them by running a tap through the bottom bracket, so that they fit easily, and then be faced. Facing ensures that the bottom bracket sides are parallel to each other and are completely flat. However, if it's genuinely impossible to get this work done GXP bearings will fit most frames without it. You can adapt the second method given for fitting Campag cranks.

Most bottom bracket shells have a width of 68mm, but Italian ones are 73mm. GXP bearings fit both, but to do so the 68mm cups require one spacer at each side.

SRAM road chainsets are roughly the same as Truvativ, with the differences described in a later section. On the latest Truvativ chainsets, the left-hand crank has the same fixing as SRAM, see the next page.

A Truvativ right-hand crank, showing the bottom bracket axle permanently fixed in the chain side. Like the Shimano design, this has a large diameter hollow axle but a much simpler left-hand crank attachment. Furthermore, the axle has shoulders, so there is no chance of smashing the bearings.

Removing a Truvativ chainset

1 Remove the dust cap using a 6mm Allen wrench. It's just like a square taper crank.

2 With the dust cap removed, you can see the end of the axle is fairly wide.

3 The extractor is the wide type. Carefully screw it into the crank, refitting if necessary.

4 Make sure that the extractor is fitted correctly before tightening into the crank.

Removing a Truvativ chainset: continued

5 Drive off the crank with the extractor using a certain amount of force to start with.

6 Remove the bearing cup, using the same tool as the Campagnolo.

7 Take out the bearing, the plastic shell and the spacer for a 68mm bearing shell.

8 Working from the other side, you can take off the chainset, but use both hands.

9 That just leaves the second bearing, which you also remove with the tool.

10 Putting back the chainset, you grease the splines, the underside of the crank bolt and the crank bolt thread.

WHEN YOU NEED TO DO THIS JOB:
■ When fitting a new chainset.
■ The old bottom bracket is showing signs of wear.

TIME:
■ 20 minutes.

DIFFICULTY:
■ Extracting the first crank is slightly difficult but it's smooth sailing from then on.

TOOLS:
■ Tool for removing the bearing cups.

GXP bearings are common to both Truvativ and SRAM. The bottom bracket axle has a slight interference fit in the inner races of the sealed bearings.

Truvativ GXP bottom bracket bearings are fitted using a large tool supplied either by Truvativ themselves or by Park Tools. It's a common fitting so it fits other bottom brackets too.

SRAM chainsets

The SRAM Force chainset, which is made of expensive carbon fiber. It is expected that cheaper SRAM chainsets will emerge later.

SRAM is the parent company of Truvativ, so it's hardly surprising that they supply the chainsets for their new groupset. They use exactly the same GXP bearings as Truvativ, so the only difference is the way the left-hand crank is attached on early Truvativ ones. On later chainsets, Truvativ has adopted the same fixing as SRAM. Apart from that, you treat the SRAM chainset exactly the same as a Truvativ with GXP bearings. Reassembly is by simply reversing the process, but the crank bolt head, the crank bolt threads and the splines are all well greased.

The Force chainset illustrated is made of carbon fiber, but the cheaper Rival is made of 7075 aluminum alloy.

It's strongly recommended that you get the frame prepared for the chainset by having it faced and chased.

1 The left-hand crank is plugged with a 16mm Allen bolt, but it's never removed.

2 Using the crank bolt as an extractor, you undo it counter-clockwise to remove the crank.

3 The crank bolt is effectively a one-key release device, so use a long 8mm Allen wrench.

4 This is the interface between the crank and the bottom bracket axle.

5 There is no adjustment because the face of the crank acts as a crank stop.

WHEN YOU NEED TO DO THIS JOB:

- When fitting a new chainset.
- The old bottom bracket is showing signs of wear.

TIME:
- 15 minutes.

DIFFICULTY:
- The left-hand crank is easier to take off than the Truvativ design.

TOOLS:
- Tool for removing the bearing cups.

NEWARK PUBLIC LIBRARY
121 HIGH STREET
NEWARK, NEW YORK 14513

Campagnolo Ultra Torque

Campagnolo has extended the Ultra Torque design right down to the reasonably priced Mirage groupset. This is a Mirage compact chainset with 50–34 rings and requires a special Campag front mech to go with it.

Shimano took the initiative by devising an alternative to the traditional bottom bracket. But by taking an unusually long time to come up with a competitive product, Campagnolo has produced a really neat system. The key to the design is the Hirth Coupling, which joins the axle in the middle and is self-centering. It only requires a 10mm bolt to hold it together. However, the cranks can be fitted offset to each other, so be careful.

Campagnolo gives two methods of fitting the chainset. One of the methods entails having access to the correct tools for tapping out the threads and facing the bottom bracket shell in the frame. That is also the method given here, and it assumes that either the frame is prepared already, or you have taken the frame to a well-equipped cycle shop and had them prepare it in the way described.

The other method is a temporary fix, because the tools for preparing the frame are not available. It is given here without any guarantee.

First of all, prepare the bracket shell by cleaning and degreasing the bracket with a cloth and a neutral soap. Then screw the cups in and out until they run freely. Take some Loctite 222 thread locking compound and one of the bearing cups. Start the bearing cup in the frame, then apply Loctite 222 as you screw it in. Loctite 222 should be applied to all of the thread. Tighten the bearing cup by hand: don't use tools.

Repeat the process for the other cup, then fit the cranks immediately, while the Loctite 222 is still fluid. Check that the cranks revolve smoothly, and leave for 48 hours while the Loctite hardens. When you eventually come to remove the cranks you will need a wrench to remove the cups, as the Loctite will prevent them from moving.

The advantages of the Ultra Torque system are lightness and rigidity, but also the same or better q factor than standard chainsets. That is to say it takes up no extra room laterally than a standard chainset, so the rider's feet stay in the same place.

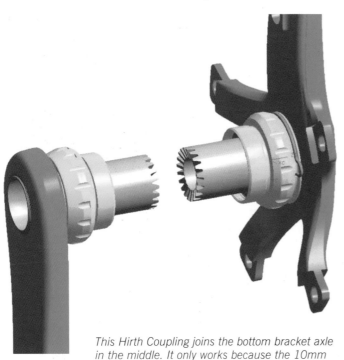

This Hirth Coupling joins the bottom bracket axle in the middle. It only works because the 10mm bolt exerts great pressure on the coupling. It can be tightened with a socket or an Allen wrench until the force required goes exponential.

Removing an Ultra Torque chainset

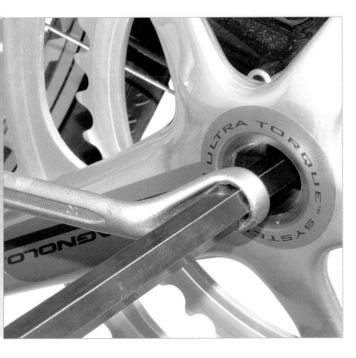

1 A 10mm Allen wrench and a 10mm wrench are required to remove the Allen bolt. Campag makes a special tool for this but this works just as well.

2 The Allen bolt is tightened to 42Nm, so it needs a lot of force to undo it.

3 Working on the opposite side of the bike, remove the crank, bearing and half-axle.

4 The crank and bearing come out, and this wavy washer has to come out too.

5 Now unscrew the bearing cup counter-clockwise with the bottom bracket tool.

6 The bearing cup comes out cleanly, especially if it was greased the last time it came out.

7 Back to the other side, click the safety spring out of the bearing cup and remove the other crank. Reassembly is the reverse of stripping down, but you must grease the inside of the bearing cups.

WHEN YOU NEED TO DO THIS JOB:

■ To fit a new Ultra Torque chainset and bracket.
■ When an Ultra Torque bottom bracket has worn out.

TIME:
■ About 10 minutes to remove the chainset and bottom bracket.

DIFFICULTY:
■ The Ultra Torque design is much easier to work on than the standard design.

TOOLS:
■ A tool for removing the bottom bracket cups is essential.

This is a picture of the chainside bottom bracket, showing how the safety spring fits into the bracket cup. Don't run the chainset without the spring in place.

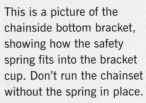

CAMPAG BEARINGS
All the Campag groupsets down to Mirage have the Ultra Torque design. But they all use the same bearings, so the cheap Mirage has the same ones as the expensive Record.

Other chainsets

A few chainsets are still fitted with cotter pins, mainly very old ones. It's sometimes possible to refit the old cotter pins but only if they've come out easily. You can improve the chances of this happening by using a drift to drive the cotter pins out, rather than just hitting them.

If new cotters have to be fitted, start off by getting the right ones. There are various types, and the best chance of getting exact replacements is to take the old ones to your bike shop and ask for new ones that match them. It's then a matter of filing them so that they go in. Don't try to fit them exactly – you need to knock them in a little to be sure they will stay in.

COTTERED CHAINSET WITH BOTTOM BRACKET

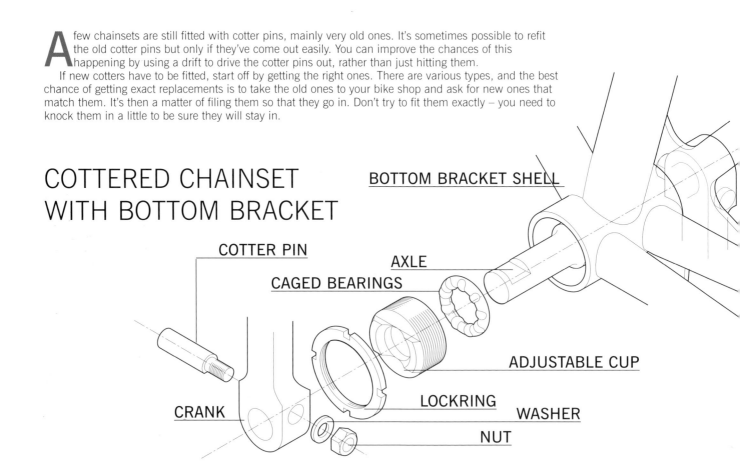

BOTTOM BRACKET SHELL

COTTER PIN

AXLE

CAGED BEARINGS

ADJUSTABLE CUP

CRANK

LOCKRING

WASHER

NUT

Cottered chainset

1 Remove the nut and washer on the cotter pin, then give it one sharp blow with a mechanic's hammer. If that does not fire the cotter pin right out, find a 1in diameter metal bar, place on the pin and hammer on that instead.

2 You can reuse the old cotter pin if it is not damaged. If you have to fit a new cotter, take the old one to the bike shop as a pattern. When you are ready to refit the chainset, test-fit the new cotter pin and see how well it fits.

3 Slip the washer on the threaded end of the new cotter pin and tighten the nut as far as it will go by hand. If there isn't enough thread to reach the end of the nut, file some metal off the flat part. Repeat if necessary.

4 Fit the cotter pin so the nut is under the crank when the crank points backward. Pound it into place with a medium hammer, then fit the washer. Tighten the nut hard with a wrench. Fit the other cotter the opposite way.

One piece cranks

This design is mainly used on kids' bikes but also on budget BMXs and adult utilities. Although designed to keep down the cost of building small bikes, one-piece cranks and the bottom bracket design that goes with them are surprisingly child-resistant. The cranks often get bent in a crash but they are made of steel. So if you have a big pair of Stillson's, you can usually straighten them up without too much difficulty. If the left-hand crank gets badly bent, consider taking the whole thing apart and straightening it in a vice.

The bottom bracket works well because it is a lot bigger in diameter than a standard one and so contains more ball bearings to share the load. The press-in bearing cups and the axle can get pitted but do not have to be replaced unless the cups are very badly damaged. Maintenance consists of removing the old grease, regreasing everything and fitting it back together with a full set of new ball bearings.

It is worth going through this procedure as a precaution, if you have just bought a second-hand bike. And judging by the way kids' bikes are often thrown together in the factory, it would not be a bad idea to strip and grease the bottom bracket on a new bike as well.

It is not easy to get spares for this type of bike, so wait until you have them in your hand before you strip the bike down. If your local bike shop cannot help, search out a specialist in kids' bikes.

To refit the bottom bracket, follow the steps given here in reverse. But take care to tap the bearing cups back in straight, not at an angle, or you will never get them in. Alternatively, use a vice to press the cups into the frame.

1 First thing is to remove the pedals, then unscrew the lockring in a clockwise direction. The lockring is very thin, so steady the wrench to prevent it from slipping off the flats. Once you have unscrewed it all the way, lift the lockring off the end of the crank.

2 Behind the lockring is a slotted bearing retainer. Position a cold chisel in the slot and tap it gently in a clockwise direction. As you unscrew the retainer, the crank assembly will tilt, so support it with one hand while you undo the retainer with the other hand.

3 Lift the bearing retainer off the end of the crank. If you then tilt the whole assembly until the plain crank is almost horizontal, you can draw it out of the opposite side of the bottom bracket shell. The crank assembly is made of steel and therefore heavy.

4 Finally, knock the bearing cups out of the frame. They are not threaded but are still a tight fit. When one side of the cup has moved a little, swap the cold chisel to the opposite side and hammer away until it also moves, otherwise the cups will jam in place. Reassembly is essentially a matter of reversing the process except for using a vice to press the bearing cups into the frame.

WHEN YOU NEED TO DO THIS JOB:
■ You have just bought a second-hand or new bike and want to check that the bottom bracket is OK.
■ There is a grinding noise as you turn the cranks.
■ The cranks have been bent in a crash.

TIME:
At least an hour to strip, clean and refit the whole assembly. Longer if you have to straighten the cranks as well.

DIFFICULTY: 🔧🔧🔧🔧
At first it is difficult to see how this assembly fits together. Once you have grasped that, you may also have problems pushing out and refitting the bearing cups. The answer is to only push one side out a little bit first. Then go to the opposite side of the bearing cup and push that out an equal amount so it stays straight.

SPECIAL TOOLS:
Large adjustable wrench, engineer's hammer and cold chisel.

CHAPTER

WHEELS

Strip down hubs

You've probably decided to strip the hubs down because of problems revealed during an inspection. But if you've been out in a downpour, especially when riding across country, it's worth checking the hub bearings during the next few days in case water has gotten in. However, provided the hubs are running smoothly it may be a year or two before they need attention.

Mountain bikes, and an increasing number of road bikes, have an external rubber seal to keep water out, but if there is no seal on the outside there may be a rubber seal or o-ring on the inside, or a labyrinth seal. Don't remove a rubber seal or similar part permanently because it will cause a severe drop in waterproofing performance.

Shimano Parallax hubs and similar designs have large diameter cones and an open side to the hub, as shown in the main picture sequence. Others have small diameter cones and a closed side. However, the two types are taken apart and reassembled in much the same way. Always strip rear hubs from the non-chain side.

On Shimano rear hubs, known as freehubs, the entire axle on some types has to be removed before the freewheel body can be taken off. Sometimes the freewheel body fixing nut is a left-hand thread, and has to be removed in the opposite direction to usual. The rear axle is often formed into an Allen wrench fitting to facilitate this.

Many bikes are now fitted with ready-made wheels, with hubs and rims made by the same manufacturer. The spoke head is at the wheel rim in some cases, but in others this is reversed. Shimano, for example, locates the spoke head at the hub, and has fewer spokes than normal. On the other hand, Mavic locates the spoke head at the rim and has roughly the traditional number of spokes.

What this amounts to is that you can usually true the wheels in the normal way, and sometimes the hubs can be treated as normal too. However, Mavic uses ball bearings, so see page 154 on dealing with their particular hubs.

Stripping down a hub

1 Remove the quick-release skewer by holding the friction nut and twisting the q/r lever until it comes to the end of the thread. Watch for the conical springs on the skewer, on each side of the hub.

2 On mountain bikes, there is sometimes a separate rubber seal around the cones, which helps to prevent water from entering the hub bearings – they usually just pull off. Internal seals are also common.

Hub seals

1 Hubs now have a recess that the rubber seals fit in. If need be, pick them out with a screwdriver or similar, lifting them over the ledge.

2 Fit the seals back into the hub by pressing them all the way around. Then spin the wheel to check that the seal fits evenly.

QUICK-RELEASE LEVER

QUICK-RELEASE SKEWER

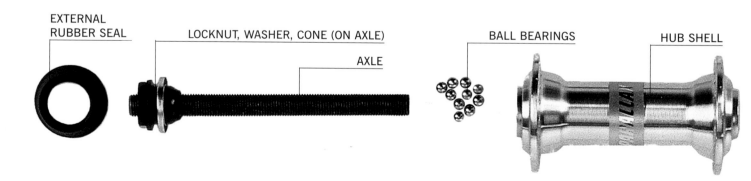

EXTERNAL RUBBER SEAL

LOCKNUT, WASHER, CONE (ON AXLE)

AXLE

BALL BEARINGS

HUB SHELL

3 Use a cone wrench to hold the axle while you undo one of the locknuts. It will take a lot of force to start with. If you are working on the back wheel, it is usually best to work on the non-chain side.

4 Undo the locknut and pull off the lock washer. This sometimes has a tag that fits into a groove in the axle, so you may have to pry it off with a screwdriver. Finally, undo the cone itself.

5 When you have removed the cone and locknut on one side of the axle, you can pull the axle out the other side. Be careful as some of the ball bearings might come with it and drop onto the floor.

6 Almost certainly some ball bearings will be left in the hub, stuck there in the grease. Dig them out with a small screwdriver or a pen top and scrape out as much of the old grease as you can.

GREASE FOR HUB BEARINGS

That old can of grease in the corner of the shed is probably intended for cars. Do not use it on your bike as it has three big drawbacks. One is that it is too heavy, so it causes a lot of drag in the bearings. Two is that it ceases to work if water gets in. Three is that it can thicken up badly and so lose most of its lubricating properties. Use grease specially formulated for bike bearings instead. It is thinner, tolerates water better and does not thicken up as much. Up to now, nobody has come up with a miracle grease for bikes but a Teflon-based grease is probably the best, although any branded waterproof bike grease will be OK for packing bearings.

WHEN YOU NEED TO DO THIS JOB:
■ When the bearings feel rough or seem to drag a bit when you turn the axle with your fingers.
■ During a big overhaul.

TIME:
■ 5 minutes to remove the axle.

DIFFICULTY:
■ This is the easy part, provided that you have a proper cone wrench.

SPECIAL TOOLS:
■ At least one cone wrench, preferably a pair of them.

A GOOD SIGN
This wheel has a metal eyelet fitted around each spoke. It is a sign of a well-made bike, as these eyelets strengthen the box section rim. However, they are limited to fairly expensive bikes.

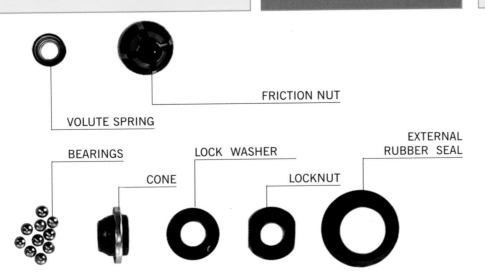

VOLUTE SPRING

FRICTION NUT

BEARINGS

CONE

LOCK WASHER

LOCKNUT

EXTERNAL RUBBER SEAL

Grease and adjust hubs

The first thing to do after stripping the hubs down is to check the cones for damage. If there is any sign of pitting or a track has been worn into the cone, it's best to fit new ones. Check also that the axle is straight – if one end of the axle appears to move up and down when you roll it along a flat surface, fit a new axle too.

Most cones have the same thread and shape, so there is usually no problem finding new ones. But if you are dealing with budget hubs, you may have to buy a complete new axle.

The core part of this job is adjusting the cones so that they apply the right amount of pressure to the bearings. Aim for the point where you cannot feel any movement at all at the end of the axle but it turns without any sign of dragging or grittiness.

Finding this exact point is mostly a process of trial and error. Even professional mechanics do not expect to hit it the first time, so do not worry if you have to readjust the cones a few times.

One problem is that when you finally tighten the locknut, it increases the pressure on the cones and through them on the bearings. So, to get the cone adjustment right, you have to leave just enough slack to make up for this.

When you think you have the adjustment right and the axle turns really smoothly, pop the wheel back into the bike and see if you can detect any movement at the wheel rim. The distance of the rim from the hub magnifies any play, so it is OK if you can detect a tiny amount of movement. Re-check the adjustment after your next ride.

If the rim is not buckled but nevertheless rubs on the brake blocks, perhaps when you are out of the saddle climbing a hill, the cones probably need tightening a fraction.

THEY ARE THE PITS

Once you have stripped the hub bearings down, you must inspect the inner surface of the cones for damage and wear. The cone above left is a brand-new, high-quality item which has a completely smooth unpitted surface. The middle one has a track worn into the metal and is pitted. Do not reuse. The right-hand cone has some wear, which will probably accelerate from now on. Re-use only to stay mobile if necessary, while you track down a replacement.

1 Having cleaned away all traces of old lubricant, coat both bearing tracks with a thin layer of waterproof grease. Do not be tempted to fill the barrel of the hub with grease or it will be forced out later and make a horrible mess.

4 If you are reusing the old cones, screw the loose one back onto the axle and tighten it down until there is just a little play left in the bearings. Spin the wheel slowly now – it should already turn much more smoothly than before.

5 When fitting new cones, adjust their position on the axle so that the axle is central in the hub. This is particularly important on quick-release hubs. Fit the lockwashers and locknuts and screw down onto the cones finger tight.

Hubs for use with disc brakes have a special mount, usually six holes, built into the left-hand flange.

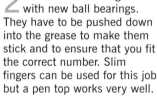

2 Now fill the bearing tracks with new ball bearings. They have to be pushed down into the grease to make them stick and to ensure that you fit the correct number. Slim fingers can be used for this job but a pen top works very well.

3 Now spread a little more grease on top of the bearings. If the old cones are OK, there is no need to undo the one still in place on the axle. But clean everything up carefully before threading the axle back into the hub.

WHEN YOU NEED TO DO THIS JOB:
■ During an inspection, you have found that the hub bearings do not run very smoothly or you can feel a significant amount of play at the rim.
■ As part of a major overhaul.

TIME:
■ 40 minutes including stripping down and de-greasing.

DIFFICULTY:
■ Provided you have proper cone wrenches, the only real problem is adjusting the cones just right. Do not forget that the grease is quite thick to start with, so the bearings will loosen off a bit later.

SPECIAL TOOLS:
■ You really need two cone wrenches. These are long wrenches slim enough to fit the narrow flats on the cones and locknuts. But if you use too much force, the jaws will distort and so become almost useless.

6 If you are reusing the old cones, the axle should already be centered and one locknut fully tightened. When fitting new cones, again check that the axle is centered, then tighten one of the locknuts hard against the cone on one side.

7 Turning to the other cone, screw it in or out until there is a tiny amount of play left, then tighten the locknut against the cone. If you judge it right, this final tightening will eliminate that last little bit of movement in the axle.

A Mavic Aksium wheel, which is light and strong yet costs about the same as getting a pair of wheels built to your specifications.

Ball bearing hubs

Most cycle hubs are fitted with cup-and-cone bearings but an increasing minority are fitted with ball bearings. These use commercially available made-up ball bearings mounted on the axle instead. However, Shimano and Campagnolo show no sign of changing, claiming that cup-and-cone bearings are the best for cycle use. On the other hand, Mavic and several other smaller makers swear by ball bearings, so there is no clear consensus.

Mavic in particular has produced high-priced wheelsets for some years, all running on ball bearings. But recently they've launched the Aksium wheelset, bringing the price down to realistic levels for the first time. It uses many of the Mavic refinements and only weighs slightly more than the expensive Ksyrium and Cosmic wheelsets. The same system is used on various Mavic mountain bike wheelsets.

Mavic uses an "expandable bearing support," which connects the bearings to the axle. However, these bearing supports can be used once only. So if you eventually have to strip the axle and renew the bearings, you must obtain a set of these expandable bearing supports as well as the bearings themselves. You also need a set of bearing pullers to remove the old bearings and Loctite.

As for play in the bearings, much depends on the amount of force exerted to tighten the quick release. So before you do anything else, just try putting the wheel into the frame and tightening the wheel as much as you reasonably can, less one quarter turn of the quick release nut. In most cases, the play will disappear. Don't exert too much force or you'll damage the bearings.

But if that fails and you have to regulate the amount of play, you can only carry out the procedure twice on each bearing So both sides of the front wheel can be adjusted, making four times in all. But the rear wheel can only be adjusted twice on the non-drive side. After that the expandable bearing supports have to be replaced. Remember to clamp the spindle in a vice when adjusting the play.

There is also a much simpler design of ball bearing hub, sold under the Formula name and various other brands. The ball bearings are mounted on a section of the axle that is ground to a slight interference fit. In this case the ball bearings are adjusted by finding the tipping point between play and no play, and they are replaced when necessary by knocking them out.

WHEN YOU NEED TO DO THIS JOB:
■ Ball bearings are showing play.

TIME:
■ 5 minutes to adjust Mavic bearings.
■ 30 minutes to replace bearings.

DIFFICULTY:
■ Both jobs are surprisingly easy.

TOOLS:
■ Mavic – 13mm thin wrench, 17mm thin wrench.
■ Formula – cone wrenches, soft-face mallet, bearing puller, drifts or pin punch.

Generic hubs

1 Loosen the locknut, holding the bearing adjuster still. Note the large knurled area of the locknut for security.

2 Remove the locknut and then the bearing adjuster. You can see the complete ball bearing now.

3 Using as little force as possible, knock out the ball bearing that is mounted directly on the axle.

4 Again using as little force as possible, use a long drift or pin punch to knock out the other ball bearing.

5 Separate the ball bearing from the axle preferably with a two-arm bearing puller. Otherwise use the mallet.

6 Reassembly is made easier if you use a suitable drift to knock in the first bearing. It should only need a tap.

7 The second bearing is fitted to the axle by a drift working on the center of the bearing. Then the hub is reassembled with the bearing adjusters and locknuts. Arrange them so that the ball bearings are held between the ridge on the axle and the bearing adjuster, with the end play just about taken up but without applying too much force.

Mavic hubs

1 Get a thin 13mm wrench and a 17mm cone wrench and put them in place on the bearing adjuster and locknut, lining them up, so far as you can, with a pair of spokes.

2 Move the bearing adjuster and the locknut clockwise simultaneously, by the space between two of the spokes. This should be enough to eliminate any play.

3 To replace a spoke, screw a nipple onto the spoke until it locks. Fit the spoke into the large part of the keyhole fixing. Then move it into the final position and tighten.

Simple wheel truing and spoke replacement

If a wheel has very loose spokes and the rim is bent, your local bike shop will sell you a replacement. They will probably offer you a choice between off-the-shelf wheels and wheels hand-built to your own specifications. If you decide on a hand-built wheel, it can be carefully tailored to suit your weight, the way you use your bike and, of course, your budget.

The spokes are usually retained in the rim by square-sided nipples, which are tightened with a nipple key. However, the square end is tiny so you must use a tightly fitting nipple key. If you use a badly fitting key, you will round off all the nipples and the wheel will be useless.

Occasionally you will find that the nipples have seized and will not move. Try loosening them with spray lube. If that does not work, the wheel will have to be rebuilt.

Any time that you tighten a nipple, the end of the spoke pokes a little further through the rim and could puncture the tube. To prevent this, file the spoke end flush with the nipple.

When replacing spokes, follow the pattern exactly, crossing the same number of spokes and alternating sides where they fit into the hub. There are many different types of spoke, so take the old one to the shop where it will act as a pattern.

Truing a wheel is a matter of increasing the spoke tension on one side to pull the rim straight and slackening it on the opposite side to make up for this. Treat each bend separately and work from the edges to the middle, a quarter-turn at a time at the edges and half-a-turn in the middle.

Fitting a new spoke

1 Spokes usually break just below the nipple or near the bend close to the hub. And they nearly all break on the drive side, as they take more load and can be damaged by the chain. It is normally easy to extract the remains but if the spoke has broken on the chain side of the back wheel, you will have to remove the sprockets.

2 Thread the new spoke into the empty spoke hole and wiggle it around so that the head seats nicely. Look at the next spoke-but-one to see if the new spoke goes over or under the spoke that it crosses and follow this pattern.

Truing a lightly buckled wheel

1 Unless you are doing a roadside repair, it is best to take off the tire and tube first. Then fit the wheel in the frame and spin it slowly, noting where exactly it wanders and how far it is out of true.

2 If the rim bends to the left, loosen the left-hand spokes a little and tighten the opposite, right-hand ones. Work from the ends of the bend toward the middle. True each bend before moving on.

3 Do not try to get it right in one attempt but work little by little, checking that you are doing it right by spinning the wheel frequently. When the wheel is true, twang the spokes to settle them in place.

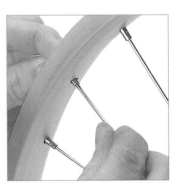

THE TRUTH MACHINE

It is OK to tighten up a loose spoke or iron out a slight bend in the rim for yourself. However, all the spokes in a wheel should be kept at a high but even tension. Once you have slackened off some and tightened up others, you may have weakened the wheel considerably. The answer is to let a bike mechanic true up your wheels as soon as they start leaving the straight and narrow. Professionals use a special jig which allows them to correct side-to-side and also up-and-down defects. They will also re-tension the spokes so that the wheel stays true.

WHEN YOU NEED TO DO THIS JOB:
■ As a roadside repair.
■ When the wheel wanders a bit but you just don't have the time to take it to a bike shop.

TIME:
■ 20 minutes to true a slightly wavy wheel.
■ 30 minutes to remove a tire and fit a new spoke.

DIFFICULTY:
■ Very difficult because you have to balance loosening and tightening spokes. Take it slowly and check frequently that you are reducing the buckle, not making it worse.

SPECIAL TOOLS:
Nipple key. The most common spoke sizes are 14, 15 and 16 but check before you buy. Do not use a combination spoke key as they are difficult to use and far more likely to damage the nipples.

3 Remove the rim tape and pull out the rest of the old spoke. Unscrew the nipple on the new spoke and bend it gently so that you can poke the end through the spoke hole. Check that the spoke head is still seated correctly.

4 Tighten nipple finger tight and check that the new spoke is following exactly the same route as the previous one. If the rim has eyelets with angled seats, make sure you tighten the nipple right down into the base of the eyelet.

5 Twang the spokes with your fingers to get an idea of how tight they are. Then progressively tighten the new spoke until it is under the same tension as the rest. File off the end of the spoke if necessary and true up the wheel.

CHAPTER

BARS AND
SADDLES

Safety check

Though the security of stems and handlebars is covered in the M Check on page 30, these components are critical to safety, so a more detailed set of tests is given here. They are not intended as a regular check but should be applied when taking over a second-hand bike, or every year or so as a bike gets older.

Rust on steel is easy enough to spot, but it seldom gets so bad that cycle components are weakened. It's just about possible that steel handlebars or a stem could get fatally weakened by rust, but that seldom happens in the real world.

Aluminium alloy also corrodes, but is much harder to pinpoint, the white flecks of oxide blending in with the silver color of the metal. Fortunately, a coat of aluminium oxide forms on the surface of the alloy, effectively sealing off components from further deterioration. It is only in exceptional conditions that aluminium alloy goes on corroding.

Unfortunately, however, there are two areas of a bike that tend to set up these exceptional conditions. These are where a quill stem fits into the front forks, and where the seat post comes into contact with the frame. In the first case the handlebars act as an effective lever, so even if corrosion forms between the stem and the fork column, it can usually be overcome by brute force.

But there is a close electrical connection between the seat post and the frame, and it's this that promotes corrosion. Furthermore, it's often uninterrupted for years at a time. So step one in prevention is to take the seat post out, remove any old grease and replace with new anti-seize grease. As a precaution you can do this with the stem as well. Step two is to repeat this process every year or so.

If the seat post does get stuck, open up the "ears" of your frame by putting in a screwdriver and wiggling it. Then spray generously with penetrating oil, wait 20 minutes and try again. If that doesn't work, spray again and leave overnight. The next day, try getting a rubber mallet and pounding the seat post. At first try to preserve the component, but if necessary destroy it. Be careful to strike downward, not across the seat post. Finally, if that still doesn't work, try clamping the seat post in a vice and using the frame as a lever. If even that doesn't work, it's probably best to leave it to an experienced cycle mechanic.

Carbon fiber and other composites should not be greased. They are notoriously difficult to check, see page 175. If there is an obvious problem, or you suspect one, replace the component.

If you have to remove the stem or the seat post, use electrical tape or something similar to mark the height of these components. Then you can reassemble them in exactly the same position.

Make sure that you've got a pair of grips or plugs to close off the handlebars. Open handlebars can gouge into the flesh and cause severe wounds, in the event of a crash.

Apply anti-seize grease to the seat post, and also to the old-fashioned quill stem. If you remove the old grease and replace with fresh every year or so, chances are you'll never have to deal with a stuck seat post or stem. This is copper-based grease, but there are other types like Corrosion Block from Worldwide Aviation that are even better.

1 Problem number one is corrosion. Second, a saddle clip can cut into the seat post and weaken it. Third is overtightening of the seat post clamp or saddle clip. Replace one or both if necessary.

2 It's right to check that the seat post clamp is tight, but do not over tighten it. If you do, it'll cause cracking if the seat post clamp is a separate component, or distortion if it's a steel frame.

4 Handlebars are usually made of thin walled tubing. If the handlebar clamp or brake lever band cuts into the metal, cracks may fan out from there. Check when you remove the handlebar tape, just in case.

5 Traditional quill stems only need a check on the main bolt, which must be tight enough to stop the handlebars from moving in the frame. On all types of stems, check that they line up exactly with the front wheel.

7 As welded stems get older, it's possible for corrosion to take hold in the welds. So check the beads of the welds and the surrounding metal for pin holes and cracks. Replace soon if anything shows up.

3 With Aheadset systems, the stem clamp bolts need checking. On triple-clamp forks, the bolts holding the legs into each clamp also need a tweak. Tighten the bolts to the maker's torque settings.

6 Handlebars can crack close to the stem in heavy use, especially if they're allowed to become loose. Run your eye slowly over the adjustment mechanism, if fitted, and also over the mounting bolts and clamp bolts as they're highly stressed.

The standard star nut fixing for Aheadset compression bolts is not a particularly good design. For tough conditions, a variety of alternatives will get a better grip on the inside of the steerer tube, without damaging it.

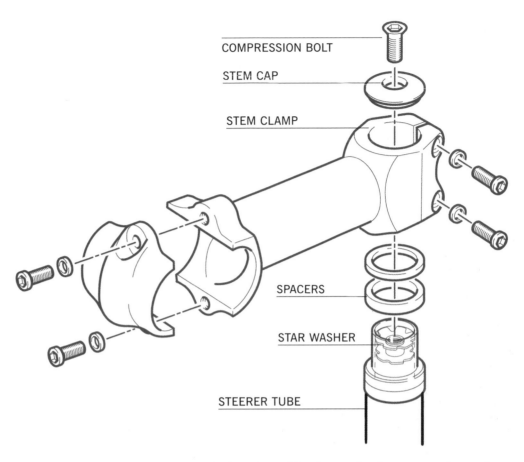

COMPRESSION BOLT

STEM CAP

STEM CLAMP

SPACERS

STAR WASHER

STEERER TUBE

The Aheadset system is lighter but more rigid than the traditional setup. But the components are all more highly stressed, so tighten all the bolts evenly. That way you will avoid distorting the clamps, or causing problems out on a ride. The top of the steerer tube must be at least 3mm below the top of the stem clamp so that the compression bolt can push the stem down onto the top bearing.

The star nut inside the steerer tube is the most vital part of the Aheadset system. It must be fitted perfectly evenly inside the steerer tube, 12 to 15mm below the top edge. There are various special tools for inserting a star nut but it can be done by hand, with care. When the compression bolt is tightened, the "petals" spread slightly and grip the inside of the steerer tube.

SAFETY LIMIT LINE

When setting up your riding position or adjusting the height of the saddle or handlebars, you must check that the limit mark is not visible. If the handlebar stem or seat post is pulled out so far that the limit marks are visible, there is a strong possibility that they will either fall out of the frame or break due to the additional stress placed on them.

If you need to set the saddle higher than permitted, just fit a longer seat post than standard. But now that there are many new ways of building a frame, you must be very careful that the new seat post is exactly the correct diameter for the frame.

You could also fit an angled stem, to raise the handlebars or even lower them, although you should avoid extreme riding positions, or you may be able to solve the problem by fitting a different style of handlebar.

Handlebars and stems

The stem and handlebars are the visible parts of the bicycle steering system, but the steerer tube is equally important, although you do not normally see it because it is concealed inside the head tube. It is the steerer tube that carries the stem, connecting it to the forks.

Quill stems are held into the steerer tube by a long binder bolt. This screws into a wedge, which locks against the inside of the steerer tube. Quill stems are so called because the the stem is cut off at an angle, which makes it look like a quill pen.

There is also an older design in which an expander bolt screws into a cone, which fits inside the stem. As you tighten the expander bolt, the cone expands the stem tube and locks it to the inside of the steerer tube.

On both of these designs, the first step when changing the height of the handlebars is to loosen the binder or expander bolt. You then tap the binder bolt and that should dislodge the wedge or cone, allowing you to adjust the stem height, or remove it. Reverse this process after adjustment.

If a modern Aheadset-style headset is fitted, the stem clamps to the outside of the steerer tube. But this can only work with threadless forks, so it is not interchangeable with either of the older types.

To remove a clamp-on stem, first take off the stem cap by undoing the compression bolt. Then loosen the clamp bolts and lift off the stem. To refit, slide the stem into place on the top headset bearing, then fit the stem cap and tighten it down to remove any slack in the headset. Only then do you tighten the clamp bolts again. See pages 182 and 183 for more on the Aheadset system.

When you have finished work in this area, always check that you have tightened all the bolts and that the stem lines up with the front wheel.

Nearly all stems are now the front loading type. This allows the handlebars to be changed, without the need to inch them around to the end. Some types have two bolts but four bolts are better.

HEIGHT ADJUSTMENT

The Aheadset system gives little height adjustment for the handlebars. If you need to raise them more, bolt a stem riser to the steerer, then fit the stem onto that. There is a similar-looking device that allows you to fit a clamp-on stem in place of a quill stem.

Removing the handlebar stem

1 Aheadset stems clamp onto the outside of the steerer tube. They are removed by removing the stem cap, then loosening the clamp bolts and lifting. Adjust the height of the stem by varying the number of spacers beneath, but for safety reasons, the steerer tube must never be more than 10mm from the top of the stem.

2 On some quill stems, the top is neatly closed off with a large rubber plug. Pull out the plug and look for the socket-headed bolt a little below it. Do not confuse a quill stem with the Aheadset type. These have a smaller socket-head bolt on top of the stem.

Adjusting handlebars

1 To adjust the handlebars, start by removing the brake levers, gear levers, light brackets and so on. But do not bother if you are only altering the angle of the bars, just remember to adjust the position of the levers as well.

2 Now undo the handlebar clamp. You only need to loosen it a few turns to adjust the position of the bars, but remove the bolt if you are separating the bars from the stem. See below for handlebar clamps with two or more bolts.

Front loading stems

1 To make it easier to swap handlebars, most stems are now front loading. Undo the clamp by loosening the clamp bolts half a turn at a time.

2 If you are trying to stop a creak, clean the adjoining surfaces with solvent. Then smooth out any minor damage with abrasive paper.

3 The socket-head bolt is sometimes buried so deep that you can only reach it with the long end of an Allen wrench. It should be inserted tightly, so slip a narrow piece of tubing over the short end of the Allen wrench to give you enough leverage to undo the bolt.

4 On older versions of the expander bolt stem, there is no rubber plug. In this case, it is much easier to undo the bolt with an Allen wrench or regular wrench. Once you have undone it about four turns, give the head of the expander a sharp blow with a medium hammer.

5 If that does not dislodge the expander bolt, cushion it with a piece of wood and hit it harder. But the stem itself may be stuck in the steerer tube. If so, apply bike oil around the top of the headset, wait, then tap the top of the stem with a hammer to help loosen it.

WHEN YOU NEED TO DO THIS JOB:
■ After fitting a new stem or handlebars.
■ If you are not comfortable.

TIME:
■ 30 minutes to fit new handlebars.
■ 5 minutes to reposition stem or handlebars.

DIFFICULTY:
■ It can be difficult to remove the handlebars without scratching them.

MIXING AND MATCHING
The International Standards Organization stipulates that the bulge in the middle of a pair of handlebars should be 25.4mm, and most bikes comply. However, the bigger the

bulge, the stiffer the handlebar, so some handlebar and stem combinations have a central bulge measuring 31.8mm. When buying replacement handlebars or stem, make sure you get the correct size.

However, there are minor variations. Fortunately, if the stem clamp is only slightly smaller than the handlebars you can gently open up the clamp with a large screwdriver. But don't use force, because you might crack it.

If you have to tighten the handlebar clamp bolts more than the minimum to stop the handlebars from moving, consider exchanging them for ones that fit more closely. This particularly applies to front-loading stems.

3 You can now try to work the handlebars out of the clamp. Be careful as there may be a separate metal sleeve around the handlebars, inside the clamp. Do not hurry as it is only too easy to scratch the bars badly, especially drops.

4 If it's impossible to pull the handlebars out of the stem, try refitting the clamp bolt the opposite way around with a coin in the slot. As you tighten the bolt, it will open up the clamp, but this trick only works when the bolt hole is threaded.

3 When you refit them, apply anti-seize compound to the clamp bolts. Tighten them with your finger tight, then give half-a-turn at a time until the 'bars will not move.

4 Make sure that the gap around the clamp is even top and bottom. If not, refit the clamp as there is a danger of it cracking otherwise.

CITY BIKES
Some city bikes are fitted with a very traditional shape of stem and handlebar, but they are adjusted in the same way as a normal quill stem, with a binder bolt.

Grips and tape

Nearly all mountain bikes are sold with flat handlebars or risers. To make sure they fit most people, manufacturers sometimes fit ones that are too wide for many riders. This is OK on short journeys but forces you to use a tiring spread-arm riding position. If you are fitting new grips, consider whether you would be more comfortable with narrower handlebars or with bar ends that give you an alternative hand position.

The simplest way to reduce the width of the bars is to cut a couple of inches off the ends. But before you do this, check that it will leave enough room for the bar ends, brake levers and shifters. If you decide to go ahead, plumber's pipe cutters will do the job very neatly. You can get these at any DIY superstore but buy good ones – the cheap types are a pain. Do not remove more than an inch of handlebar each side at a time, otherwise it might be difficult to retain full control of the steering.

There are many different types and styles of bar end but the cheaper ones made of aluminium alloy suit most riders. When you are fitting them, do not overtighten the fixing bolts or the light aluminum handlebar tube might collapse under the pressure.

Handlebar tape is always used with drop handlebars, perhaps with extra padding to reduce the shock reaching the hands. Tape is available in various materials and lots of different colors and patterns. The most popular type is slightly padded plastic. But cork ribbon, which gives a cool sweat-free grip, is very pleasant to the feel and so is cloth tape. This ages fast, but feels good. When you reach the brake levers, mold the tape neatly around the clip and the hood. But with combined brake and gear levers, use a short length of tape to cover the fixing bands.

Drop handlebars often have a groove for the brake and gear cables. Use a few short lengths of tape to retain each cable in the correct groove, before you apply the handlebar tape.

BAR END CLAMPS

Bar ends come in only one size and should fit any normal handlebar. But if you have problems getting the clamp onto the handlebars, try filing a slight chamfer on the end of the bar and lightly greasing the inside of the clamp. If that does not work, it may be possible to cautiously open up the clamp with a screwdriver. But do not use a serious amount of force as you could crack the clamp and that is potentially very dangerous.

Fitting new grips

1 Get ready by breaking the bond, using a screwdriver aided by WD-40 or similar.

2 Remove the grips by a straight pull, or by turning them around and pulling.

Taping drop handlebars

1 Pull out the handlebar end plugs first. Some have a central screw that must be loosened first to ease off the pressure, but most just pull out or pry out with a screwdriver.

2 Undo all the old tape, cutting it with a utility knife if necessary. Then roll back the rubber brake hood and use a short length of tape to cover the edge of the lever.

Shortening handlebars

1 With a plumber's pipe cutter, decide how much you want to cut off each side.

2 Turn the pipe cutter to cut a groove in the bar, tightening it as you progress.

3 Pour some methylated spirit into the new grips so that they will go on fairly easily.

4 Quickly push the new grips on, so the methylated spirit doesn't have time to evaporate.

5 To complete the job, fit the end plugs supplied if you aren't going to fit bar ends.

ADJUSTABLE STEMS

3 Start taping close to the center of the handlebars, overlapping about one third and stretching it around the brake levers. When you get to the end, tuck it in neatly.

4 Fit new bar end plugs as a final touch. Sometimes they go in easily but you may have to use the palm of your hand to screw them around and around until they are flush.

5 Cork handlebar tape often comes in a set. The tape itself has an open texture and feels cool and grippy but slightly rubberized. Short lengths are supplied to cover the brake/gear levers, plus end plugs. And if you start taping from the end of the handlebars, you can use the adhesive plastic tape to trap the ends of the cork tape to prevent it from unwinding.

Many hybrid and leisure bikes now come with an adjustable stem to make it even easier to get the right riding position. To alter the angle of the stem to lift the handlebars, loosen the clamp bolt that holds the stem to the steerer tube. Next, undo the socket head bolt on top of the stem until it is loose, lift the handlebar assembly and re-tighten the top bolt. Then re-tighten the clamp bolt in front of the stem, making sure that it is exactly in line with the front wheel. If you are having trouble with your riding position, it is certainly worth fitting an adjustable stem to other types of bikes as well. The type shown above right is suitable for use with an Aheadset-style setup and threadless forks. The type shown on the

3 Eventually the end will fall off. Then use abrasive paper to take off the rough edges.

WHEN YOU NEED TO DO THIS JOB:
■ Grips or tape are old and worn.
■ Handlebars are too wide for comfort.
■ You want to fit bar ends to give a better riding position.

TIME:
■ 15 minutes to fit new grips.
■ 30 minutes to cut down handlebars with pipe cutter.
■ 15 minutes to remove old handlebar tape and fit new.

DIFFICULTY:
■ Pretty easy, even if you decide to reduce the width of the handlebar.

SPECIAL TOOLS:
■ Plumber's pipe cutter.

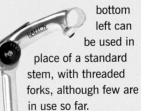

bottom left can be used in place of a standard stem, with threaded forks, although few are in use so far.

Saddles with seat post fixing

Saddles have almost become a fashion item, with new designs appearing almost weekly. Cut-outs to avoid contact with the most delicate tissues, designs that enable the saddle to rock with the shifting of the weight, saddles that suit a female anatomy. The trick is to distinguish genuine advances in saddle design from the marketing and the hype. As ever, the saddle to go for is the one that makes you feel comfortable, so you may have to try various types before you find what suits you.

Seat posts with a built-in clip are far superior to those with a separate one. They look better, weigh less and are not so fiddly. Most have a good range of adjustment but this varies between different types and makes. So if you are unusually tall or short, you may have to change your seat post to get the correct riding position. Take a look at the "layback" design pictured below if you want to get the saddle far back over the back wheel.

There are many variations on the basic design, some of which are not micro-adjusting because there may be 2mm or 3mm difference between each possible saddle position. Other types have a two-bolt "see-saw" design where you undo one bolt and tighten the other to adjust the saddle angle.

However, the latest design is completely different. It's based on a flanged beam, which replaces the rails in a conventional design. The clip wraps around the flange of the beam and allows adjustment of both position and angle. It is both lighter and easier to adjust, but faces a lot of hurdles before it replaces the standard design.

There are two important dimensions to watch when you are buying a seat post – diameter and length. Diameter is more important because there are at least 14 sizes you could come across. These vary between 25.4mm and 31.8mm, so the differences in diameter are very small. Instead of making all possible variations, manufacturers often supply shims so that one basic seat post covers a variety of seat tube sizes. But be careful – if you try to fit the wrong size seat post, it will either seize in place, or it will always be too loose unless you can find the correct size shim.

So when buying, either take the old seat post or, better still, the frame with you. Get the bike shop to check the correct size with calipers or by using a micrometer before buying.

Most road bikes have a seat post 220mm long, but MTBs use a 300mm length, because of the smaller frame sizes. Provided the diameter is correct, you can use an MTB-length seat post in a road frame, cutting it to length if necessary. BMX bikes use a steel seat post, 400mm long.

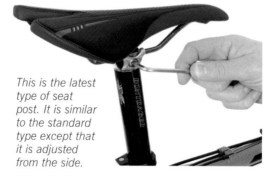

This is the latest type of seat post. It is similar to the standard type except that it is adjusted from the side.

Saddle with I-beam

1 Undo the clip on the bottom of the saddle, ready for the adjustment.

2 With the clip undone, the saddle can be adjusted for angle as well as fore-and-aft.

3 Tighten the clip, which clamps it around the beam once more.

CREAKING NOISES
It is quite common for a saddle to make creaking noises, most often when you are climbing a hill or sprinting. If this annoys you, try thoroughly cleaning the seat post clamp and replacing it dry, without any grease. Do not be tempted to overtighten the alloy clamp bolt as it will snap quite easily, or you could damage the thread.

WHEN YOU NEED TO DO THIS JOB:
■ When fitting a new saddle or seat post.
■ To adjust your riding position.

TIME:
■ 10 minutes to fit a new saddle or seat pin.
■ 2 minutes to make a change to the saddle position.

DIFFICULTY: 🔧🔧
■ You should find it very much easier with a micro-adjuster seat post than working on one with a separate clip, whether you are fitting a new seat post or adjusting the saddle position.

Fitting the saddle

1 On the standard-design single-bolt seat post, the saddle clamp is held in place by a bolt through the cradle. In the type shown, the cradle is part of the seat post, but it's usually separate. Always use anti-seize on the clamp bolt.

2 Fitting the saddle is usually easier if you take the seat post out of the frame. Turn the saddle upside down, support the top part of the cradle with two fingers and lay the square nut under the cut-out portion, supported by your fingers.

3 Now lay the other part of the cradle on the saddle rails. Then lower the saddle and clip onto a firm surface and check that the cut-outs in both parts of the cradle line up with the square nut. Do not worry about saddle position.

4 Finally, fit the clamp bolt through the hole in the seat post, through both parts of the clip and screw it into the square nut. Then tighten the clamp bolt until the cradle grips the rails, allowing you to remove your fingers at last.

Adjusting saddle position

1 When getting a new bike ready or bringing an old one back into action, coat the bottom of the seat post with anti-seize grease to prevent corrosion. Then set the saddle height using the guidelines way back on page 10.

2 For fore-and-aft adjustment, undo the clamp bolt one turn. But to adjust the angle, hold the cradle together with one hand while you undo the clamp bolt several turns. Lift and rock the saddle to change the angle, and then tighten.

3 Do not try to slide the saddle to a new position because there is too much friction in the cradle for you to do that accurately. Tap it with the palm of your hand instead, moving it only a couple of millimeters or so at a time.

4 When you are satisfied with the new saddle position, check that the clamp bolt is tight – not over tight – and that the saddle is exactly aligned with the frame. Finally, do a short test ride to make sure you are comfortable.

SHOCK POSTS
For extra comfort, consider fitting a shock post. These have approximately 50mm of up-and-down movement to absorb bumps. The Allen wrench adjuster allows you to alter the tension of the spring.

VARIATION
Some seat posts are fitted with a device to compensate for wear. When wear is detected, undo the locknut, adjust the Allen wrench fitting and retighten.

Saddles with clip fixing

There is seldom any need to separate a saddle clip from the saddle, but if you have to do so for some reason, reassemble all the parts in the correct order on the through bolt. Then hold the assembly together by tightening both nuts an equal amount. This keeps the through bolt in the center of the clip. Tighten the nuts with your fingers.

Position the saddle rail retainers facing outward and slip them onto the saddle rails from the rear. Then loosen one of the nuts a little and rotate the curved outer retainer so that it closes off the saddle rail retainer. Repeat on the other side and tighten both nuts.

With the clip fitted to the saddle, push it onto the slimmer section of the seat post, then tighten both nuts equally. Fit the circular part of the saddle clip above the point where the thin section of the seat post bulges out to the main part, otherwise it will eventually cut deep into the metal. Occasionally the seat post will either suddenly fail or the saddle will fall off altogether.

To allow you to adjust the riding position, the saddle slides backward and forward on the rails. You can also change the angle of the saddle. This is best done by undoing both nuts a little at a time until they are loose enough to allow the ridges on the outer retainers and the saddle rail retainers to jump over each other. Retighten the nuts as soon as you have completed the adjustment.

TRADITIONAL SADDLES

The traditional saddle is staging a comeback. It's broader than most modern types and has a pair of springs, so it particularly suits a female rider who just uses a bike for short journeys. The clip is slightly different from normal types. That's because it has to take into account the two wires that form the underside of the saddle. However, it can be dealt with in roughly the same way as a standard clip.

SADDLE

SADDLE RAILS

SEAT POST

SADDLE CLIP

SEAT POST CLAMP

SEAT POST HEIGHT

Most seat posts are marked with a line showing the minimum length that should be inside the frame at any time. To put it another way, you should never see the line on the seat post when the bike is in use. As a rule of thumb, at least one third of the seat post length must stay inside the frame.

Final saddle adjustment

1 It is very important to get the angle of the saddle right, otherwise too much of your weight will rest on the most sensitive part of your anatomy. Undo the nut on one side of the saddle clip first.

2 Do not undo the nuts too far or it will be impossible to make fine adjustments to the saddle angle. To tilt the nose downward, lean on the front of the saddle and lift the back with your hand.

3 A saddle clip also allows adjustment backward and forward. Loosen the nut slightly on one side and thump the back of the saddle with the heel of your hand to move it forward and vice versa.

LEATHER SADDLES

Solid leather saddles must be allowed to dry out naturally, whenever they get wet. If the rain soaks right into the saddle, apply a dressing to feed the leather and build up water resistance. Tighten the nose bolt if the leather sags – the makers supply a special wrench.

Altering saddle height

1 Saddle height is adjusted by undoing the saddle clamp bolt until it is fairly loose. The seat post can sometimes be a tight fit in the frame, so it may not move easily. Turn it from side to side to get it to move. Then pull the seat post right out and coat with copper-based anti-seize grease to prevent it from seizing in the frame.

2 Turn the saddle 2in or 3in each way and lean on it to adjust downward. To raise the saddle, move it from side to side and lift at the same time. Then tighten the saddle clamp bolt fairly hard.

SEAT POST BINDER

Lots of mountain bikes have a seat post binder instead of a bolt. They are similar to the quick release on a hub so, when you tighten the binder, you might have to make a definite effort to lock it. If not, tighten the nut on the other side from the lever. Once you get used to whipping the seat post in and out, you can use it for security. Removing the saddle also makes it easier to load your bike into a car.

WHEN YOU NEED TO DO THIS JOB:
■ Fitting a saddle to a standard seat pin, usually on an older type of bike.
■ Swapping a saddle from a new bike to an old one.
■ Adjusting the riding position.

TIME:
■ Fitting a saddle clip can take 5 minutes or drive you crazy and take 15 minutes.
■ Adjusting saddle height is easy, unless the seat post is stuck in the frame.

DIFFICULTY: 🔧🔧🔧🔧
■ Refitting a saddle clip is one of those jobs where you need three hands – one to hold the clip, one to hold the saddle and the other to use the wrench. It is best to assemble the clip away from the saddle and fit it back on all in one piece. If that does not work, get a bike mechanic to fix it. Spray light lube or penetrating oil around the base of the seat post if it seems to be stuck in the frame. Wait a while, then try to move it from side to side to break the seal.

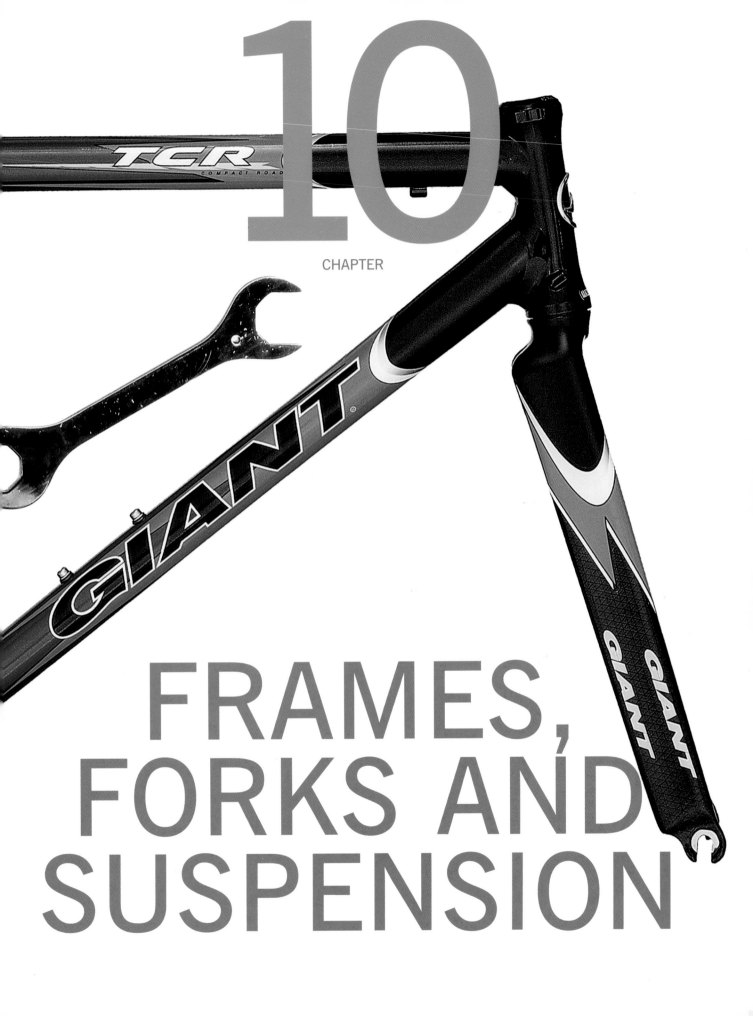

FRAMES,
FORKS AND
SUSPENSION

Frame materials and design

The most affordable bikes are made of steel. Unfortunately the low price means that the tubes have to be very thick, so they don't have the liveliness and comfort that more expensive steel tubes offer. What's more, details like the front and rear ends border on the crude, so standard operations like fitting the wheels are a bit of a struggle. Finally, they don't have items like built-in hangers for the gears. They'll do to start you off but if possible, spend a little bit more.

Happily, one price range up from this, aluminum frames become the norm. Even the cheapest ones are lighter than a cheap steel frame, but if possible go for one that tells you what quality of aluminum is used. The most common is 7005 heat-treated alloy but various other 6000 and 7000 grades are used as well.

The source of these frames is the Far East but the consistent quality is very impressive. If you look at the welding on them you'll see that it's very neat and even. This is due to the automated machinery used, which also controls the temperature very accurately. Furthermore the welding is carried out by the TIG (tungsten inert gas) process, which envelops the weld in an inert gas. This prevents the formation of oxides and cools the weld. So although previous experience might suggest that these welds are brittle and have a limited life, in fact these frames are probably no more likely to fail than steel.

Mountain bikes will mostly be fitted with "no name" forks at the lower end of the market, but when only slightly more expensive they tend to have Suntour. However, if possible go for a frame that has either RockShox, Marzocchi or Manitou. These will still be very reasonably priced but the know-how gained at the expensive end of the market inevitably rubs off. Don't buy a cheap bike with front and rear suspension, because it's inevitably been built down to a price.

As far as city bikes, hybrids and road bikes are concerned, the cheaper aluminum frames have cromoly steel forks, as aluminum ones tend to feel dead. Only the more expensive types have carbon fiber, which is not only lighter but also tends to filter out vibration. These have very much come down in price, so you can start looking for this material at the top end of the affordable range.

Apart from full-suspension mountain bikes, bike frames are made up of triangles, which concentrate the stresses where one tube is joined to the next. So all good-quality frame tubing is thicker at the ends, where the stresses are concentrated, and thinner in the middle to save weight. The thicker ends are butts, so tubes with two thicker ends are known as double-butted.

In addition, the frame tubes are frequently manipulated so that although they start off round, the down tube will be more-or-less triangular over its whole length by the time it has been worked, with two equal length sides facing upward. Or it will be a flattened doughnut shape where it meets the bottom bracket but much more nearly square at the head tube end.

On the other hand the top tube may well be nearly square over its whole length, but flare out toward the head tube end. There it is as big as possible to stiffen up the joint. The seat tube may well be a large diameter tube as well, flaring out to an even larger diameter at the bottom bracket.

Finally, the chain and seat stays are especially likely candidates for manipulation. Keyhole-shaped seat stays to introduce a certain amount of give in the rear are well known. But the chain stays can be shaped to keep them out of the mud on mountain bikes, or to give the same amount of compliance as the chain stays.

Hybrid or City Bikes

The hybrid bike invariably has an aluminum frame, sometimes with a simple suspension fork. But it can have cromoly steel forks at the bottom of the price range, or carbon fiber forks at the top end of what most people are prepared to pay.

Mountain Bikes

Mountain bikes are available with full suspension, but way above what most people are prepared to pay, so a reasonable "hardtail" is the best compromise. Ideally choose one with an oil-damped fork, rather than elastomers.

Design features

1 The better MTB frames are gusseted to make them stronger. So it's worth checking the welds every year, to make sure they aren't showing signs of pinholes or even total failure.

2 Most mountain bike frames now have 1⅛in headsets. The head tube is shaped to allow for this. They are much better-suited to carrying the weight and stresses of the fork.

3 Ride on aluminum frames is harsh, so the seat stays are shaped into a keyhole pattern to introduce some give. This frame is also fitted with wishbone seat stays.

4 Any reasonable-quality MTB frame should have two sets of bottle mounts and a well-thought-out set of cable eyes along the top tube. There should also be a built-in gear hanger.

5 Aluminum road frames are often fitted with carbon fiber forks. They filter out road shocks and vibration. At the next price point they also have carbon fiber seat stays.

6 All good quality road frames have semi-vertical drop-outs with a gear hanger that is renewable. In addition they have brazed-on fittings for bottle cages and gear, brake cables and possibly a pump.

7 Aluminum frame tubes are usually double butted, but they can also be shaped so that they take the stresses at the end of the tube. In this frame the tubes are hydroformed, or shaped by water pressure.

8 Touring frames need more brazed-on parts than any other type. There should be rack-mounting eyes at the top of the chainstays, on the rear drop outs and on the forks, and chain stay pump pegs.

Racing Bikes

This is a full-blown carbon fiber racing bike, complete with the latest groupset. But similar bikes are available with a higher build at the front end, so riders can enjoy the racing experience but with a less extreme riding position.

Touring Bikes

Traditional touring bikes are built with 631 steel tubing and look like racing bikes with mudguards. However, an MTB influence is creeping in with the use of vee brakes or cantilever brakes and very wide-range 27- or 30-speed gearing.

Safety inspection

Most bike frames have plenty of reserve strength, so they are more likely to go out of alignment than to fail. When this happens, the wheels sit at an angle to each other and the bike won't steer straight. It also interferes with the gear change, particularly the indexing.

Sometimes you'll be able to spot this by eye alone, especially if you check the frame from different directions. Comparing the front and back views can also help, especially if you tie string to each side, running from the head tube to the rear ends.

If you suspect that something is wrong, there is a choice. With a cheap frame, you can obtain a replacement very cheaply, so it's not worth asking a cycle shop to take a look. But if it's a good machine it may be possible to get the frame realigned.

The forks are by far the most vulnerable part of the frame, often taking the brunt of minor crashes. However, it's now easy to get replacement forks for a road bike, although you should try to obtain ones that roughly match the dimensions of the original. You can get forks in cromoly steel or aluminum, and you can also get carbon fiber if the rest of the frame is worth upgrading.

As for a mountain bike with suspension forks, you should be able to see if they need replacement. You can get a professional to assess the damage but the cheapest solution may well be just to replace the whole thing.

The aging of aluminum frame shows up, in theory, in a deterioration of the welds. Either pinholes appear, indicating air bubbles, or the welds actually crack. So far, if these things have happened at all, they have happened extremely rarely. Nevertheless, it's worth keeping an eye open for them, especially when the frame is more than five years old. That is when any guarantee runs out and we're in unknown territory.

Aging can also result in a loss of strength, in both steel and aluminum. This shows up as a high-speed wobble when going downhill. If you ever experience this kind of thing, the frame is scrap.

If your frame is worth getting resprayed, or you intend to fit a chainset with external bottom bracket bearings, get the bottom bracket faced and the threads chased. Facing ensures that both faces are parallel, which allows the bearings to run properly, while chased threads make installation easy.

DESIGNER FRAME TUBING

Some frames have tubes supplied by a known maker, but most of them are the more expensive types of steel tube and therefore out of our price range, unless you are buying second-hand.

REYNOLDS
500 – Plain-gauge cro-mo (chrome-molybdenum alloy steel) tubes for budget mass-produced bikes.
525 – Butted cromoly tubing, for brazed frames with lugs and for TIG welding. For good-quality mass-produced bikes.
531 – Famous since 1935. Alloyed with manganese and molybdenum so it can only be joined using brazing or silver soldering. No high temperatures so TIG welding is out. Tube sets now available for racing (531C) and touring (531ST).
631 – Upgraded version of 531. Air hardening, so it gets stronger after TIG welding or brazing. Strong, with a good ride.

COLUMBUS
Aelle – Heavy, budget-priced cromoly.
Gara – Still a budget product but butted.
SL and **SLX** – Roughly equivalent to 531. No longer used for new frames.
Thron – Quality tubes for mass production.
Foco – Top-quality steel tubing.
Columbus Altec – Drawn from 7005 aluminum, alloyed with zinc and magnesium.

DEDACCIAI
Scandium – Very advanced aluminum tubeset, maybe the best. Mostly used as oversize tubes.

ALUMINUM ALLOY TUBE SETS
Easton – An American firm supplying various good-quality aluminum tubesets.
6000 – Aluminum alloyed with magnesium. Easy to extrude, so good for components like handlebars. Also used for frames.
7000 series – The most popular aluminum frame tubing, used for almost all budget aluminum bikes. Easy to weld but a bit prone to cracking near welds. Even if the tubes are butted, they have to be very thick-walled. 7020 is probably the best grade.

Checking for crash damage

1 Position yourself at the front of the bike and look along the frame. You should be able to see if the short head tube and the seat tube that carries the saddle line up.

2 Stand over the bike looking down. You will be able to see if the horizontal top tube lines up with the down tube. Check also that the forks splay out an equal amount.

3 Now look along the frame from the back. The rear mech should hang straight down and the seat tube align with the head tube. Check also that the seat stays are straight.

4 Most important: run your fingers down the back and front of the forks, checking for ripples in the tubing. Next, take a look to make sure that the fork curves smoothly. Then take the front wheel out, so you can see if it fits back in easily and is centered exactly between the fork blades.

CARBON FIBER CARE

Bikes with carbon fiber components are, in theory, more susceptible to damage than all-metal bikes, it will fail catastrophically if hit hard enough. Any carbon fiber frame that has been involved in a big accident should be thoroughly checked.

They are also susceptible to deterioration due to age; here is a three-point test:
1. VISUAL TEST. Inspect the carbon fiber component for scratches, gouges, cracks, loose fibers or any other visual faults.
2. AUDIBLE TEST. Listen for unusual noises when riding: creaks, groans, pops or any other weird noises that you haven't heard before.
3. TACTILE TEST. When out riding, take note of how the bike shifts gears, brakes, corners and accelerates, and also any strange changes to the ride or handling. Pay particular attention to whether the bike pulls one way or the other, or if it suddenly starts changing gear by itself.

IF ANY OF THESE TESTS HAS A POSITIVE RESULT, HOWEVER SMALL, STOP USING THE COMPONENT.

Carbon fiber components do not necessarily give warning of impending failure. However, there are plenty of components around that are five years old, and so far they aren't showing a high failure rate.

5 Finally, run your fingers along the underside of all the tubes. Damage like the tiny ripples in the tubes arrowed in the picture below often goes unnoticed during a purely visual inspection. Luckily, your sense of touch will often pick up defects that the eyes just skate over and miss.

Neither the tubes nor the welds have cracked on the crashed frame in the picture, showing the amazing strength of a really well-built frame.

WHEN YOU NEED TO DO THIS JOB:
■ When buying second-hand.
■ After a crash.
■ If the bike is not running or steering straight.

TIME:
■ 10 minutes is enough for a thorough inspection from several different angles. Always try to look along the frame against the light.

DIFFICULTY:
■ When you first start, you will think you are going cross-eyed, but you will get the hang of it.

Suspension set-up

When setting up a full-suspension bike, you have to adjust the force needed to compress the springs. The idea is that when you put your weight on the bike, the suspension should sag by about 25% of the total travel. Total travel does not refer to the length of the springs themselves but the distance the front or rear wheel moves between the fully extended and the fully compressed positions, within the limits of the design. If the forks or rear suspension reach the end of their travel when riding over rough ground, this is known as bottoming out. It should be avoided because it tends to shake your eyeballs out and can damage your bike, particularly the suspension itself. The opposite of bottoming out is called topping out and occurs when the suspension reaches its fully extended position, for instance when the wheels leave the ground. The 25% of spring travel allocated to sag is intended to allow the wheels to drop down into holes, allowing them to follow the shape of the ground more efficiently, particularly at the rear when braking hard going down a hill.

Hardtail mountain bikes with suspension forks only, as well as hybrids and leisure bikes with sprung forks, should also be set up for the same 25% sag.

When adjusting any kind of forks, try to adjust both legs evenly. If there is a difference between the springing of the legs, it will tend to produce uneven wear and possibly lead to distortion. Although many suspension forks now have the spring in one leg and the damping in the other, eliminating this problem.

Many of the suspension forks fitted to budget hardtails and full suspension bikes have steel coil springs but no form of damping. So the bike tends to bob up and down because there is nothing to control the springs or dissipate the energy of the bumps. When riding a suspension bike, try to develop a smooth pedaling style to stop the bike from bobbing up and down. And on hills, change down to the lower gears early so that you do not have to get out of the saddle. This will help reduce the amount of bob, allowing the suspension to react more efficiently to the terrain instead of to rider-induced movement.

REBOUND DAMPING ADJUSTMENT

If you sit on the saddle and press down on the handlebars, the forks compress. When you take your weight off the 'bars, the forks extend once more. This is the rebound.

On many forks, the rebound is not controlled. So the forks compress and rebound a couple of times before they settle. If this happens when you are out riding, the forks will not be able to react properly to the next bump. They may be rebounding when they should be compressing, or the other way around.

Quality forks usually have oil damping to control the rebound. In addition to the pre-load dial, they usually have an extra control for the rebound at the bottom of one of the fork legs. Set this so that when you push the handlebars down, they only come back up once. Adjust it again, if you find the front of the bike still bobbles around when you are out on a ride.

Front suspension

1 To set up the suspension, you must know what the total travel is. This figure should be in the handbook but if not, you will have to measure it. If you have air forks, remove the air valve completely. With coil forks, remove the spring or springs. Once the fork has no springing it can be fully compressed and extended. Now lift the handlebars upward and get a friend to pull the wheel down to make sure that the forks are fully extended. While you support the bike, ask your friend to tie a piece of string or, better still, a tie wrap around the upper fork leg where it disappears into the lower fork leg. If you now compress the forks fully, the tie wrap will be pushed up the fork leg. Pull the forks out to their full extent again and measure the distance between the top of the lower fork leg and the tie wrap. This gives you total fork travel. Leave the tie wrap in position.

2 Refit the spring or the air valve and pump up the fork to the pressure given for your weight in the owner's manual. Work out 25% of the total travel. Then sit on the bike in the normal way, with your feet on the pedals and bounce the fork up and down a few times, then get your friend to measure the distance between the tie wrap and the top of the fork legs again. Subtracting this figure from the first measurement gives you the amount of sag. If that figure is less than 25% of total fork travel, the forks are too stiff. To correct that, turn the adjuster counter-clockwise one turn, or on an air-sprung fork, reduce the air pressure. Turn the adjuster the other way if sag is over 25%, or increase the air pressure. Repeat until the amount of sag is correct. If you are unusually heavy or unusually light, you may have to change the coil spring to one of a higher or lower poundage (strength) to get the sag right.

Rear suspension

REAR SUSPENSION PIVOT

When buying a full-suspension bike, check that the pivots are large and meaty looking. They should also have some kind of built-in protection against water but you should still keep the area free of dust and mud. In normal circumstances, no maintenance is required.

1 Coil-sprung rear suspension sag is adjusted by turning the spring seat on the suspension unit. If sag is less than 25%, turn the spring seat counter-clockwise to increase it and clockwise to decrease it. Keep adjusting the spring seat until you get around 25% of the total travel as sag.

2 If you are unusually heavy or light, adjusting the spring seat adjustment alone may not work. You can change the spring to one with a higher or lower poundage (strength). There are several specialized companies that stock springs of all shapes, sizes, and poundage.

3 Some bikes have two or more mountings for the rear shock unit. This changes the leverage between the rear wheel and the shock, and can increase or reduce the total travel. For example fitting in the lower position here increased travel by one inch at the rear wheel.

Suspension fork: strip

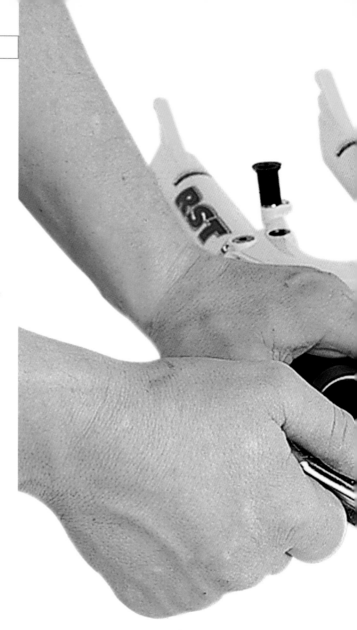

Crashing up and down over rough ground, suspension forks take more of a beating than any other component on a bike. What is more, unless the sliding parts are protected by gaiters in sound condition, dirt will get between the moving parts and cause rapid wear. So day-to-day, keep an eye on the gaiters and do not ride cross-country if they are defective.

If no gaiters are fitted, keep the sliders clean and give them a squirt of aerosol lube every time you go out on a ride. That will certainly lengthen the life of the working parts.

Every couple of months, the forks must be stripped so you can check the bushings and regrease the stanchions. The bushings are plastic tubes that fit in the tops of the fork legs. The fork stanchions are a close fit in the bushes, so they can slide up and down smoothly, without any judder.

When the bushings are regreased frequently, the stanchions will slide more smoothly and wear on the plastic bushing will be kept to a minimum. However, depending on how fast you ride and the terrain, the bushings will have to be replaced sooner or later.

You only apply a fairly thin smear of grease to the bushings, spring or elastomer stack, and upper stanchions. But you must use a synthetic type because mineral grease will attack the rubber parts. RST recommends Sylkolene Pro RG2, available from their dealers but any fully synthetic grease will do. Teflon-based grease is particularly suitable for the elastomers.

Upgrade kits are available for some forks, offering better quality gaiters and bushings. Soft rubber gaiters will always outlast hard plastic ones, but the bottom end of the gaiter must be held in place with a cable tie to stop dirt from getting in.

You can usually get alternative springs to help you set up the suspension and you can change elastomers too. Cream ones are hard and blue ones soft. But fit the same stack of elastomers in each fork leg to avoid problems. The elastomers themselves damp down movement pretty well but many bikes are sold with spring forks but no damping at all. Consider upgrading to forks with oil or air damping if you find the front of the bike bobs around a lot or tends to act like a pogo stick.

SUSPENSION FORKS
The instructions on how to strip a suspension fork on this spread, and the next spread explaining how to change the oil, show these jobs being done on typical and popular examples. But there are many different designs, so check the manufacturer's instructions or their website for exact details before starting work. And remember, all these components are critical to safety, so it could affect your own safety if you get things wrong.

Sprung forks

1 Before starting the actual strip down, degrease the forks with solvent and water and dry them off. Then undo the countersunk Phillips screws or bolts holding the fork brace to the fork legs.

2 Check the brake pivots next to see if they are bent or cracked. Then unscrew them using a ring wrench right at the base of the pivot hexagon, in case the wrench slips. Lift the fork brace out of the way.

Triple-clamp forks

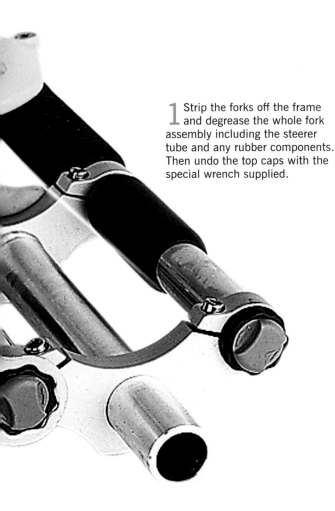

1 Strip the forks off the frame and degrease the whole fork assembly including the steerer tube and any rubber components. Then undo the top caps with the special wrench supplied.

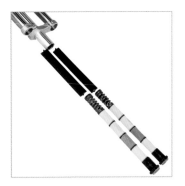

2 Once you have undone the top caps, withdraw the complete elastomer stack and wipe off any grease. Check that none of the elastomers is damaged in any way.

3 Lift the wheel end of the forks and undo the socket-head bolt buried in the end of each fork leg. You can then pull the lower legs off the stanchions and degrease them inside.

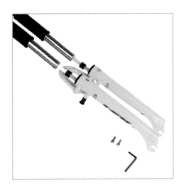

4 With the forks stripped and degreased, carefully inspect the plastic bushings at the top of the lower legs. If some areas of the bushing look shiny or scored, they need changing.

5 During a major overhaul, pull the compression rod out of the stanchions, degrease, and inspect for damage. Finally, reassemble by reversing the previous procedure.

3 Pull back the rubber gaiter and grasp the steerer tube with one hand. With the other, turn the lower leg counter-clockwise and pull it right off. Use Stillson's cushioned with a rag to start it turning if necessary.

4 Wipe away any surplus grease and unscrew the spring using long-nosed pliers. Use your thumbs to push off the bush around the top of the fork legs, then clean and degrease this area as well.

5 Degrease inside the fork leg and all the parts. Place the new bush on a hard surface, sit the lip of the fork leg on the seal and lean on it with all your weight. Grease the springs and lower legs, then reassemble.

Suspension fork: oil change

The oil in a suspension fork has two jobs. First, it lubricates all the various parts as they slide past each other, which slows down wear. Second, it flows through the damper valves, absorbing the energy that each bump puts into the fork.

When acting as a lubricant, bits of metal and rubber worn off by use are carried in the oil. Changing the oil then flushes all these abrasive pieces away, which substantially extends the life of the fork. But when acting as a shock absorber, the additives in the oil slowly get broken down by the action of the fork. Eventually, the oil will start to foam, which reduces the damping effect.

New forks do not become fully effective until they have been ridden for a couple of hundred miles or so. After that, you should notice that the fork moves up and down much more smoothly. That is the signal that the period of "breaking in" has finished, which is a good time to change the oil.

After that point, change the oil every 750 miles or 100 hours but more frequently in severe or very dusty conditions. If you are short of time, it is OK to just change the oil but a full service including regreasing the spring is worth the extra effort. In between services, keep the fork clean, especially the exposed chrome slider tubes. And every 250 miles or so, peel back the rubber seals and apply a squirt of the lubricant specified by the manufacturer at the top of the fork legs.

Bear in mind that the fork shown here is only one typical example among many. Check the manufacturer's instruction booklet or website for specific details about the forks on your own bike.

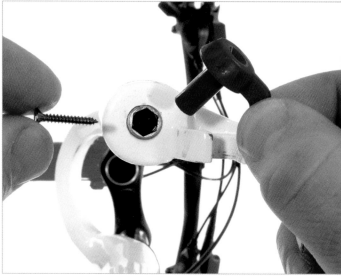

1 Remove the fork from the frame, as shown on pages 182–183. Brush off any loose dirt and mud, then degrease with a solvent cleaner. Rinse with warm water and dry. Then turn the fork upside down and rest the steerer tube on a bench or a Workmate. Undo the countersunk screw holding the rebound adjuster knob in place, then pull the knob away.

Oil for suspension forks is usually synthetic. The most important components are the anti-foam additives and lubrication properties. If they were left out, the churning of the oil would whip up a foam, making the oil thinner and providing too little damping. Various "weights" of oil are available, to help you tailor the fork to your preferences. For example, if you change from 5 to 10 weight oil, the fork will have more damping.

Most oil-damped forks are fitted with a lockout control, which prevents the fork from compressing. It is used uphill, when the rider wishes to save energy.

9 Empty out the remaining oil in the fork tube, allow to drain for a couple of minutes, then wipe out. Check all the parts for wear, especially the fork leg seals, and inspect the fork legs themselves for cracks.

2 Turn the forks the right way up, then loosen the plain top cap with a close-fitting ring wrench. You should be able to unscrew the top cap the rest of the way with just your fingers.

3 Pull the top cap away from the fork, wiggling it slightly from side to side to prevent the damper assembly from sticking in place. Lay it down on some clean rags so that the rest of the oil can drain off.

4 With an Allen wrench, remove the adjuster knob on the other fork cap. Unscrew the adjuster assembly, then pull out the spring. It will probably be covered in old grease, so wipe it all off carefully.

5 Pour the old oil out of the other fork leg, catching it in a suitable container. Do not dispose of the old oil by pouring it into the drains or onto the ground as that will damage the environment.

6 Work the fork up and down several times to release the oil trapped at the bottom, then pour off into a container again. Repeat this process a few times until all the old oil is emptied out of the fork.

7 Turn the fork upside down again and undo the small socket head screw at the bottom of the right fork leg. This holds the rest of the damper assembly in place in the middle of the fork leg.

8 You can now pull the fork crown assembly away from the fork legs. Lay the fork crown assembly on some clean rag to absorb the oil as it drains off. After a few minutes, wipe the rest of the oil away.

10 Replace any parts past their prime, then slide the fork crown assembly back into the legs. Refit the adjuster and the socket head screw. Move the damper assembly around with a screwdriver if necessary.

11 Pour fresh oil into the fork until you can just see the surface when peering down into the fork leg. Work the fork up and down a few times so that the bottom of the fork fills up with fresh oil.

12 Fully compress the fork, then check the level with a tape measure. Adjust according to the maker's instructions. The lower level makes the fork softer at the end of its travel, the higher makes it stiffer.

AIR FORKS

Most air-sprung forks are very sensitive to the height of the oil. The air above the oil is used as a spring, and when air is compressed inside the fork it behaves in a manner known as "inversely proportional." This means that if you start with 50psi, and halve the fork travel, you will have 100psi. If you then halve the remaining travel you will have 200psi, and so on. The oil height is crucial to the performance of the fork throughout the whole range of travel of the fork. Raising the oil height makes the fork more progressive – stiffer toward the end of its travel. Lowering it makes it softer at the end of its travel. But always stick to the manufacturer's instructions, otherwise you could damage the fork internals.

Aheadset headsets

A headset and similar systems are very different from threaded headsets. The biggest difference is that they are held together by the handlebar stem, which clamps onto the unthreaded steerer tube and presses downward onto the top bearing. See page 161 for a diagram.

To adjust the bearings on an Aheadset, you first loosen the compression bolt that holds the stem cap in place. Then loosen the clamp bolts on the stem and press it down onto the top bearing race. To get the pressure right, the bearing has to be "pre-loaded."

This is done by tightening the compression bolt, which forces the stem cap down onto the stem. The stem then presses down onto the bearing, applying the pre-load. Ideally, the amount of pre-load should be set with a torque wrench. But using two fingers only to apply a moderate force to the compression bolt works

nearly as well. Anyway, you always have to balance between too much pre-load, making the steering feel tight, and not enough pre-load, causing the forks to knock over bumps.

After applying the pre-load, check that the forks turn easily, without any play or movement. Loosen the compression bolt and then re-apply the pre-load if there seems to be a problem. Finally, tighten the clamp bolts on the stem to lock in the pre-load.

Mountain bikes are usually fitted with $1\frac{1}{8}$ in Aheadset components, road bikes with 1in. But, increasingly, road bikes also use $1\frac{1}{4}$ in headsets and a few bikes use other rarer sizes.

The only drawbacks of the Aheadset system are that the star washer in the steerer tube is not very strong, although better systems are available – see page 161. And it is impossible to adjust the handlebar height more than about 1in. For more adjustment, you have to fit an angled stem or an extension.

To keep out water and dirt, cartridge bearings are now supplied with good-quality Aheadsets. Fitting and adjustment is the same, but be careful to fit the cartridge the right way up.

STEM CAP

COMPRESSION BOLT

STAR NUT

CLAMP BOLT

SPACERS

TOP BEARING RACE

BOTTOM BEARING RACE

CROWN RACE

Cartridge bearings

1 When stripping a headset, check that the cartridge bearings are OK by turning the top and bottom halves in opposite directions with your thumb. If it feels gritty or sticky, pry out the seal using the blade of a utility knife and lift it away.

2 Then separate the two halves and wipe away the old grease. Clean all the parts with solvent, then check for indentations and severe wear in the bearing tracks. If all is well, reassemble with fresh grease and press the seal back.

VARIATIONS ON THE BASIC DESIGN

Within the basic Aheadset design, there are many small differences. Sometimes the compression bolt is neatly hidden by a rubber plug, and there may be a cover for the top race fastened to the steerer tube with three tiny socket-headed grub screws.

Stripping and refitting an Aheadset

1 Remove the stem cap, which is held in place with a compression bolt that screws into the star nut inside the steerer tube. Loosen the clamp bolts, usually located at the back of the stem itself.

2 Lift the stem away and then take off any spacers and the top bearing cover, often fitted with cartridge bearings. The only thing stopping the forks from dropping out now is the compression ring, so be careful.

3 The compression ring is usually split. If it will not move, pry it out using the tip of a blade. Hold the fork in place as you do so, or the weight will make it difficult to shift the compression ring.

4 Push the compression ring up the steerer tube. This will give you enough room to lift away the cartridge bearing, or the top bearing race, whichever is fitted. There may also be a seal for the bearing.

5 Now let the forks drop down out of the frame. Remove the bottom bearings or cartridge and clean away the old grease so you can examine all the bearing races and bearings for pitting and wear.

6 Check that the cartridge bearings (if fitted) turn smoothly. But if caged bearings are fitted, pack them and the bearing races with fresh grease. Fit the bearings into the races, then grease the fork race.

7 Lift the forks back into position. Fit the top bearings or cartridge and hold the forks in the frame by pushing the compression ring back down into the angle of the bearing. See below for the final stages.

WHEN YOU NEED TO DO THIS JOB:
- During a major overhaul.
- If the steering is stiff.
- When the forks seem to judder in the frame.

TIME:
- 30 minutes. This type of headset is simpler to work on, so you probably will not need to take the brake levers and shifters off.

DIFFICULTY:
- The hardest thing about this job is grasping how it is all held together.

Fitting a clamp-on stem

1 You may find it easier to fit the stem if you tie the forks in place. Slip any spacers onto the steerer tube, then hold the forks with one hand and press the stem down onto the top bearing with the other.

2 Clean and grease the thread of the compression bolt, then screw it into the star nut. At this stage, leave the clamp bolts loose but check again that the stem is pressing evenly onto the top bearing.

3 Tighten up the compression bolt using two fingers. Check that the forks turn easily, and that you cannot feel any slack or play in the headset if you wiggle the forks. Re-set the pre-load if necessary.

4 Tighten the clamp bolts lightly, then line up the stem with the front wheel. Once you are sure that the steering is exactly aligned, tighten the clamp bolts fully. Check again, then road test.

Threaded headsets

When a bike is past its first youth, you may find the steering is not as smooth as it was. This could be because the headset needs stripping down and cleaning, although this should not be necessary more than once every couple of years, unless you ride the bike across country a lot.

But if the bike is a few years old, it is possible that the headset needs changing. Every time you go over a bump, the bearing race on top of the fork lifts and smashes the ball bearings into the bottom ball race. At the same time, the top bearing race is lifted away from the bearings, so it does not get battered in the same way. After this has happened many thousands of times,

tiny depressions form in the bottom races. The ball bearings then have to climb in and out of the depressions when you turn the steering, making it feel stiff and notchy. It can only be fixed by fitting a new headset. It will also be difficult to wheel your bike straight.

Fitting a new headset is a job for your local bike shop because a special headset press is needed to remove and refit any type of headset.

Riding a bike with any amount of play in the headset increases the force with which the ball bearings smash into the top race. So if the front brakes start juddering or the bike "knocks" over bumps, check for play and adjust immediately, otherwise the headset will wear out much faster.

TOP BEARING RACE

LOCKNUT

LOCKWASHER

HEAD TUBE

BOTTOM BEARING CUP

FORK RACE

FORK CROWN

FORK

CAGED BEARINGS

Most budget headsets are supplied with caged ball bearings instead of loose ones. Unless the cage is badly distorted, it is OK to reuse a caged bearing, although replacements are widely available.

Before refitting, clean the bearings with solvent, then rinse in water and carefully dry. Apply a little grease to the bearing race and press the caged bearing into it. The ball bearings must contact the bearing race, with the cage facing away from the bearing track. Finally, pack the space between the bearings, plus the cage itself, with grease.

Removing and replacing

1 When stripping the headset on an MTB, disconnect the front brake. On a road bike, unbolt the front brake from the fork. Then undo the quill bolt, and lift the stem out of the frame. Let them hang down beside the bike.

2 Your next move is to undo the locknut. A tight-fitting wrench is best but a pair of Stillsons or a big adjustable wrench will do. Most quality bikes have a soft alloy headset, which you will damage if you do not use the right wrench.

3 Below the locknut is a tagged washer or spacer, or there may be a flat on one side of the steerer tube with a matching flat on the washer. Use a small screwdriver to pry the washer away from the top bearing race if necessary.

4 Unscrew the top race next. If the bike is standing on the floor, the steerer tube will stay in place. But if the bike is in a workstand, the forks will drop out as you undo the top race. Try to catch any loose bearings as they fall away.

5 If caged bearings are fitted, they will probably stay in place, so pry them out. Clean all the parts with solvent and a rag, then inspect all four bearing tracks for wear. Look very closely for dimpling on the bottom race and fork race.

6 Stick the bearings in the races with waterproof grease, and grease the crown race. Thread the steerer tube up through the head tube and then screw on the top race to hold it there. Adjust the top race to eliminate any play.

7 If the bearings cannot be removed from the races, flush the old grease and dirt out with solvent, then dry and grease. A grease injector is ideal because it will force the grease into the bearings better than your finger can.

8 Fit the washer and locknut, then screw it down. Turn the forks to check that there is no friction. Adjust the top race to take out any movement in the forks. Then tighten the locknut and check again for friction and play in the forks.

WHEN YOU NEED TO DO THIS JOB:
- The bike is due for a general overhaul.
- There is a judder when you turn a sharp corner or apply the brakes hard.
- Turning the handlebars requires effort or the steering is not smooth and accurate.

TIME:
- 30 minutes if you just lift the handlebars and let them hang down.
- 40 minutes if you decide to remove the handlebars completely.

DIFFICULTY: 🔧🔧🔧
- It's not too difficult to strip down, grease and adjust a headset, especially if you've got suitable wrenches. Don't try fitting a new headset because you need a proper headset press to position the bearing races accurately in the frame.

SPECIAL TOOLS:
- Headset wrenches.

O-RINGS AND SEALS
Watch out for very thin rubber O-rings in grooves around the bearing cups. These are very effective at keeping water out but must not be stretched or broken because you will not get replacements. Off-road and touring bikes should be fitted with the additional external seals available at bike shops.

WHAT DOES THAT MEAN?

This section explains the meaning of words often used by bike enthusiasts, including any technical words that the author has been forced to use in this book.

A

AHEADSET: a design and brand of headset that has now largely taken over from the traditional threaded type. Can only be used with threadless forks and a clamp-on stem. Similar designs are produced by many other firms under license.

ALLEN WRENCH: six-sided, I-shaped tool that fits into the socket of a socket-head bolt. Somtimes referred to as a hexagon key in this book.

ALLOY: usually short for aluminum alloy. A mixture of metals, often including copper and zinc, with better characteristics than a pure one.

ALLOY RIMS: nearly all bikes have wheel rims made of aluminum alloy. Steel is the cheaper alternative material but the braking surface is so smooth that it is hard to stop quickly.

ANTI-SEIZE GREASE: a light grease often with powdered metal, usually copper. It is used to separate different metals, preventing them from seizing together.

AXLE: the central part of a hub or some other bearing assembly.

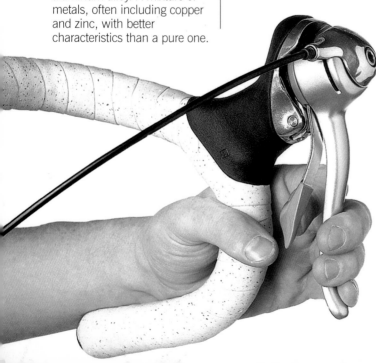

B

BALL BEARING: usually a hard-chromed, perfectly round, steel ball that fits between the cup and cone in bike bearings. Also means the complete assembly of inner and outer race plus ball bearings, as used in a cartridge bottom bracket and some hubs.

BAR ENDS: look like cow horns bolted to the ends of straight handlebars. Now mainly replaced by raised handlebars on cross-country MTBs.

BEADS: stiff inner edge of a tire that engages with the hook on the inside edge of a clincher rim. Usually made of wire or Kevlar.

BEARINGS: any part designed to minimize the friction and wear in a rotating or sliding assembly. On a bike, the main bearings are the headset, bottom bracket and hub bearings.

BOTTLE BOSS: threaded insert used for attaching bottle cages and other items to the frame.

BOTTOM BRACKET: the bearings, bearing cups and axle that carry the chainset.

BOTTOM BRACKET SHELL: the housing at the bottom of the seat and down tubes into which the bottom bracket is fitted.

BRAKE MODULATOR: adjusts the amount of force needed to apply the brake. Not normally used.

BRAZED-ON FITTING: items like bottle bosses and lever bosses fixed to the frame.

BUTT: the thickened end of a tube. See *double-butted*.

C

CABLE CAP: a soft metal sleeve that is crimped onto the end of a cable to prevent it from fraying.

CABLE STOP: a hollow tube or socket brazed onto the frame. The outer cable fits into one end, while the inner cable passes out of the other. Often slotted so that you can pull the outer cable out, without disconnecting the inner.

CANTILEVER BRAKES: attached to the frame via brazed-on pivots on the fork blades and chain stays. Fitted to many older mountain bikes because mud does not build up around them. Replaced by vee brakes.

CARBON FIBER: high-strength, high-cost material mainly used for making forks for road bikes. Also used for complete frames, seat posts and many other high-end components.

CARTRIDGE BOTTOM BRACKET: bottom bracket bearing in which the axle runs on two or three sealed ball bearings, enclosed in a metal sleeve.

CASSETTE: a set of 7, 8, 9 or 10 sprockets that mount onto a freehub body. A freewheel mechanism fits inside the freehub body.

CENTER PULL BRAKES: a brake with two separate arms independently mounted on a backplate. Powerful and reliable, but no longer made.

CENTER-TO-CENTER: usual way of measuring frame size. Distance from center of the bottom bracket axle to center of top tube. Given in either inches or centimeters.

CENTERING: usually refers to adjusting the position of a brake in such a way that the brake pads are equally spaced from the braking surface. Centering screws for this purpose are fitted to vee and dual pivot brakes. Can also refer to fitting a back wheel so that it is equally spaced between the chain stays.

CHAIN CAGE: on a rear mech, the chain cage consists of both jockey wheels and the side plates. Tensions and guides the chain.

CHAIN STAY: the small diameter tube that runs between the bottom bracket and the drop-out. It is usually oval near the bottom bracket but some modern frames use square-section tubes. May be curved or S-shaped.

CHAINRING: the toothed part of the chainset that engages with the chain. Usually removable.

CHAINSET: together the chainrings and cranks are known as the chainset.

CHROME MOLYBDENUM OR CRO-MOLY: a steel alloy often used for frames and forks. Can be welded, so cro-moly tubing is ideal for budget bikes.

CLINCHERS: detachable tires that are held onto the wheel rim by stiff beads that clinch under the raised edges of the rim.

CLUSTER: usually short for sprocket cluster. Cassette.

COGS: non-cyclists often speak of the chainring and sprockets as cogs because they are toothed.

COLUMBUS: Italian maker of high-quality frame tubing.

COTTERLESS CRANKS: cranks that bolt onto the shaped end of the bottom bracket axle.

COTTER PINS: slightly tapered steel pins with one flat side that hold the cranks onto the bottom bracket axle. Little used in modern times.

CRANKS: long arms that carry the pedals and transmit the rider's energy to the chainring.

CUP AND CONE BEARING: the standard bike bearing, which consists of loose or caged ball bearings between a semi-circular cup and a tapered cone. They are adjusted by moving the threaded part in or out until they turn freely, without play.

D

DEGREASER: any solvent that will dissolve grease. Includes paraffin, diesel fuel and various ecologically acceptable brand-name products.

DERAILLEUR: French word for gearing sytems that work by "derailling" the chain from one sprocket to another.

DIAMOND FRAME: the standard shape for a bike frame since about 1890. Mountain bikes usually have a modified diamond frame.

DISC BRAKE: a brake using a flat rotor fitted to the hub and a caliper that carries the pads on the fork leg or chain stay.

DOUBLE-BUTTED: lightweight frame tubing that is thin in the middle for lightness, and thicker at the ends where maximum strength is required.

DOWN TUBE: usually the largest diameter part of the frame. Runs from the head tube to the bottom bracket.

DROP-OUT: part of the frame that carries the front or back wheel.

DUAL-PIVOT BRAKES: a brake for road bikes using a Y arm and a C arm mounted on a backplate. More compact than center pulls and more powerful than side pulls.

E

EXPANDER BOLT: long bolt carried by the upright part of the stem. Screws into the cone that expands the base of the stem and holds it into the steerer.

F

FAST ROAD BIKE: a bike with flat handlebars but built like a sports bike in nearly every other way. Faster and more agile than a hybrid.

FIXED WHEEL: single sprocket on the rear hub, without a freewheel. Whenever the bike is moving, the rider has to pedal.

FORK CROWN: the top part of the forks, where they join the steerer tube. Often formed out of the fork blade itself.

FORK END: the part of the fork that carries the front wheel.

FORKS: the steerable part of the frame that holds the front wheel.

FRAME ANGLES: the angle between the top tube and seat tube; and between the top tube and head tube. Greatly influences how the bike behaves on the road.

FREEHUB: rear hub with the freewheel mechanism in the cassette body. Replaced hubs with separate freewheels to allow 7, 8, 9 and 10 sprockets without weakening the axle.

FREEWHEEL: most sprockets are mounted on a freewheel mechanism, which allows you to coast along without pedaling.

FRONT MECH: short for front-gear mechanism. Also called the front derailleur. Swaps the chain from one chainring to another. Two chainrings multiplies the number of gears by two. Three chainrings multiplies the number by three.

G

GEAR HANGER: part of the rear drop out that provides a mounting for the rear mech. Can be separate from, or part of, the frame.

GEAR RANGE: the gap between the lowest gear and the highest.

GEAR RATIO: the distance that a bike moves for each revolution of the cranks. In a low gear, this is about 1m (40in) per revolution and around 2.7m (110in) in a high one.

H

HAMMER: a tool of desperation and last resort.

HEADSET: the top and bottom bearings pressed into the head tube to support the forks and allow them to steer. The bottom bearing is subject to very heavy impact loads, so the races eventually become indented.

HEAD TUBE: the shortest frame tube. Fits between the top and down tubes. Can be almost non-existent on very small frames.

HIGH GEAR: a gear ratio in which you travel a long way for every revolution of the cranks. In high, the chain is on the largest chainring and one of the smaller sprockets.

HUB GEARS: alternative gearing system for city and leisure bikes. Contained within an enlarged rear hub. 3-, 5- and 7-speed versions are now available but they all tend to be heavy and absorb a lot of energy.

HYBRID: bike combining some mountain bike components and often sprung front forks with larger 700c or 650c wheels and a fairly upright design of frame. Faster than an MTB but purely for road use.

I

INDEXED GEARS: derailleur gears and changers designed together so that the changer has a definite position for each gear. Click stops usually indicate each gear position but STi and Ergopower levers work on strokes of the changer levers.

J

JOCKEY WHEELS: small wheels in the chain cage of the rear mech that guide the chain round the sprockets.

K

KEVLAR: high-strength artificial fiber used for reinforcing tires, saddles and other components.

KNOBBLIES: deeply treaded MTB tires for high grip in mud.

L

LEISURE BIKE: an often heavily styled bike for short distance use on hard surfaces. Can be fitted with hub gears. Also known as a cruiser bike or city bike.

LOW GEAR: a gear ratio in which you move a short distance for every revolution of the cranks. Used for climbing hills and off-road riding.

LUBE: short for lubricant, especially when packed in an aerosol can or grease gun.

LUG: a complex steel sleeve mostly used to join the main tubes of a steel frame.

N

NIPPLE: square metal nut that passes through the rim and screws onto the spoke, allowing the wheel to be tensioned by tightening up the nipple.

P

PHILLIPS SCREWDRIVER: screwdriver with cross-shaped tip. Sizes 1 and 2 are both used on bikes but not interchangeable.

PLAY: unwanted movement in a bearing due to wear or incorrect adjustment. Sometimes spoken of as "a couple of millimeters' play" or similar.

PRESTA VALVE: found mainly on sports and racing bike tires. Has a knurled brass nut on the stalk to keep the valve shut.

Q

QUICK-RELEASE: a mechanism that allows you to remove a bike wheel by operating the quick-release lever. Also refers to other quick-release (q/r) items like seat post clamps and panniers.

QUILL STEM: handlebar stem with wedge fixing, only suitable for use with threaded forks.

R

RACE: the part of a bearing assembly in contact with the ball bearings. Can be fixed or not.

REAR MECH: short for rear gear mechanism or rear derailleur.

ROADSTER: old-fashioned bike usually seen in the hands of old ladies and the police force.

S

SCHRADER VALVE: car-type tire valve with a separate insert. Larger than a Presta valve.

SEAT POST: tube that fits into the seat tube and supports the saddle.

SEAT STAY: the small-diameter tube that runs between the seat lug and the drop-out. Key-hole stays are S-curved for resiliance.

SEAT TUBE: the large-diameter frame tube that supports the saddle and bottom bracket.

SHIFTER: gear changer. Any mechanism for changing gear.

SIDE-PULL BRAKE: brake used on road bikes. The brake cable is connected to both brake arms at the side of the brake assembly.

SLICKS: smooth tires used on mountain bikes for road riding.

SPIDER: the part of the chainset that the chainrings are bolted to.

SPOKE: round or flat wire that connects the hub to the rim.

SPRINTS: very light wheels and tires used for road and track racing. The tube is sewn into the tire and the whole thing is then stuck to the rim.

SPRAY LUBE: a silicon or Teflon-based aerosol lubricant. Types for general use and specialized bike lubes with a solid lubricant particularly for chains are both used on bikes.

SPROCKET: a toothed wheel or wheels that take drive from the chain to the hub.

SPROCKET CLUSTER: collective name for all the sprockets on a back wheel. Also cassette.

STEERER TUBE: tube connecting the handlebar stem to the fork crown, inside the head tube. Turns with the handlebars.

STEM: connects to the steerer tube, supports the handlebars. Various lengths are available to suit the build of the rider.

STI: combined brake and gear levers for sports and racing bikes, made by Shimano.

STRADDLE CABLE: short cable that joins two independent brake arms. Found on center pull and cantilever brakes.

SUSPENSION FORKS: forks that allow the front wheel to move up and down to absorb bumps. Usually controlled by some sort of spring and a gas or fluid damper mechanism to minimize bounce and rebound.

T

TIRE VALVE: device that holds air pressure in a tire. Part of the tube unless tubeless tires and wheels are fitted.

TIRE WALL: also sidewall. The thinner part of a tire between the tread and the bead. Often colored to contrast with the black of the tread.

TIRE – 700c: the type of tire normally fitted to sports/racers, and hybrids. Thin and light.

TOE-IN: usually measured in millimeters. Refers to fitting brake pads closer to the rim at the front than at the back.

TOP TUBE: the tube joining the seat tube to the head tube. It is usually horizontal but compact road frames and most MTBs have a sloping top tube.

TRANSMISSION: all the components that deal with transmitting power from the rider's legs to the back wheel. Chainset, chain and sprockets, plus the front and rear mechs.

TUBULARS: a tire where the tube is sewn inside the tread and carcass. Used with sprints only.

V

VEE BRAKE: standard design of cantilever brake for MTBs. The long brake arms bolt onto standard pivot bosses but are vertical, which increases leverage and allows the cable to pull directly on the brake arm.

W

WHEEL RIM: the outer part of a bike wheel that carries the tire. Also the braking surfaces. Made of steel, alloy or carbon fiber.

WISHBONE STAY: design of chainstay in which the two tubes from the rear drop-outs join above the back wheel. They are then connected to the seat tube by a larger single tube. Often made in carbon fiber in one piece with the chain stays.

INDEX

Written and edited by:	Fred Milson
Technical editor:	Ian Pearson
Studio photography:	Steve Behr
	Tim Ridley
	Polly Wreford
	Paul Buckland
Illustrations:	Ian Bott
Page make-up:	David Notley
Project manager:	Louise McIntyre

For this new and updated edition, the author and publisher would like to thank

◆ Various persons at Madison / Shimano
◆ Graham Snodden and Ian Young of SRAM
◆ Cedric Chicken, Chicken & Sons
◆ Select Cycle Components (Campagnolo)
◆ Hamish Stewart of Weldtite
◆ Simon Ford of Extra (UK) Ltd
◆ Andy Wigmore of Felt Cycles
◆ Fibrax Ltd
◆ Ruth Casson of Amba Marketing
◆ Frank van Rooijen of Koga Miyata
◆ Chris Hearn of Schwalbe
◆ Martin Kirton of Lyon Equipment
◆ Chris Compton, Compton Cycles
◆ Nick Lumb
◆ Gary Mather of Moore Large
◆ Ali and Chris Boon of Yeovil Cycle Centre/Tri UK
◆ Pasq Bianchi of Cycleurope
◆ Edwards Cycles of Camberwell
◆ Sturmey Archer

From the author, particular thanks to Louise McIntyre, James Robertson, David Notley, and Pete Shoemark of Haynes. And to Paul Buckland and Peter Trott of the Haynes Project Workshop, who put up with a lot.

Above all, to my partner, Sally Mitchell, grateful thanks for the unlimited support she gave me when writing this book.

First published in 2011 by MVP Books, an imprint of MBI Publishing Company, 400 First Avenue North, Suite 300, Minneapolis, MN 55401 USA

Copyright © 2002, 2011 by MVP Books, an imprint of MBI Publishing Company

Originally published by Haynes Publishing, Sparkford, Yeovil, Somerset BA22 7JJ, UK

All rights reserved. With the exception of quoting brief passages for the purposes of review, no part of this publication may be reproduced without prior written permission from the Publisher.

The information in this book is true and complete to the best of our knowledge. All recommendations are made without any guarantee on the part of the author or Publisher, who also disclaims any liability incurred in connection with the use of this data or specific details.

MVP Books titles are also available at discounts in bulk quantity for industrial or sales-promotional use. For details write to Special Sales Manager at MBI Publishing Company, 400 First Avenue North, Suite 300, Minneapolis, MN 55401 USA.

To find out more about our books, visit us online at www.mvpBooks.com.

ISBN-13: 978-0-7603-4025-7

Design manager: Kou Lor
Cover designed by: Rick Korab, Korab Company Design, Inc.

On the front cover: © *Mike Tittel/Photolibrary*

Printed in China